Mathematics Teacher Education

Studies in Mathematics Education Series

Series Editor: Paul Ernest, University of Exeter, UK

Studies in Mathematics Education Series: 12

Mathematics Teacher Education:
Critical International Perspectives

Edited by

Barbara Jaworski
Terry Wood
and Sandy Dawson

UK   Falmer Press, 1 Gunpowder Square, London, EC4A 3DE
USA   Falmer Press, Taylor & Francis Inc., 325 Chestnut Street, 8th Floor,
        Philadelphia, PA 19106

First published in 1999

A catalogue record for this book is available from the British Library

ISBN 0 7507 0809 3 cased
ISBN 0 7507 0808 5 paper

Library of Congress Cataloging-in-Publication Data are available on request

Jacket design by Caroline Archer

Typeset in 10/12 pt Times by
Graphicraft Limited, Hong Kong

Printed in Great Britain by Biddles Ltd., Guildford and King's Lynn on paper which has a specified pH value on final paper manufacture of not less than 7.5 and is therefore 'acid free'.

Contents

Contents

List of Figures and Tables

Series Editor's Preface

Mathematics education is established world-wide as a major area of study, with numerous dedicated journals and conferences serving ever-growing national and international communities of scholars. As it develops, research in mathematics education is becoming more theoretically orientated. Although originally rooted in mathematics and psychology, vigorous new perspectives are pervading it from disciplines and fields as diverse as philosophy, logic, sociology, anthropology, history, women's studies, cognitive science, semiotics, hermeneutics, post-structuralism and post-modernism. These new research perspectives are providing fresh lenses through which teachers and researchers can view the theory and practice of mathematics teaching and learning.

The series *Studies in Mathematics Education* aims to encourage the development and dissemination of theoretical perspectives in mathematics education as well as their critical scrutiny. It is a series of research contributions to the field based on disciplined perspectives that link theory with practice. The series is founded on the philosophy that theory is the practitioner's most powerful tool in understanding and changing practice. Whether the practice concerns the teaching and learning of mathematics, teacher education, or educational research, the series offers new perspectives to help clarify issues, pose and solve problems, and stimulate debate. It aims to have a major impact on the development of mathematics education as a field of study in the third millennium.

Currently, world-wide attention is being given to the development and enhancement of mathematics teaching and mathematics teacher education. As this volume illustrates, many states and countries in the Americas, Europe, Africa, Asia and the Pacific region are implementing programmes of inservice teacher education and development. In England and Wales, for example, a new legal framework for a National Curriculum for Teacher Training has been established, together with strict guidelines on the funding and accreditation of inservice teacher education.

Just as more diverse practices than ever can now be identified in this area, so too research in teacher education has grown in volume. Furthermore, the lack of attention to specific subject matter in research on teaching and teacher education, as decried by Lee Shulman in his AERA presidential address of 1986, is no longer true for the area of mathematics. One might even say there has been a renaissance of research on mathematics teaching and teacher education since then. For as well as many scores of research reports and papers in this area a new international journal in mathematics teacher education has been founded (edited by Tom Cooney). The present volume is part of this renaissance.

These developments in an increasingly lively area of activity suggest that now is an appropriate time to take stock and reflect on progress so far. To accomplish this, the present volume offers three kinds of research contributions. First, it provides a state of the art review of international developments in inservice teacher education. This alone constitutes a valuable contribution, as international overviews are not easily obtained. Second, in extended chapters by its editors, it considers some of the key underlying theoretical positions that are driving research in the area, and relates them to the research projects reported here, as well as to further projects and developments. Third, the volume includes chapters that reflect critically on the nature of research in the field and some of the assumptions and problems involved. This critical evaluation of, and reflection on, research in the area makes the volume an invaluable tool for researchers.

The outcome overall is a coordinated set of perspectives that makes clear the multiplicity inherent in the field, while addressing all of the key substantive issues. The book is a welcome and valuable contribution from three of the leading practitioners in the field. In straddling both the theory and practice of inservice teacher education, the book embodies the philosophy of the series *Studies in Mathematics Education*, by extending the theoretical and critical understanding of mathematics teacher education research and through firmly linking it with practice.

Paul Ernest
University of Exeter
1999

Section One

Openings

Introduction

Barbara Jaworski, Terry Wood and Sandy Dawson

This book is written by practising mathematics teacher educators around the world. It is written for all people engaged in the inservice education of mathematics teachers in both elementary and secondary education. You will find it documenting practices, recognizing problems, identifying themes, highlighting differences, raising issues and challenging conceptions.

Background of the Book

The first ideas for this book arose in a Psychology of Mathematics Education (PME) International Working Group entitled, 'The Psychology of Inservice Education of Mathematics Teachers'. This working group met first in 1986 in London, and each year thereafter until 1994 in Lisbon. The last four years were particularly significant in an ongoing programme of work in a culturally diverse group with leaders Sandy Dawson, Barbara Jaworski and Terry Wood. Most of the authors of chapters in this book were at one time, or for several years, members of the group. The work of the group evolved out of issues of concern and critical questions about mathematics inservice teaching education (known by the acronym INSET in many parts of the world[1]) that were raised by members of the group. Members created a forum for the discussion of teacher inservice education and wrote papers on a variety of topics related to the issues that arose (although not all members wrote a paper). It is this international collection of papers that forms Section Two of the book.

From these core contributions, the group leaders, as editors, identified themes and issues which seemed pervasive in the practices documented. In doing so, we attempted to fill a gap in the mathematics teacher education literature identified by Cooney (1994) wherein he indicated that:

> . . . few articles provide any quantitative or qualitative basis for comparing inservice programs . . . [and he failed to] uncover any recently published books that address the improvement of inservice teacher education programs. (Chapter 8, p. 1)

There is no intention here, however, to provide a review of inservice programmes for mathematics teachers, or indeed to suggest improvements to programmes. The themes and issues identified might be seen to *represent* the status quo of mathematics teacher education internationally, and need to be seen in relation to national characteristics and sociocultural issues in a period of great political and economic change throughout the world. What we present here (in Section Three) is a critical analysis of the themes emerging from some selected international mathematics teacher education projects as reported by those who designed and implemented them.

We debated long and hard about our own contributions to the book. Eventually we settled on three chapters, one from each of us which tried, firstly, to represent our own work and thinking in mathematics teacher education; and, secondly, to take a rather wider, and more critical, perspective on theoretical issues than had been appropriate in the earlier contributions. These three chapters complete Section Three of the book.

Overall we introduce readers to a range of practices that they can set against their own teacher education programmes and compare issues and outcomes, a critical analysis of themes and issues emerging from these practices, and a critical view of theoretical perspectives which inform mathematics teacher education. We leave the reader with the challenge of taking further the search for a more unified theoretical conceptualization of mathematics teacher education.

Organization of the Book

Section One: Openings

Following this introduction is a historical perspective on teacher inservice education in mathematics from the personal viewpoint of one of the group leaders. This is designed to set the scene for the sections which follow.

Section Two: International Perspectives in Mathematics Teacher Education

This book describes some of the recent work in mathematics teaching inservice development taking place in countries around the globe, although it is not intended to be an international review. Papers were offered by participants in the PME Working Group, mentioned above, who had joined the group from reasons of personal and professional interest. Their papers form this section of the book and represent current practices within the international community of mathematics teacher educators. They offer not only an awareness of prevailing practices, but also an insight into the underlying beliefs and philosophy of teacher education in a variety of countries across several continents. Each of the papers describes ways of working with mathematics teachers and the associated outcomes and issues for teachers and teacher educators. Not surprisingly, these practices are characterized by both unity and diversity and reflect the work being accomplished in mathematics teacher education from countries with widely differing national characteristics.

As editors we have seen some progression of ideas and methods across the papers and this is indicated briefly in remarks which preface the papers. The reader is invited to review each paper, to draw personal insights and conjectures as to current international practices, and to raise questions.

Section Three: Critical Perspectives Linking Theory and Practice in Mathematics Teacher Education

From the collection of papers we first identify common themes in practices across the countries and raise issues related to these themes. Readers can compare their conclusions with those extracted. From the analysis of these themes and issues, we were able to discern a shift in the underlying perspectives that guide mathematics teacher development across countries. Analysis suggests that these changes in approaches can be viewed as a shift from traditional methods of delivering courses to teachers, often involving direct instruction, to approaches influenced by a constructivist philosophy in which teachers take more responsibility for developing their own teaching. One current position in this shift might be seen in programmes where teaching development arises from teachers taking on the mantle of researchers in their own classrooms and engaging in practical inquiry.

However, analysis also shows diversity in the practices, reflective of the specific cultural contexts in which they are embedded. Although common themes in the practices exist, they are nonetheless interpreted relative to the cultural and/or political situation for each country. Thus, issues relating to the cultural contexts of the papers, in a rapidly changing political world, enhance the international perspective.

Following the discussion of themes and issues, are three further chapters, each written by one of the editors. Our purpose here has been to offer personal perspectives which are related to our own current work in teacher education and to some extent to our own national contexts. In addition we have tried to indicate, critically, the theoretical perpectives on which we have drawn and which underlie our analyses of the programmes we discuss. In debating our various theoretical positions it became clear that these are diverse, not only in their particularities but in the nature of what we count as theory. We resisted trying to develop some overall theoretical synthesis, rather leaving it to readers to make their own interpretation of what is presented. Inevitably it is hard to make a detached critique of theoretical positions in which our work is embedded. It will therefore be up to readers to judge what we offer in relation to other practices and theoretical perspectives with which they are familiar.

We hope the book will play a role in a wider debate about the nature of mathematics teacher education and whether there are ways in which it can move to a more unified theoretical approach with common practices; indeed whether this is even desirable.

Note

1 Where we have used the adjective 'inservice' alone, it is taken to mean the 'inservice education of teachers'.

Reference

COONEY, T.J. (1994) 'Inservice programs in mathematics education', in FITZSIMMONS, S.J. and KERPELMAN, L.C. (eds) *Teacher Enhancement for Elementary and Secondary Science and Mathematics: Status, Issues, and Problems* (Chapter 8), Washington, DC: National Science Foundation.

1   Charting a Historical Perspective

Sandy Dawson, Canada

A part of the process of composing this book included conversations and debates with mathematics inservice teacher educators, among whom we include ourselves. Invariably we posed questions and expressed concerns regarding the programs we develop and present to teachers, many of which are exemplified in the practices described in Section Two. Issues and questions which arose from these debates, and which offer us professional and theoretical challenges, include the following:

- How can our inservice programs connect to what teachers do in their classrooms?
- How can we simultaneously deal with pedagogy, mathematical content and the reality of teachers' instructional situations when the length of contact with teachers is severely limited?
- Do we take cognizance of teachers' realities at the same time as we entreat teachers to take cognizance of their students' realities? Are our inservice programs true models of what is being espoused?
- Often teachers are criticized for seeing children as being deficient, but are our own inservice programs designed to overcome teacher deficiencies? Are we being hypocritical if we operate in such a fashion?

Some of these questions and concerns are new, yet some go back a number of decades to the time when mathematics education as a field of study originated. Since those days, there has been a movement away from the dominant positivistic view of the learning and teaching process to a time where constructivism has acquired a position of philosophical dominance in educational discourse. Where once the process–product research paradigm was paramount, qualitative studies are now central to most research in mathematics education. In order to understand these changes better, let us sketch a history of how we got to where we are today. Although these reflections are about inservice education in North America over the past 30 years, the underlying issues identified are universal.

Early Stages of Inservice Education

It was just the third month of my first year of teaching. I had a teaching job back in the high school I had graduated from five short years before. The year was 1963. On this particular November day, along with my new colleagues (men and women who had taught me during my three years as a high school student), I was headed for the cafeteria to be given the latest word on the New Math by representatives of the Scott Foresman Publishing Company. For the next two hours, the two reps told us the 'wonder' of their new texts, and how the learning of mathematics would be revolutionized because now we would be teaching sets! Like it was yesterday, I can recall and picture in my mind's eye one colleague saying sincerely and enthusiastically, 'I like the New Math. I will be able to make tests up easily by asking for the definitions of a set, the union of two sets, the intersection of sets, and so on. And the tests will be quick and easy to mark'. 'But,' he added, 'I might have to learn some new mathematics before I can do that.' Looking at me, he said, laughing somewhat derisively, 'Dawson, you're the big expert who has been away studying all this stuff for the past year. You can teach us in our spare periods'. Thus began my career in teaching, and more germane to this book, my career in inservice teacher education.

This small vignette highlights a number of issues and assumptions which were central to inservice education in the 1960s and early 1970s, not least of which was the suspicion which greeted those who were eager to proselytize about the New Math. I was seen as one of the New Math advocates. In the year prior to beginning to teach I completed a Masters degree in which I had focused on the new mathematics curriculum. Even I had more experience in just three short months than did the two publishing company representatives, who were not viewed as authentic teachers, as persons who knew what it was like to teach mathematics to adolescents. Even I was sceptical of what they said, which was that we teachers needed to know more mathematics, and that if we just learned this new mathematics, many, if not all, of our teaching difficulties would diminish or disappear altogether. They suggested that we organize study groups, and perhaps get some professors from the university to come and teach us the mathematics. If we filled the gap in our mathematical knowledge, all else would fall into place, or so they claimed.

It seemed clear that teaching for them, and for many of my colleagues at that time, was a matter of: 1) knowing one's material; 2) presenting it clearly and concisely to one's students, preferably but not necessarily, with accompanying explanatory diagrams; 3) having the students do exercises, by-and-large identical to the examples the teacher had presented; and 4) which the students then re-presented to the teacher on the chapter, unit, or term end test. If a student did not do well, then there was something deficient about the student, because, clearly, the material had been well presented by a knowledgable and well-prepared teacher. Teaching methodology, or pedagogy in current parlance, was not problematic for these teachers and teacher educators.

The view at that time was one which said if teachers were given more mathematics, this was sufficient to guarantee changes to the teaching and learning of mathematics in schools. The view today, as will be seen from the analysis presented later in the book, is that improved mathematical knowledge is a necessary but far from sufficient condition to foster change in the teaching and learning of mathematics.

The goal of many curriculum revisionists three decades ago was to create a so-called teacher-proof curriculum, one that most teachers with (or without) the proper mathematics background could teach and the students would learn. This was the period when teaching machines — programmed learning — were being advocated as a tool to replace teachers whose mathematical background might be deficient to the task of presenting mathematics correctly, precisely, and concisely.

The mood was one of seeing teachers and students as being deficient — following the disease model of medicine. If students did not score well on national and international tests, then the teachers were blamed for having deficits; teachers in turn laid the responsibility at the feet of their deficient students. Inservice programs of the era were designed to rectify the mathematical deficiencies of the teachers. This view fitted well, firstly, with a positivistic world view, one in which knowledge exists outside the learner, and which is funnelled into learners by knowledgable teachers — the trick was to get the knowledge packaged in sufficiently comprehensible and digestible bite-size pieces so that learners would be able to have a veritable feast from the table of knowledge. Secondly, if fitted with the dominant research paradigm of the day, a reductionistic, process-product, experimental mode which tried to atomize teaching into constituent elements which were then to be taught to teachers.

But some educators were troubled by this view of teaching and of teacher development. As one of those, I knew from my work with the Madison Project people in the early and mid-1960s (Davis, 1963) that there was an alternative view of children, one which did not see them as deficient learners, nor their teachers as deficient instructors. Even before Lakatos' articles appeared in the *British Journal for the Philosophy of Science* (Lakatos, 1963–64) in the late 1960s, and 15 years in advance of the appearance of his book *Proof and Refutations* (Lakatos, 1976), the Madison Project was advancing a view of mathematics and its teaching and learning which can aptly be described as fallibilistic. The students' voices and those of teachers were being heard by a few mathematics educators. Gradually, more and more mathematics teachers joined the chorus singing to be recognized as committed and dedicated educators who knew there was more to the preparation for teaching than just knowledge of subject matter. By the mid-1970s, cries were being heard for changes to the focus, manner and underlying assumptions of teacher development programs. Along with this, the philosophical underpinning of mathematics was becoming the subject of debate in the mathematics education community. Reconceptualization of teaching and of teacher inservice education was beginning.

The Middle Years: Mathematics Teaching and Learning Reconceptualized

I vowed I would never attend another INSET day so long as I lived. I was not even one of the teachers sitting through the particular session which provoked this declaration. It was one of many sessions teachers attended during the two-day inservice program. I wondered what thoughts were occurring inside those teachers' heads as they endured speaker after speaker telling them what was wrong with the teaching in schools, and how 'you' teachers only need buy this or that magic elixir to solve these problems.

I was so disturbed about all this, and about my own part in perpetuating that system, that I wrote a paper (Dawson, 1978) in which I argued:

> Inservice education activities which are imposed on teachers from above, whether by well intentioned school board officials or through the auspices of a university, are destined for failure if they do not take into account the teachers' perception of reality. If some group external to the people for whom the inservice training is designed decides a priori what teachers need, without taking account of the teachers' own view of what is relevant to them, then the chances are extremely good that teachers will ignore the inservice activity. They may attend. They may even get involved to a certain degree, but if the activities do not deal directly with the teachers' perceived reality the activities will have little permanent effect on the teachers. (p. 50)
>
> *Inservice education, to be successful, has to be generated dynamically by the teachers themselves, from their view of classroom reality.* (p. 51)

And so I stopped giving 'one-shot' inservice sessions. I sought different ways to work with teachers, to talk with teachers, to provide opportunities for teachers to talk with each other, and I tried to find ways to come to know teachers' realities as they saw them, not as I imagined or remembered those realities to be.

Central to my thinking was a growing recognition of the key role played by teachers in whatever learning might take place in classrooms, and of how the multitude of decisions teachers make daily impacts on the opportunities of students' learning. As teacher education began to take the reality of the teacher into account, Cooney (1994b) noted that this research path focused 'not just on what teachers did, but on the kinds of decisions they made and on what influenced those decisions' (p. 624). Concomitantly with this development was a dawning recognition of just how difficult and complex the teaching task was. The centrality of teachers in the educational process was finally being acknowledged. They were no longer seen as just distributors and dispensers of mathematical knowledge. The kind and number of decisions they had to make, typically under pressures of time and exhortations to 'cover the curriculum', came under close but empathetic study. This was the positive outcome of this research direction (Cooney, 1994b).

Not all the implications of these insights were positive for the professional development of teachers. Some teacher educators and curriculum developers believed that teachers were not adequately educated to carry out this difficult and complex task of teaching the young, and concluded that the best way to counteract this state of affairs was to develop curriculum which was as 'teacher proof' as possible, and to then assess student outcomes endlessly in order to be sure that the teachers were teaching to that curriculum. The back-to-the-basics movement, and the competency-based teacher education movements are approaches which tried to eliminate the teacher variable from the educational equation. Teacher 'accountability' was the buzz word and teacher development programs were generated to make sure that teachers taught in the manner that outside experts deemed they should. These approaches, though they received a lot of notoriety in the late 1970s and early 1980s, were doomed to oblivion largely because they did not take teachers' realities into account. They did not deal with the questions, issues and concerns that were central to teachers' work in their classrooms. Further, such approaches were increasingly seen as being 'out of tune' with the growing constructivist thrust in education, a development which directed sharp attention to how learners created their own mathematical knowledge (Cooney, 1994b).

Researchers were beginning to recognize that effective teachers focused on their students' learning, subordinating the instructional process — the lesson plans and so on, all those things we usually call teaching — to the learning process of students (Gattegno, 1970). This shift in attention led to a focus on inservice in which teachers were provided opportunities to understand how children thought about mathematics in ways that were personally meaningful. The earlier approach of inservice programs that focused on increasing teacher knowledge of mathematics declined, and was replaced by a desire to increase teacher knowledge of how their students learned mathematics. The shift, then, was to teachers learning about learning, rather than learning about mathematics.

Gradually this somewhat narrow shift broadened and deepened. Indeed, the either–or approach itself was challenged: the question concerning whether teacher development should focus on increasing teacher knowledge of mathematics, or whether it should focus on learning about learners was increasingly seen as being the wrong question to ask. It finally came to be recognized that both aspects were important. A more global view of the teaching and learning environment was emerging, one where the total context in which mathematics, teachers and students interacted needed to be accounted for in teacher development programs. Cooney (1994b) summarized the variety of intellectual forces which gave rise to this shift:

> Primary among them was an increasing dissatisfaction with the positivistic paradigm and the perception that the atomization of teaching behaviors would yield productive results, the calling into question about the notion of objectivity and the infallibility of mathematical knowledge, and an increasing acceptance of the constructive paradigm. (p. 625)

Concerns about and investigation of teacher decision-making, and student learning strategies, took their place alongside the previous focus on the acquisition of and dispensing of mathematical knowledge. Moreover, the context in which these concerns were examined became that of the classroom, where variables are hard to identify let alone control, where spontaneity is the only prediction possible, and where the interactions among teachers, students and curriculum are multi-faceted and extremely complex.

The Current Scene: Teacher Research and Reflection

'That was great stuff,' Pushpa exclaimed as she handed me back Gattegno's book (Gattegno, 1974). 'Why didn't you give that to me sooner, to read before now? It fits so well with what I was doing with the kids in my class last spring, with what I was thinking for months, and with what I was trying to write in my thesis.'

It was an excellent question, as they say. It arose during the spring of 1995 when Pushpa and I were meeting weekly to discuss the Master's thesis she was writing. My answer to her went something like this. 'If you were already thinking about those ideas, if you were already trying those kinds of activities with your kids, and clearly you were writing about them in your thesis, then you really didn't need Gattegno to tell you what you already knew!' Pushpa was quick to respond, 'Maybe not, but it was great to get the confirmation, the validation. And I might have just reached those ideas more quickly if you had given me Gattegno to read sooner.'

Of course, the fact that it was some of Gattegno's writings is not the point here. The issue I raise is really about the dialectic seen to exist between teacher and student, and the reflective process which typifies teaching in the 1990s. Teachers are reflecting more about their classroom work, they are experimenting more in their classes with various teaching and learning strategies, they are developing instructional materials which seem to stand a good chance of 'hooking' the interest and motivations of their students, and they do all these demanding tasks whilst still being (perhaps) parents, partners, children, colleagues, leaders, and taking care of their own personal needs and wishes.

Some teachers seem to be discarding distinctions and dichotomies which once seemed central to the teaching and learning process. They no longer see a separation between theory and practice, or between content and pedagogy, or between teacher and learner, or between teacher and researcher. Indeed, many see a seamless web of life with no firm distinctions among the various aspects of their life. They see their teaching co-evolving with their students' learning, an evolution which occurs within and is influenced by the instructional setting. The influence is bi-directional — teachers ↔ learners, teachers ↔ curriculum, learners ↔ curriculum — though not in the sense of a Venn diagram composed of three intersecting circles (teachers, learners, and curriculum), because the three aspects blend and meld together to such a degree that it is not possible to distinguish the teacher from the learners from the curriculum.

And it is into this situation that teacher educators are finding themselves immersed. What this means is that inservice leaders cannot just 'deliver' a course, or a workshop, or a session as they might once have done. Now the pressure is for inservice providers to become part of the learning community, to live with the teachers and the learners and the realities of their situation. In doing so, inservice providers will necessarily influence and be influenced by that situation, and be an intimate part of any research the inservice providers might be engaged in as part of the development work.

The study of teacher development in mathematics education seems to finally have come of age. Cooney (1994b) suggests that:

Although it has been 30 years coming, it appears that the field of mathematics education is poised to seriously consider teacher education as a legitimate field of inquiry. The emphasis on cognition and context and the rise in popularity of constructivism provide a foundation for systematic inquiry into the processes of teacher education. (p. 626)

He further suggests that individual descriptions of these practices and processes are important. To this end, the international teacher development programs and projects presented in Section Two offer such descriptions. Cooney further advises that, while these illustrations are most valuable, there is still a need to a more general theory of teacher education derived from 'naturalistic generalizations' from research studies. The individual papers in the book provide a wealth of insight and understanding about particular attempts to modify the teaching and thus the learning process in mathematics. But the need to go beyond description is paramount. Two things seem required. First, the common themes found in the individual papers need to be culled out, critiqued, and the practices they report made problematic. Second, once this is accomplished, generalizations derived from the papers need to be elucidated. These are tasks which we, as editors, attempt in Section Three of this book.

Still, something more is required. We need to go beyond collecting and reporting on 'insightful stories', as Cooney (1994b) calls them, so that we begin to develop '. . . theoretical perspectives . . . that allow us to see how those stories begin to tell a larger story' (p. 627). In Section Three, we inspect the diversity of theoretical positions which influence and underpin teacher education programs in an attempt to chart the theoretical diversity which prevails. We also provide our own, individual, suggestions for what might be productive and fruitful theoretical frameworks for research in the field of teacher development in mathematics education.

References

COONEY, T.J. (1994a) 'Inservice programs in mathematics education', in FITZSIMMONS, S.J. and KERPELMAN, L.C. (eds) *Teacher Enhancement for Elementary and Secondary Science and Mathematics: Status, Issues, and Problems* (Chapter 8), Washington, DC: National Science Foundation.

COONEY, T.J. (1994b) 'Research and teacher education: In search of common ground', *Journal for Research in Mathematics Education*, **25**, pp. 608–36.

DAVIS, R.B. (1963) *A Modern Mathematics Program as it Pertains to the Interrelationship of Mathematical Content, Teaching Methods, and Classroom Atmosphere: The Madison Project*. Washington, DC: Commissioner of Education, U.S. Department of Health, Education, and Welfare.

DAWSON, A.J. (1978) 'Criteria for the creation of inservice education programs', *Canadian Journal of Education*, **3**, pp. 49–60.

GATTEGNO, C. (1970) *What We Owe Children: The Subordination of Teaching to Learning*, New York, NY: Outerbridge & Dienstfrey.

GATTEGNO, C. (1974) *The Common Sense of Teaching Mathematics*, New York, NY: Educational Solutions, Inc.

LAKATOS, I. (1963–64) *British Journal for the Philosophy of Science*, **14**, pp. 1–25, 120–39, 221–43, 315–417.

LAKATOS, I. (1976) *Proofs and Refutations*, Cambridge, UK: Cambridge University Press.

International Perspectives in Mathematics Teacher Education

In reading through the contributions in Section Two, it will become clear that a transition is taking place in the learning and teaching of mathematics in a direction considered to be influenced by the cognitive revolution in learning and a constructivist philosophy. This is revealed in the papers as a movement from a traditional approach which emphasized doing paper-and-pencil routine exercises in teacher-centred classes to a focus on student-centred lessons involving problematic mathematical activities. Moreover, a corresponding shift to a constructivist view is also occurring in the approaches taken in mathematics teacher inservice education.

The approaches described in these chapters reveal the prevailing attempts to relate a constructivist philosophy, and the corresponding perspective on learning, to mathematics teacher education. But, more importantly, these papers reveal the current dilemma in attempts to transform constructivism to practice which is pervasive and global. That is, the papers reveal the necessity for mathematics teacher educators to develop common ground for the meanings of constructivism and the implications this perspective has for developing mathematics teaching and teacher education.

Editors' comment

The first four chapters in the collection have in common a focus on the discipline of mathematics. For Amit and Hillman, the focus is on mathematizing and modelling situations, and the need for ways to assess students' performance. Weinzweig's emphasis is on the processes involved in mathematical activity as a human event. While Murray, Olivier, and Human, and Farah-Sarkis create situations to direct teachers' attention to the ways in which students are experiencing doing mathematics in their classes.

2 Changing Mathematics Instruction and Assessment: Challenging Teachers' Conceptions

Miriam Amit, Israel and Susan Hillman, USA

Introduction

The current reform in mathematics education calls for changes in classroom instructional practice and assessment. From a proliferation of exercises practicing basic skills in an isolated way, there is a shift toward using more open-ended, real-world problems for learning in context (NCTM, 1989). Changes for assessment include a decreased emphasis on 'counting correct answers on tests for the sole purpose of assigning grades' and increased emphasis on 'multiple assessment techniques, including written, oral, and demonstration formats' (NCTM, 1989, p. 191). Performance assessment activities are one way to diversify assessment techniques while providing an opportunity to contextualize learning mathematics through the use of open-ended, real-world problems.

Teachers' conceptions of mathematics, instruction, and assessment seem to have a significant influence on what happens in classrooms. Changing teachers' conceptions and the impact on instruction is a difficult and complex phenomenon. One step towards changing teachers' conceptions is to provide experiences where those conceptions are challenged and teachers have opportunities to reflect on and rethink their conceptions about mathematics, instruction, and assessment. Teacher education opportunities where teachers participate in new approaches to instruction and assessment as learners and then reflect upon and discuss their experiences have the potential to facilitate new insight and understanding (Aichele and Castle, 1994; Fosnot, 1989; Thompson, 1985). Although Fosnot (1989) focuses on preservice teachers, the argument for modeling new approaches 'to engage the [teachers] in experiences that are meaningful and confront their traditional schemes of teaching' (p. 16) for the purpose of critique and analysis would seem to hold for practicing teachers as well.

This chapter will describe the similar inservice experiences of middle school teachers in Israel and the United States, and the impact on changing the teachers' conceptions of mathematics, instruction, and assessment. The intent of the inservice was to acquaint teachers with new approaches to instruction and assessment using performance assessment activities. To elicit and challenge their conceptions, teachers experienced the new approaches as students and then engaged in discussion designed to question and rethink existing conceptions.

Performance Assessment and Mathematical Models

Performance assessment requires the students to perform a task rather than select an answer to a multiple choice item (Zimmermann, 1992). As an athlete or actor might use their knowledge and skills in ways to create a winning or convincing performance, a mathematics student performs by actually demonstrating knowledge and skills through construction of a solution to a task. The actual performance of constructing the solution may provide valuable information about what the student knows and understands, as well as the final product. Performance assessment activities may include mathematical contexts or real-world contexts for problem situations. Open-ended problem situations generally allow for multiple levels and types of solutions. Currently, performance assessment tasks are being developed for at least two purposes: on-demand performance for accountability; and instructional tools with the potential to integrate instruction and assessment (Katims, Nash, and Tocci, 1993). The performance assessment tasks used for the teacher inservice described in this chapter were designed as instructional tools based on open-ended, real-world problem situations.

Real-world problem situations are realistic, not contrived illustrations (Burkhardt, 1981). They create the need for a mathematical model (Lesh and Akerstrom, 1982), and allow for multiple solutions and solution paths (de Lange, 1987). Since real-life problem situations are usually complex and not well-defined, they require some mathematization of the situation for solution. A mathematical model is a situated mathematical system that contains mathematical objects, operations on those objects, and the relations between them for 'describing, explaining, constructing, modifying, manipulating, and predicting' (Lesh and Lamon, 1992, p. 21). The real-world situation must be simplified by identifying key elements and relationships. A mathematical model of those elements and their relationships is constructed and manipulated so that the results can be interpreted and validated in terms of the original situation. The mathematical modeling of real-world problem situations is generally thought of as having the potential to contribute to the development of higher order thinking and provide information about students' usable mathematical knowledge.

Kulm (1991) found that teachers who are part of the mathematics education reform and believe that problem-solving provides important opportunities for students to use higher order thinking, are not always able to accomplish this goal. He offers several possible-explanations that include teachers who 'think that they are teaching problem solving' but are actually providing students with algorithms, and teachers who would like to teach problem-solving but do not 'because they don't know how, student competency tests don't include problem-solving items, or there isn't time' (p. 73).

To align instruction with the new directions in mathematics education and promote the implementation of mathematical modeling in the classroom, teachers should have clear ideas about how to mathematize problem situations, the characteristics of appropriate mathematical models, and how to assess them. To assist teachers in clarifying their ideas and challenging their conceptions, it seems reasonable to have teachers experience a new model of instruction and assessment. This experience could then be used to provide the context for discussions about what it means to 'do' mathematics in the context of performance assessment.

Teacher Education

Inservice for Teachers in Israel

The aim of teacher education in Israel is to enhance mathematical knowledge and pedagogical content knowledge to empower teachers. Two innovative models for teacher training are currently being used. One model involves a two-year training for elementary teachers. A second model involves a series of mini-conferences designed and funded as part of an initiative by the Ministry of Education and Culture called 'Tomorrow 1998' to promote mathematics and science education in Israel and prepare students for the technological society of the twenty-first century. The mini-conferences aim to expose new ideas about mathematics instruction and assessment to 'tutor teachers', each with a different focus on relevant topics, issues, or concerns in mathematics education. These tutor teachers then have the responsibility to educate other teachers with whom they work throughout Israel. The tutor teachers are an important link to making changes in instruction and assessment in this centralized educational system.

A tutor teacher has additional training in mathematics, methods of teaching mathematics, and tutoring skills, from ordinary teachers. Typically, a tutor teacher spends half of every week as a regular classroom teacher and works the rest of the week with other teachers from the same school and from two to five other schools. The tutor teacher works one-on-one or in small groups to help teachers with planning, teaching strategies, and developing assessment tools. For the experience described in this chapter, 124 middle school tutor teachers participated in a series of workshops that formed a mini-conference with a focus on performance assessment activities. These teachers participated on two levels: as classroom teachers themselves; and as tutors of other teachers.

Inservice for Teachers in the United States

In the United States, teachers are being encouraged to reform their practice with respect to the Curriculum and Evaluation Standards for School Mathematics (NCTM, 1989), the Professional Standards for Teaching Mathematics (NCTM, 1991), and the Assessment Standards for School Mathematics (NCTM, 1995). Several teacher enhancement projects have been funded by the National Science Foundation to provide inservice support for practicing teachers. The Delaware Teacher Enhancement Partnership[1] (TEP) was one such project which has a main goal of developing mathematical power in teachers for grades seven through nine. The TEP uses 'situation-centered learning' to enhance the teachers' own mathematical knowledge, to provide a model for new approaches to instruction and assessment, and to support teachers to make changes in their classrooms that are consistent with the Standards. Situation-centered learning involves using open-ended, real-world problem situations, where small groups of teachers work together to mathematize the situations and then share solutions. Follow-up discussions include formalizing the mathematics involved and making connections with curriculum, instruction, and assessment issues.

The workshop described in this chapter was part of a three-week summer institute, sponsored by the TEP. The 15 middle school teachers who participated in the workshop represented several school districts throughout the state of Delaware. Their teaching experience ranged from first year teachers to those with more than 20 years of teaching, and mathematics backgrounds varied from the minimal mathematics required for elementary certification to the more substantial mathematics requirements for secondary certification.

Inservice with Teachers: Performance Assessment

The workshops in Israel and the United States had a common purpose and similar format. The goals of the workshops were to identify and challenge the conceptions of the participating teachers with respect to mathematics, mathematical modeling, the use of real-world problem situations, and assessment in the teaching of mathematics in the middle school. The workshops were designed so that teachers would first experience the problem activity as students and then reflect on this experience both as students and as teachers. Initial discussions included specific questions to provide the opportunity for teachers to share their conceptions. Teams of three to four teachers then worked for approximately one hour on a performance assessment activity. Each team presented their solution process and product to the whole group, and then the whole group reflected on the solutions to the problem activity. A reflective discussion of the whole experience revealed how teachers were beginning to rethink initial conceptions.

The performance assessment activity, SHAPE, was selected from 24 activities based on open-ended, real-world problem situations developed as a part of the *PACKETS®Program: Performance Assessment for Middle School Mathematics* (Katims, Lesh, Hole, Hoover, and Tocci, 1995). Each teacher received a newspaper article discussing the United States 1990 census information. The article included a 'map' of the United States that distorted the size of each state according to the size of its population; for example, California appeared much larger on this map than Texas since the population of California is much larger than the population of Texas. An attempt was made to retain the relative shape and placement of each state as much as possible so that the map was recognizable. All teachers in the United States and Israel were presented with a regular map of the United States for comparison with the distorted map. The problem situation was to produce a similar map so that a friend could write an article about the 22 countries in North, Central, and South Americas. The task included constructing the map and writing an explanation of how the map was created. Each teacher was given an authentic map of the Americas and a list of the populations for the 22 countries. Other tools and materials, such as calculators and graph paper, were available upon request.

Teachers' Initial Conceptions

Teachers' comments during the initial discussions were grouped to identify conceptions about the nature of mathematics, mathematical models, mathematics instruction and assessment. Examples of teachers' comments about the nature of mathematics include: 'The most important thing in mathematics is skills and this is what teachers should be accountable for'; 'mathematics is made up of rules and procedures'; 'there is always a best way to solve a problem and there is one correct answer'; 'in mathematics, the answer must be precise and very accurate regardless of the context of the problem situation'; and 'real-life situations are not "real" mathematics'. These comments reflect a narrow view of mathematics as knowing rules, applying procedures, making precise calculations, and accumulating skills and procedures. Consistent with this view are the conceptions that mathematics is composed of distinct topics taught in isolation from one another, contextual circumstances have no bearing on the required degree of accuracy, and 'real' mathematics is abstract with no relation to real life. Also consistent with this view is the conception that correct answers are checked by appealing to mathematical authorities (e.g. the textbook or mathematicians who 'know') rather than validated through reasoning and logical argument.

A common conception among the teachers was that mathematical models are formulas and certain models are used to solve specific types of problems. For example, if a problem is identified as a 'distance, rate, and time' problem, then the formula $D = R \times T$ is the only appropriate model to solve that problem (i.e. the best way to arrive at the one correct answer). Other teachers' comments indicated that a mathematical model was something concrete like manipulatives (e.g. base ten blocks, or an abacus). Some teachers commented, 'only great mathematicians can create models, we just learn what they are and how to apply them'. This comment seems to make sense with respect to their conception of specific mathematical models related to certain classes of problems. From the teachers' point of view, these models could not be assessed but just 'used'.

Comments from the teachers related to instruction and assessment included 'first you teach the skills, then you test them to see if they've mastered those skills and, if they have, then they can apply those skills in problem solving'; and 'this kind of problem solving takes too much time, I'd use it for enrichment, or with the higher level kids if there's time'. These statements reflect the view that teaching and assessing are disjointed activities. The issue of accessibility is clearly evident in that problem-solving is considered appropriate for 'higher level' students, but that 'lower level' students need the structure of practice with skills. The conception that skills must be mastered before posing problems involving higher order thinking seems to be related to the view that using real-world problems takes time away from 'real' teaching where teachers lead students through procedures and students dutifully practice what was presented.

Teachers' Conceptions Challenged

While working on the SHAPE problem activity, each teacher team constructed a product. Each team was given the opportunity to present their product to the whole group and justify their approach as a solution to the task. Their products reflected a variety of approaches to solve the problem that led to the creation of several different mathematical models. The models were characterized by the mathematical objects, relationships, and operations used in the construction of the solution. These models were not mutually exclusive, in the sense that the same objects appeared in more than one model, but the models differed in their use of relationships between, and operations on, the objects. For a more complete discussion of the models created by teacher teams see Amit and Hillman (1995).

Two common models from teachers in both the United States and Israel were based on proportional reasoning. One model used an arbitrary unit (e.g. one square on the graph paper equals one-tenth of a per cent of the total population, so that using this scale required 360 squares for the United States since its population was approximately 36 per cent of the total population of the Americas). A second model involved a correspondence between two ratios: the population of a particular country to the total population of the Americas, and the area of the country to the total land area available on the map (e.g. the population of the United States to the total population of the Americas was approximately one-third, so that one-third of the total land available on the constructed map represented the United States). Some products showed an attempt to maintain the relative shape and placement of countries, while others did not. A third model that was constructed by a team of teachers from Israel used discrete ranking to create a bar graph. The countries were ranked in order from the smallest population to the largest population, and the height of each bar represented the size of the population for each country. This particular representation did not allow for retaining either the shape or the relative placement of the countries. Although this particular model was not used by any of the teacher teams in the United States, this product was shared in the reflective discussion as a possible solution.

During the initial discussion, teachers were not sure that solving a real-world problem was 'doing mathematics', and as they worked on the activity several teachers asked, 'Where is the mathematics?' To answer this question, the teachers were asked (after completing the activity) to make a list of the mathematical objects and operations used in their solutions. The teachers listed mathematical objects such as units, scales, areas, proportions, fractions, percentages, and estimations of whole numbers; and identified the operations of comparing, ranking, multiplying, dividing, and estimating. Reflecting on these lists convinced the teachers that they were doing real mathematics. Moreover, it was clear from the discussion that they were making connections between domains of mathematics that they usually perceived, and taught, as disjointed topics, such as area and percentages.

To encourage the teachers to reconsider their notion of a mathematical model as a formula or concrete object, they were asked, 'Is there a mathematical model in your product?' Initially the teachers were unable to articulate such a model. They were then challenged to explain how they mathematized the situation using the terms generated from their lists of mathematical objects, operations, and relations. Reflecting on their explanations, the teachers seemed to indicate that their solutions contained a 'prototype system' or a 'prototype model' that could be manipulated and used to help construct solutions in other situations. Other examples where this prototype model could be used (e.g. creating a map to represent the amount of rainfall in the different districts of Israel, or the amount of income generated by various exports from each of the original 13 colonies in North America) were suggested by teachers and accepted by the rest of the group as valid situations. The teachers seemed to indicate that they could manipulate and adjust the system to new situations. Although they were unable to verbalize a concise definition, the teachers did agree with a definition from the literature used in the earlier part of this chapter. This discussion seemed to broaden their conception of a mathematical model from a concrete representation or formula to include mathematical systems that could be constructed from mathematical objects, operations and relations. Several teachers seemed thrilled that they could actually create a model, and some teachers commented that they may have created mathematical models in the past without knowing that was what they were doing.

To focus the discussion toward issues related to assessment, we posed the following question to the teachers, 'How would you assess and evaluate the products you generated in your attempts to solve the problem?' A heated discussion ensued among the teachers about whose model was the best, and this gave rise to a more general discussion of whether it made sense to talk about a 'best model'. As the teachers discussed the variety of models and levels of mathematics, and differences in precision and utility (usefulness of the product in the context of the problem situation), they began to feel uncomfortable about their conceptions of what counts in mathematics assessment. For example, one product that used the model based on corresponding ratios was drawn very precisely but did not reflect any attempt to retain the relative shape or placement of the countries whereas another product used the model based on an arbitrary unit and was not drawn very precisely but did retain the shape and placement of countries. Most of the teachers agreed that the second product might better fit the needs of the client in the problem situation even though it was not drawn as precisely as the first product. Context was recognized by the teachers as an important factor in considering the appropriate levels of precision. During the discussion, the teachers acknowledged that rather than looking for a single, correct answer, there were several valid models that could be constructed to meet the needs of the client. They also seemed to recognize that each model had advantages and limitations, and could be revised for a better fit with the actual problem situation.

During the discussion of assessment related issues, the teachers voiced a concern about how their final products did not reflect the whole process of what they had learned or thought about as they were constructing solutions. There seemed to be general agreement that it would be helpful to know something of how the process of constructing the solution contributed to the final product, and that a grade based just on a final product might not accurately reflect the mathematical knowledge and understanding of the students involved. From the final product, it was not obvious to those who were not involved in the construction what misconceptions, great ideas, or dead ends inhibited or contributed to each team's mathematical understanding. The teachers acknowledged a need for a broader view of assessment that would provide a better integration of assessment with instruction.

Conclusions

The similarity of teachers' conceptions, construction of mathematical models, and reflective comments about the experience by teachers from two different cultures, using different languages, in different settings, illustrates the robustness of this experience. The workshops provided a way for teachers to participate in a new approach to instruction and assessment, and then took advantage of that common experience to confront their conceptions about using such performance assessment activities in their own classrooms. While we do not claim that the experiences described in this chapter entirely reshaped the teachers' conceptions, there is evidence that some of their conceptions were challenged. The time for reflection and discussion encouraged the teachers to think about their conceptions with respect to their direct experience with the performance assessment activities. Inservice teacher education that provides experiences to do, reflect, and discuss new approaches to instruction and assessment are a step in the right direction for challenging and reshaping teachers' conceptions of mathematics, instruction, and assessment.

Note

1   The Delaware Teacher Enhancement Partnership was funded by NSF grant number TPE9155307.

References

AICHELE, D.B. and CASTLE, K. (1994) 'Professional development and teacher autonomy', in AICHELE, D.B. and COXFORD, A.F. (eds) *Professional Development for Teachers of Mathematics* (pp. 1–8), Reston, VA: National Council of Teachers of Mathematics.

AMIT, M. and HILLMAN, S. (1995) 'Remodeling mathematics teachers' conceptions using performance assessment activities', in SLOYER, C., BLUM, W. and HUNTLEY, I. (eds) *Advances and Perspectives on the Teaching of Mathematical Modelling and Applications* (pp. 107–17), Yorklyn, DE: Water Street Mathematics.

BURKHARDT, H. (1981) *The Real World and Mathematics*, London: Blackie and Son Limited.

DE LANGE, J. (1987) *Mathematics, Insight and Meaning: Teaching, Learning and Testing of Mathematics for the Life and Social Sciences*, Utrecht: Rijksuniversiteit Utrecht.

FOSNOT, C.T. (1989) *Enquiring Teachers, Enquiring Learners: A Constructivist Approach for Teaching*, New York: Teachers College Press.

KATIMS, N., LESH, R., HOLE, B., HOOVER, M. and TOCCI, C. (1995) *The PACKETS®program: Performance Assessment for Middle School Mathematics*, Lexington, MA: D.C. Heath.

KATIMS, N., NASH, P. and TOCCI, C. (1993) 'Linking instruction and assessment in a middle school mathematics classroom', *Middle School Journal*, November, pp. 28–35.

KULM, G. (1991) 'New directions for assessment', in KULM, G. (ed.) *Assessing Higher Order Thinking in Mathematics* (pp. 71–8), Washington, D.C.: American Association for the Advancement of Science.

LESH, R. and AKERSTROM, M. (1982) 'Applied problem solving: Priorities for mathematics education research', in LESTER, F. and GAROFALO, J. (eds) *Mathematical Problem Solving: Issues in Research* (pp. 117–29), Philadelphia: The Franklin Institute Press.

LESH, R. and LAMON, S. (1992) 'Assessing authentic mathematical performance', in LESH, R. and LAMON, S. (eds) *Assessment of Authentic Performance in School Mathematics* (pp. 17–62), Washington, D.C.: American Association for the Advancement of Science.

NATIONAL COUNCIL OF TEACHERS OF MATHEMATICS (1989) *Curriculum and Evaluation Standards for School Mathematics*, Reston, VA: National Council of Teachers of Mathematics.

NATIONAL COUNCIL OF TEACHERS OF MATHEMATICS (1991) *Professional Standards for Teaching Mathematics*, Reston, VA: National Council of Teachers of Mathematics.

NATIONAL COUNCIL OF TEACHERS OF MATHEMATICS (1995) *Assessment Standards for School Mathematics*, Reston, VA: National Council of Teachers of Mathematics.

THOMPSON, A. (1985) 'Teachers' conceptions of mathematics and the teaching of problem solving', in SILVER, E.A. (ed.) *Teaching and Learning Mathematical Problem Solving: Multiple Research Perspectives* (pp. 281–94), Hillsdale, NJ: Lawrence Erlbaum Associates.

ZIMMERMANN, J. (1992) *Performance Assessment. Education Research Consumer Guide, 2*, Washington D.C.: Office of Educational Research and Improvement, U.S. Department of Education.

3   The Institute for the Learning and Teaching of Mathematics

A.I. Weinzweig, USA

Introduction

The Institute for the Learning and Teaching of Mathematics is located at the University of Illinois in Chicago. Chicago is a large city with a diverse population — culturally, ethnically, racially and economically. This diversity is reflected in the schools. Most teachers' major experience of a classroom is that of a transmission line where the teacher is the center, the source of knowledge that is to be transmitted to the students, and the students are passive receivers. The initial objective of the Institute, then, was to provide teachers with the opportunity to experience mathematics as an activity, something you do rather than something you learn, a way of thinking, and a way of looking at and solving problems. We believed that we must present mathematics to teachers so that problem-solving and mathematical thinking are integral components of concept development. If teachers are to recognize that there are many problems in mathematics that have more than one answer and usually many different paths to arriving at an answer, then they need to meet problems of this nature. We must provide them with experiences in problem-solving that require them to use all of their mathematical resources, including executive control and other metacognitive skills. If we want them to understand how children learn and how that learning can be facilitated, we must give them a context to observe these processes in action. Moreover, if we want them to adopt a classroom model different from the transmission model then we must provide them with the experience of the classroom as a dynamic learning environment involving the interaction of three interrelated components — the learner, what is to be learned, and the learning facilitator. They must understand: how learning takes place; mathematics, the nature of the content under study; and how the learning of the mathematics is facilitated. This can only be achieved by experience, in the context of developing and doing mathematics.

School principals were asked to solicit volunteers for the Institute from among their teachers and recommend a minimum of three so that they could support each other in their efforts to effect change. The involvement of the principal was important so that she or he would have a stake in the outcome. The city of Chicago is divided into 20 elementary school districts. From 10 of these we chose one school. Within each school, three teachers — one from the early grades, one from the middle grades and one from the upper grades — became part of the study. In this way, 30 teachers were chosen out of 400 applicants. For the most part, these teachers were from inner-city schools with many minority students, and with many students from families below the poverty level who were achieving poorly. We believed that the changes in the practice of participating teachers induced by the Institute would result in improvement in the attitudes, motivation and achievements of their students. It was our hope that this would entice other teachers in that school to participate in similar programs — a hope that was born out.

Underlying Perspectives

Concepts in mathematics arise within a specific context in response to a particular recurring problem situation. The recurring nature of the problem situation makes it useful to seek a more effective technique for dealing with it. To this end, we create or invent a concept. It is essential to communicate about the problem and about the solution and for this we need language, both written and spoken, and terminology.[1] To deal effectively usually involves determining the outcome of a certain action without actually carrying out the action. For example, I have a bag of cookies and would like to give one to each child in a room. If I start distributing the cookies and run out of cookies before I run out of children, I will have an extremely unpleasant social condition on my hands. How can I determine what would happen if I distribute the cookies without actually distributing them?[2] I could determine the outcome by counting the children, counting the cookies and comparing the number of children to the number of cookies. If the number of children does not exceed the number of cookies, I can safely distribute one cookie to each child.

Once a concept has been developed, we often broaden the scope of applicability of the concept to apply to new situations, that is, we generalize. Subsequently several different concepts are subsumed under a new, single, more abstract concept, one level removed from the original contexts. This is the process of abstraction.

As we move up a level of abstraction, we move further away from the contexts that initially gave rise to the concept. This process of generalization and abstraction continues — the more abstract, the further removed from any context. Eventually, this leads to an abstract, context-free concept. The mathematical notions of number in general and rational numbers in particular are examples of such context-free concepts. The power of mathematics stems to a large extent from this abstraction — the development of these context-free concepts. A problem in one context can be formulated in terms of the context-free concepts and then shifted down to another, more familiar context and there solved. The solution can be reformulated in terms of the context-free concept and then shifted back down to the original context. This is the process of modelling.

Mathematics educators and teachers tend to view mathematics in terms of these context-free formulations of the concepts, as a mathematician might view them, as something that exists outside the child and must somehow or other be ingested by the child. The use of different embodiments to assist the child's learning of a concept implies that the concept already exists and must be learned rather than constructed. Moreover, we experience these concepts in different contexts and as adults are often unaware of their differences in different contexts. Children are very aware of these differences and are confused when teachers seem to imply that there are no differences.

It is our view that children do not receive a concept from without, but construct it from within. Each child must reinvent the wheel. This is a manageable task because it occurs in a milieu in which wheels are used everywhere. Experiences alone are not enough. These must be focused. In much the same way, teachers must be given the opportunity to experience this construction of knowledge.

Our approach has been to focus on what mathematics a child can learn and how we can help this learning. It begins with a careful analysis of some concept or process that we would like children to learn, not from the perspective of the mathematician, but from the primitives of the child. In the analysis of the concept, we ask: Why was this concept invented? What kind of problem situations gave rise to this concept? How is it used? Once this analysis has been completed and these questions answered, the next step is to create a suitable problem situation. This must be interesting to the student, and the student must have the necessary tools to deal with it. It should not be a single problem but a field of problems with connections to other problems. During the course of working in groups on the problem situation they discuss improvements and refinements of their solutions and in this way construct the concept. Determining appropriate problem situations is not a trivial task and should not be done in a vacuum. The ones used in the Institute were developed in collaboration with teachers and children over many years.

Background

The Institute, which ran for five years, with a different group of teachers each year, met for three weeks in the summer, every day, all day, and then for one evening a month during the school year. One of the main features of the Institute was that teachers became active participants in the process of constructing knowledge rather than passive recipients of knowledge. They were challenged with problem situations on which they worked in small collaborative groups. The role of the instructor was not to transmit knowledge, but to create opportunities for the teachers to construct their own knowledge together, to encourage them to think, to question their hypotheses and conjectures, and to make them confront the consequences of their reasoning. These problem situations usually were presented as a group activity and were designed to provide a context for the development of specific concepts by providing a need for and application of the concept and to establish connections between different concepts.

On the completion of an activity, the dynamics of what occurred were discussed as a whole group. This provided an opportunity for the teachers to confront and articulate their own feelings during the course of the activity, and to think about their own thinking as well as the dynamics of the group process. It also provided a context to discuss various theories of learning and teaching that were relevant to that activity. Specific events or actions were brought out to illustrate the theories.

The participants voiced their concerns, raised objections, and asked questions. They argued about the different theories and the research, but in doing so they confronted and modified their own beliefs and ideas about mathematics and the learning and teaching of mathematics. They had an opportunity to do mathematics and to experience collaborative problem-solving. They discovered that often they were able to synthesize collaboratively a solution to a difficult problem that none of them could solve separately. This experience enabled them to participate in solving more complex and interesting problems that were nevertheless within their 'zone of proximal development' (Vygotsky, 1978). Above all, they experienced the learning of mathematics in a context that we wanted them to practice — they experienced mathematics as ideas to be applied in specific situations to solve problems. They ended up seeing mathematics not as a discrete sequence of topics, but as a dynamic network of interconnected ideas. They discovered the complexity of the mathematical ideas that even a young child must confront and learn.

Ideas generated in the project were immediately applied in their classrooms during the school year. We received many reports from the participants that their students looked forward to the day after our classes since their teacher brought back new and interesting activities. Another important outcome of the project has been the collegiality fostered among the participants. This has led to an informal network among 'graduates' of the project that has served as an effective peer support group. The original objective of the program was to improve and deepen their understanding of the mathematics they were teaching. However, another important outcome turned out to be the changes in their attitudes, fears, and beliefs towards mathematics. They were surprised to discover that not only could they understand mathematics, but they could have fun actively doing mathematics.

The Problem Situations

The problem situations or case studies were an integral component of the project. For the most part, they were based upon our work with children, pre-teachers and teachers. Some of these provide a specific context from which a network of concepts can arise. The problem situations or case studies involve a sequence of activities to engage the participants in the construction of knowledge that is really new to them. In many instances these concepts involve 'familiar material' that they think they know. In the course of the activity, teachers deepen their understanding in a non-threatening, supportive atmosphere. They experience the active construction of knowledge. In the discussion that follows each activity, the teachers become aware of how much more effective it is for children also to engage in the construction of their knowledge rather than to have it told to them.

In other problem situations the main focus is on the complexities of a particular concept from the point of view of the child. These are particularly important for 'simple' concepts like counting, addition, and subtraction where prospective teachers feel their knowledge is adequate. They provide an opportunity to point out some of the informal knowledge that children bring with them when they begin formal schooling, and to discuss relevant research.

An Example

The following case-study problem situation allows the participants to discover connections between seemingly unrelated mathematical concepts and to realize the problems that children encounter when learning these same concepts.

> *The product of the ages of a group of teenagers is 649,967,409,000. How many teenagers are there of each age?*

The problem is presented to the whole class, but they are expected to work in collaborative groups. The activity of a typical group is discussed below. Their first response is complete bafflement; they have no idea where to begin. The instructor rarely answers questions directly, but asks other questions to focus the group's activities. After some discussion, someone observes that the number ends with three zeros. What significance, if any, does this have? The zero at the end indicates that 10 is a factor. Is 10 a teen age? This raises a question as to what is a teenager. Is a 13-year-old a teenager? (This provides an opportunity to focus attention on the importance of definitions in mathematics.) In the context of this discussion they become more aware of what it means to understand a problem, and of the importance of the language in a problem. The term 'teenager', in the English language, often refers to a behavior or maturity level of adolescents, rather than a chronological age which is the meaning intended in the problem. It is just this sort of situation which often arises and impedes understanding of 'word' problems. After some discussion, they understand that the ages of the individuals in the group can only be 13, 14, 15, 16, 17, 18 or 19 — these are the teen ages. Ten is not a teen age. What, then, is the significance of the fact that 10 is a factor? (We have noticed that novice problem-solvers initially disregard this helpful information.) After further discussion, someone recognizes that since 10 is a factor of the product, 5 must also be a factor of the product. However, since the given number is a product of teen ages, 5 must therefore be a factor of one of the teen ages. The only teen age with 5 as a factor is 15. Hence 15 must be one of the factors of the product, and so there must be a 15-year-old in the group. At this point, someone will usually observe that there are three factors of 10 so there must be three 15-year-olds. They soon realize that dividing 649,967,409,000 by 15 will, in effect, eliminate one 15-year-old and yield the product of the ages of remaining youths in the group. However, since there are at least three 15-year-olds in the group (three factors of 10) it would be better to divide by 15.15.15 and remove all the 15-year-olds from the product. 'Can we use a calculator?' is always asked. The answer is always affirmative; however, they soon recognize that most calculators will handle only 8 digits, but the number to be divided has 12 digits. They carry out the division by hand and conclude that the product of the ages of the remaining teenagers is 192,582,936. Can there be any more 15-year-olds? Only if 5 and 3 are factors. Since the last digit is neither a 5 nor a 0, 5 is not a factor. Someone observes that this number is even and divisible by 9 — using the sum of the digits test for divisibility by 9^3 — so that 18 is a factor and there is an 18-year-old in the group. Dividing by 18 we get 10,699,052. This is not divisible by 3. Where does this leave us? There can be no 15-year-olds and no more 18-year-olds, since these are the only teen ages divisible by 3. That leaves the possibility of 13- , 14- , 16- , 17- , and 19-year-olds. At this point, they use a calculator to complete the problem.

Another collaborative group took a different approach. They divided the original number by 1000 and then tried to factor the quotient without recognizing that 27 must also be a factor. Another group tried to divide the original number by 13, 14, 15, etc., and solve the problem by brute force. Yet another group obtained the prime factorizations by dividing by 2, 3, 5, etc. — $2^3 3^5 5^3 7^2 13^2 17^1 19^1$. From this they recognized that 16 is not one of the factors. Combining two of the 2s with four of the 3s gives two teen age factors of 18. This leaves one 3 and three 5s. However the 5s must be multiplied with 3s (as 15 is the only teen age with 5 as a factor). They have now arrived at a dead end. This led to a discussion of a better strategy. Someone suggested that they should get rid of the 7s first. The only way to get a teen age with 7 is to multiply it with 2. This yields two 14-year-olds and uses up two of the 2s. Similarly, the 5s will only occur as factors of 15 and must be multiplied with 3s. This gives three 15-year-olds and uses up three of the 3s. The two remaining 3s must then be combined with the remaining 2 to yield an 18-year-old, leaving two 13-year-olds, one 17-year-old and one 19-year-old.

In the discussion that follows they are surprised to discover that although they knew all the necessary mathematics, there was no obvious formula or rule that they could use and there were several different ways to solve the problem. This is an experience of mathematics that is in great contrast to anything in their background. At this point we encourage them to discuss their fears and apprehensions at the beginning of the activity and how convinced they were that they could not solve the problem. They get very excited over the fact that they did solve it. Although their initial apprehension was a familiar experience, the excitement of solving an unusual problem is a new and exhilarating one. They are amazed to realize how little it took to get them on the road to a solution once they understood the significance of the zero at the end. Most were surprised at how many different ways there were to solve this problem and discovered, from their own experience, what problem-solving is about.

This problem presents an opportunity to bring together a number of mathematical concepts and provides a context for them to practice and understand these important concepts. It makes them aware of some simple number theory and how it can be used. They become conscious of connections between what they know and how to use it. Above all, they have experienced problem-solving and mathematical thinking.

Integral to this case study is what is often referred to as 'looking back' — often overlooked by teachers. Our approach stresses this 'post mortem' stage of problem-solving. This not only makes the participants better problem-solvers, but also makes them better teachers by providing a shared experience to facilitate group examination of learning and teaching issues. Problems are often revisited, generalized, and extended.

An extension appropriate for many elementary school students, is to revisit the problem of dividing a 12 digit number, 649,967,409,000 by 3375 (= 15.15.15) on an 8 digit (or even a 4 digit) calculator. If one understands long division (as opposed to being proficient in doing long division) then one can use the calculator.

Conclusion

It is difficult to measure the impact of such a project for ultimately we need to assess the change in classroom behavior of the participating teachers, or, even more importantly, any improvement in the achievements of the students in their classes. One indication of success is that half of the teachers who participated wrote competitive proposals and received grants from the State of Illinois to purchase manipulative materials for their schools. Many developed the confidence to become involved in the State and the National Council of Teachers of Mathematics, as participants, presiders and presenters. Many went on to become mathematics specialists, conducting inservice programs in their schools and districts. Most importantly, having discovered that they can do mathematics and that they enjoyed doing it, they demanded additional opportunities to learn more mathematics. This led to the development of additional courses within the Mathematics Department, specifically geared to the needs of elementary school mathematics teachers. This demand was a key factor in ultimately creating a Master of Science in Teaching Mathematics Program for elementary school teachers. Approximately 70 per cent of the participants in the Institute for the Learning and Teaching of Mathematics completed this MST program.

Notes

1   We feel that this question of language, often overlooked, is of crucial importance in the learning of mathematics. Failure to deal with this question often leads to serious obstacles in learning.
2   Implicit in this is that there is a well-determined outcome independent of the way that the cookies are distributed. Thus, if all the children line up randomly, or according to some algorithm — such as alphabetically, or girls first, etc. — before I distributed the cookies, the result would be the same. For very young children this fact is not obvious and is of course related to what Piaget refers to as conservation of number.
3   This provides an opportunity to discuss divisibility rules and why they work.

Reference

VYGOTSKY, L.S. (1978) *Mind in Society: The Development of the Higher Psychological Processes*, London: Harvard University Press

4   Teachers' Mathematical Experiences as Links to Children's Needs

Hanlie Murray, Alwyn Olivier, and Piet Human,
South Africa

Circumstances have forced us to design a two-day workshop programme for teachers with very weak mathematical backgrounds and very rigid and instrumental perceptions of the nature of mathematics and mathematics teaching. The two-day time limit arose from the education authorities' unwillingness to allow teachers more than two days' absence from school even for official workshops, and teachers' disinclination to attend longer workshops during their holidays. The aim of such a workshop is both to change these perceptions in teachers and to equip teachers for radically different classroom practice in line with their new perceptions. The technique of posing problems that are challenging to the teachers themselves and then encouraging reflection on their experiences has proved to provide a driving force and a network of connections that enable us to cover a number of major issues in a limited time.

Introduction

There are different ways in which an inservice programme may attempt to address these two issues, depending on which perceptions and which skills are addressed. We believe that, for mathematics teachers from kindergarten to 12th grade, the perceptions that radically influence their classroom practice concern:

- the nature of mathematics;
- the way mathematics is both learnt and applied in life;
- children's mathematical thinking;
- the aims of school mathematics;
- how children best learn mathematics, given particular aims.

The necessary skills are clearly those that enable the teacher to create and sustain on a daily basis the learning environment which will support the type of learning in children the teacher has come to accept as desirable.

Our own perspectives of the above matters are based on a socio-constructive view of knowledge, and on our continuing research into young children's thinking and on environments which seem to support their thinking. We try to implement these ideas in the classroom through a problem-centred approach to mathematics

learning and teaching, where students are presented with problems that are meaningful to them but which they cannot solve with ease using routinized procedures,
and where students are expected to discuss, critique, explain and justify their interpretations and strategies (Murray, Olivier and Human, 1993).

Inservice programmes with views similar to ours on mathematics education
may use a particular technique as part of their programmes: such programmes
expose teachers to doing mathematics at their own level in the hope that this will
encourage teachers to reflect on the nature of mathematics and mathematics learning (e.g. Davidson, Weisglass and Robertson, 1990; Simon and Schifter, 1991; Hadar
and Hadass, 1990; Corwin, 1993). However, much like the Educational Leaders in
Mathematics (ELM) Project (Simon and Schifter, 1991), we take it one step further:
we actively use the mathematical experiences to which we expose teachers as the
core around which we construct the rest of the programme. Because of practical
considerations, the format for inservice programmes which is usually requested by
teachers and school principals has been a two-day workshop, in some cases with
the expectations from both teachers as well as supervisors (school principals included)
that such a workshop should bring about not only a paradigm shift in the teachers'
perceptions about learning and teaching, but also equip the teacher to establish and
maintain on a daily basis a completely different classroom culture.

Although we therefore use techniques that are common to other inservice programmes, we labour under a severe time constraint, which makes essential careful
selection of the main issues to be covered and the most economical way in which
they can be covered. For the purposes of this paper, we limit our discussion to two-
day inservice workshops for lower elementary teachers with a very low perception
of their own mathematical abilities, and indeed only limited skills and little explicit
understanding of basic whole number arithmetic. Where knowledge has been retained
in a formalized fashion by some teachers, it is mostly of a highly instrumental nature.

It could be anticipated that these teachers would find it even more problematic
to broaden their perceptions about the nature of mathematics and how mathematics
is learnt than better educated teachers, yet this is only partly the case, as we shall
indicate later. It is, however, the case that the time constraint has a much more severe
(and negative) impact on these teachers than on other teacher groups, mainly because
more time has to be spent on basic teaching skills such as classroom organization
and making workcards.

The workshop format that we use at present has remained constant for the past
six workshops of this type, and has provided us with valuable insights. We shall,
however, have to start planning inservice programmes that are less dependent on
a particular workshop presenter and that can easily and safely be expanded to reach
larger numbers of teachers.

Organizational Information

Each workshop runs for two consecutive days from 8am to 3.15pm, with breaks for
tea and lunch. The number of participants has varied from 34 to 47, and consisted

mainly of K-3 teachers, with a sprinkling of upper elementary teachers who function as subject heads for mathematics. Most of the teachers had only had school mathematics up to 9th grade, and some had left school after 10th grade. They all had at least a three-year teachers' diploma. During their school and college years they had been exposed to quite rigidly traditional views of mathematics as a series of set formulae which had to be memorized and then applied to the appropriate word problems. Although it appeared during the workshops that, especially, the K-3 teachers possessed strong intuitive powers for solving problems they could not identify as school-type problems, these thinking skills had never been sanctioned. Initially most teachers were embarrassed to explain their reasoning processes, saying that their strategies were not mathematically 'correct'.

One advantage is that with this group of teachers we were only dealing with K-3 mathematics, and we have much anecdotal evidence from other K-3 teachers who found that their own number sense and general arithmetic skills developed simultaneously with those of their students when they started to follow a problem-centred approach to mathematics teaching and learning. For the K-3 workshop, therefore, we believe that it is sufficient to attempt only the following:

1. Addressing teachers' perceptions about the nature of mathematics and how mathematics is learnt and practised (used).
2. Addressing teachers' perceptions about their own mathematical abilities and how they (can) do mathematics.
3. Describing and justifying a problem-centred approach to mathematics learning and teaching.
4. Sharing information on some basic guidelines for establishing a problem-centred learning environment in the classroom. This includes dealing with matters that are seldom perceived as issues in classrooms where transmission-type teaching is the norm, but which in our longitudinal research have shown to be crucial for problem-centred classrooms.

According to our basic technique of providing teachers with their own mathematical experiences, the activities that address teachers' personal views (points 1 and 2 above) also supply us with direct links to children's thinking and children's needs (which we present by means of many examples of children's work and videos of children solving computational problems), which lead directly to points 3 and 4. We now briefly elaborate on the main ideas to be covered under points 3 and 4.

A Problem-centred Approach

In brief, the approach implies that the teacher regularly (i.e. on most days) poses problems to her students that they do not experience as routine problems and that they cannot solve with ease. Students are expected to construct solution methods for the problems with the tools that they have available (theorems in action, number knowledge at different levels of development). Students are also expected to share ideas, to discuss, justify and explain among themselves. Although students may (and should) experience classroom events as informal and child-centred, the teacher has to plan the classroom activities and tasks in accordance with a simple but important set of guidelines that we have been able to formulate through monitoring the development of students' computational strategies in selected classrooms over the past nine years (e.g. Murray, Olivier and Human, 1994).

The guidelines consist of:

- Certain simple but powerful activities that help students to develop a flexible number knowledge, which directly influences the solution methods they construct.
- A variety of word problems that suggest different computational methods — if some problem-types are omitted, certain methods may not be constructed. Teachers therefore choose their word problems from a list of basic problem-types so that the different meanings of the four basic operations and fractions are all covered.
- Students mainly learn through voluntary interaction with each other, and not through listening to the teacher, but the teacher has to know that social-type information still has to be supplied to her students (e.g. recording skills, and knowledge involving the measurements). The ability to distinguish between the logic of a solution method and the way in which it is recorded is essential for a teacher.

The Problems Posed to Teachers in the Workshops

When we use the teachers' own mathematical experiences and their reflections on these experiences as a laboratory to provide clues to (or empathy with) children's needs, the basic assumption is that adults' and young children's responses to novel mathematical situations are sufficiently similar to use in such a way. Simon and Schifter (1991) state this categorically: 'Teachers' learning can be viewed in much the same way as mathematics students' learning' (p. 312). Although we accept this as probably generally true, it is clear from experience that teachers (and other adults) only respond in ways that can be used as departure points for children's thinking when the mathematical problems posed are of such a type that the adults involved cannot solve them automatically (or mechanically), but actually have to construct solution strategies for them.

The choice of problem for a particular audience is therefore crucial. It is important that the problem situation makes sense, even though it may be ambiguous (this is referred to later). We have never used a puzzle-type problem or investigations, since we do not know whether a situation that has no clear connection with any syllabus content will have the same powerful effect on the teachers. We know of inservice programmes where investigations have been used very effectively, but the informal lore among the teachers themselves has it that when teachers only experience enjoyment with problems that they do not relate to a syllabus, they view these experiences as add-ons, 'something you do every Friday'. We cannot afford this to happen, since there is no time to correct this impression.

Furthermore, it should be possible to solve at least the initially posed problem(s) by direct modelling — i.e. by drawing or a sketch — because direct modelling enables a person to easily resolve an incorrect choice of a drilled method at a deep level. At this stage in the workshop, a logical refutation only serves to strengthen existing beliefs about the nature of mathematics! It should be kept in mind that the problems used create powerful situations only because they suit these particular audiences and other audiences will need other problems.

An Example to Show How Problems are Used

In the workshop, the problem is always presented to the group as a whole. Teachers are encouraged to consult with each other, to leave their seats and move around if needed. The presenter moves around, trying to maintain a very low profile, but identifying a variety of different conceptualizations of the problem. Different teachers are then requested to explain on the overhead projector how they had conceptualized and then solved the problem. This is followed up with a general discussion, eliciting from the teachers the links that need to be established to future topics, or illuminating and emphasizing points that will be referred to again. It must be emphasized that these discussions are very thorough and that the teachers really share not only their mathematical thinking but also especially their feelings and fears; i.e. all the factors which could have inhibited or supported their thinking.

The Apple Tarts

> *Mrs Daku bakes small apple tarts. For each apple tart she uses $\frac{3}{4}$ of an apple. She has twenty apples. How many apple tarts can she bake?*

This is posed as the very first problem, immediately after the opening and welcome on the first day. The most common solution methods generated by the teachers are:

1. *Incorrect choice of a drilled method.*

    $20 * \frac{3}{4} = 15$

2. *Direct modelling of the situation.*

    Twenty apples are drawn and each is divided into $\frac{3}{4}$ and a $\frac{1}{4}$; the $\frac{3}{4}$ pieces are counted (giving twenty tarts), then the remaining quarters are grouped. Sometimes the remaining quarters are grouped into threes, giving another six tarts with two quarters left; sometimes the remaining quarters from each group of three apples are immediately dealt with.

    Lillian solves the problem in this way, having first reduced the problem to ten apples and afterwards doubling the answer.

Figure 4.1   *Lillian's approach*

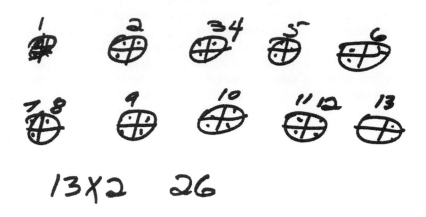

13X2   26

3.   *Numerical approaches which closely model the problem structure.*

Cassius: 'Twenty apples give me at least twenty tarts. With the twenty quarters I make five apples. Five apples give me at least five tarts. With the five quarters left I make one apple. There are two quarters left. I have twenty plus five plus one tarts, and half an apple left.'

Sibongile: 'Three apples give four tarts. How many groups of three in twenty? Six groups of three is eighteen. So eighteen apples is equal to 6 ∗ 4 tarts. That is twenty-four. There are two apples left. That's another two tarts and half an apple left.'

Beauty: 'I thought about the kitchen. First I cut all the apples into quarters and then I find out how many groups of three I can make. So I do 20 ∗ 4 = 80; 80 ÷ 3 = 26 remainder 2.'

Beauty knew she could make twenty-six tarts, but she needed prolonged discussion and an inspection of one of the direct modeler's drawings to decide what the remainder of two signified.

These discussions generate a great deal of excitement among the teachers, especially when they are informed that from the formal point of view the problem involves division with a fraction, which is only specified in the local 7th grade school syllabus. The following important perspectives arise naturally out of the whole episode:

1.   Attempts to classify the problem type and choose an operation made the problem more difficult for some teachers, and an incorrect choice of operation prevented some teachers from solving the problem. Teachers who simply responded to the structure of the problem itself and who tried to make sense of the situation, using the tools they had available and felt confident with, were invariably successful.

This very important perspective serves as a link to the next session during which examples of young children's responses to problems are studied, and comparisons made between the child's view and the adult's view of problems which seem quite routine to adults. Mistakes that children make when they feel forced to 'choose an operation and apply a procedure' are discussed extensively.

2.   The tools that were used to solve the problem are identified: a knowledge of fractions, of whole numbers and of some recording skill. This is elaborated on during a session where the development of young children's number concept is studied, and a practical demonstration, with some teachers acting as children, and videotaped classroom scenes give some ideas of suitable number concept development activities. The role of the teacher regarding the 'social knowledge' component of mathematics, and the development of communication skills, both verbal and written, are also discussed.

3.   The teachers are asked to reflect on how they went about solving the problem: when did they talk to one another, about what did they talk, what was the main effect of these discussions on their thinking processes and why, etc. These issues touch on the classroom culture, the didactical contract between teacher and students, the nature of knowledge and how knowledge is constructed (individually as well as socially), some characteristics of a good learning environment for mathematics, research-based information on young students' own perceptions of what constitutes a good learning environment, etc. These topics take up most of the morning of the second day, and four or five video episodes of children interacting are shown and discussed.

The other problems posed to the teachers in the course of the workshop introduce other important issues. A proportional sharing problem involving three workmen generates discussion on the role that the context of the word problem plays, as regards the ambiguity of interpretation, its influence on the level of complexity of the problem, etc. Teachers are asked to reflect on how students may respond to some word problems, and are then asked to make up word problems for particular problem types, keeping in mind variables that affect young children's understanding of a particular word problem. Consensus is reached that different cultures and different backgrounds should not be ignored in the mathematics classroom, but should actually be subjected to discussion. Other problems lead to the idea that children themselves can generate mathematical ideas that are sufficiently rich to initiate and support discussions about new topics, given appropriate problems to think about.

Evaluation

Free-format evaluations invited from teachers at the end of every workshop were unanimously positive and enthusiastic. Most of the teachers mentioned that they now 'knew where to begin' in their own classrooms, but that they desired a follow-up workshop in approximately six months' time. About 10 per cent of the teachers involved suggested that the workshop be spread over three days, not to deal with more issues but to give them more opportunity for discussion and reflection. About half the teachers responded in person as well, stating that the workshop was the most meaningful and radical training experience that they had ever had. We mentioned in the beginning that workshops with any chance of lasting influence probably need to address the two main issues of beliefs and skills. Since the teachers' free comments mentioned both these issues extensively, there is at least the possibility that the workshops were to some extent successful. It is, unfortunately, the case that no workshop can really be evaluated until its effects on classroom practice can be observed. Changed classroom practice is yet again heavily dependent not only on the quality of the workshops given, but also on factors like peer, principal and supervisor attitudes and support.

Conclusion

It has been proved possible to identify some problems which, when posed to teachers during a workshop, will supply them with mathematical experiences that can serve as links to both the basic principles of a problem-centred approach, as well as to the practicalities of classroom organization and the flow of classroom activities. The teacher's own experiences when solving problems can encourage reflection on what mathematics is, how mathematics-related learning takes place, and the factors that encourage or hinder such learning. These reflections can then help the teacher to understand his or her students' needs.

We would also like to draw attention to a point that we regard as potentially even more important than the above. It was stated earlier that these teachers perceived themselves as mathematically weak, and had been exposed to years of formalized mathematics instruction, and that it may be hypothesized that this background would make it more difficult for them to broaden their perspectives. It may be that these teachers actually respond very readily and at a very deep level to a workshop that is geared to providing them with personal experiences of their own thinking, sense-making abilities. We would therefore suggest that personal feelings of incompetence and anxiety which have been caused by formalist mathematics teaching may be turned to good account if handled correctly, and need not be a liability at all. We believe that these teachers can actually be brought to identify with and understand children's needs more deeply and truly during such a workshop than some of the more advantaged teachers.

Concluding on a personal note, we quote Marilyn, who at the beginning of the second day of a workshop, came up to the presenter and said with great excitement: 'I thought and thought right through the evening and almost couldn't sleep last night. I have learnt the one thing I think is the most important thing I have learnt as a teacher; that is that if you show somebody how to do a problem, you stop him thinking. This is what happened to my mathematics.'

Note

1   An earlier version of this paper was presented at the 1995 International Conference of the Psychology of Mathematics Education and can be found in the proceedings for that meeting.

References

CORWIN, R.B. (1993) 'Doing mathematics together: Creating a mathematical culture, *Arithmetic Teacher*, **40** n 6, pp. 338–41.

DAVIDSON, N., WEISGLASS, J. and ROBERTSON, L. (1990) 'Staff development for cooperative learning in mathematics', *Journal of Staff Development*, **11**, pp. 12–17.

HADAR, N.M. and HADASS, R. (1990) 'Preservice education of math teachers using paradoxes', *Educational Studies in Mathematics*, **21**, pp. 265–87.

MURRAY, H., OLIVIER, A., and HUMAN, P. (1993) 'Voluntary interaction groups for problem-centered learning', in HIRABAYASHI, I., NOHDA, N., SHIGEMATSU, K. and LIN, F. (eds) *Proceedings of the Seventeenth International Conference for the Psychology of Mathematics Education, Vol. 2*, (pp. II-73–II-80), Tsukuba, Japan: Psychology of Mathematics Education.

MURRAY, H., OLIVIER, A. and HUMAN, P. (1994) 'Fifth graders' multi-digit multiplication and division strategies after five years' problem centered learning', in DA PONTE, J.P. and MATOS, J.F. (eds) *Proceedings of the Eighteenth International Conference for the Psychology of Mathematics Education, Vol. 3*, (pp. 399–406), Lisbon, Portugal: Psychology of Mathematics Education.

SIMON, M. and SCHIFTER, D. (1991) 'Towards a constructivist perspective: An intervention study of mathematics teacher development', *Educational Studies in Mathematics*, **22**, pp. 309–31.

5   Inservice in Lebanon

Fairouz Farah-Sarkis, Lebanon

With increased pressure for educational reform, and with more emphasis on teachers' roles, additional attention has been given to teacher education as a field of study. While several studies investigated teachers' beliefs and its effects on their practices, more work is needed to be done on methods that help teachers reflect on their practice. As Yackel (1994) stated, '. . . a first priority when working with teachers is to help them become aware of and make problematic aspects of their current practice'. But to become reflective depends on many factors which are related not only to teachers' beliefs and conceptions but also to the teacher's educational background (i.e. university degree, pre- and inservice training), school pedagogical culture and the educational system as a whole. Ponte (1994) wrote, 'Beliefs and conceptions cannot be viewed as determining practice, since it is the nature of the social institutions in which we move — including schools — that mostly shapes them.' Thus designing inservice training programs that might help get teachers to reflect is not an easy task, particularly in pedagogical communities and school systems such as Lebanon which have restricted conceptions of mathematics teaching.

Educational System in Lebanon

The Lebanese educational system is influenced by the French one. As a result of reform in 1997, the educational ladder now includes five cycles: kindergarten (2 years), elementary (6 years, 2 cycles), intermediate (3 years), and secondary (3 years). At the end of the intermediate cycle, students take the Brevet official exam which is a prerequisite to get into the secondary school. Three years later, i.e. at the end of the secondary cycle, students take the Baccalaureate exam which is a prerequisite for entering a university. The five cycles are subject to a national curriculum prepared by the Ministry of Education. The present curriculum has been used since 1970. It included a great deal of modern mathematics as defined in 1970. A new curriculum will be implemented in the school year 1998–99. The new curriculum has deleted modern mathematics topics, especially at the intermediate level, and introduced new topics such as statistics, calculator use and a new approach for dealing with geometry.

Teachers' Qualifications

In the public schools, requirements for full-time teaching at the intermediate and secondary levels is a university degree with a teaching diploma, while for teaching at the elementary level, a high school certificate is enough plus one year of preservice training. On the other hand, in the private schools where students' enrolment is 60 per cent of the total student population, no restrictions are made on the qualifications of teachers. However, most intermediate and secondary school teachers in private schools either hold a university degree or have done one or two years of university work. Many secondary teachers work part time in several schools so as to augment their income.

Preservice Training

Teacher training institutions in the country are attached mainly to universities and colleges except for the Center for Educational Research and Development (CERD). CERD is a state center for preparing teachers for the elementary and intermediate levels in the public schools. There are also some private institutes which offer two years of training after grade 10 level for those who intend to become elementary school teachers.

The program of preservice training in the universities comprises theoretical and practical parts with more weight given to the theoretical part. In fact, the number of hours spent in class observation by student-teachers in the entire preservice training program ranges between 15–30 hours while the number of teaching hours does not exceed 10 at its best. There is one state university which is tuition free, while the rest are private universities and colleges with relatively high tuition fees. The high fees means that the majority of teachers, especially at the secondary level, work in private schools without preservice training. As for the elementary teacher training institutes, though the tuition fees are not high, the quality of training is quite poor since most trainers are not qualified for the job. As a result, most mathematics teachers at the different levels are in need of training.

Inservice Training

Inservice training of mathematics teachers in Lebanon started in the early 1970s when modern mathematics was introduced to the Lebanese schools. Training programs at that time focused on the subject matter area which was mainly set theory and algebraic structure. The target groups were intermediate and elementary mathematics teachers. It was assumed that most secondary mathematics teachers had taken modern mathematics in their university programs. The war broke out in the mid-1970s and all inservice training in the public schools stopped until quite recently. During this period a few private educational institutes took the responsibility of inservice training but their target was mainly the elementary school teachers with little emphasis on training intermediate and secondary school teachers.

With the end of the war, more emphasis is now being put on inservice training on the different cycles and especially by the private schools. With respect to inservice strategies, teachers were in two groups: intermediate and secondary teachers in one group; and elementary teachers in the other.

Intermediate and Secondary School Teachers

Teachers' concerns in this group were to have their students pass the official exams because the results of these exams reflect on their career opportunities (average success in the Brevet exam is 45 per cent while for the Baccalaureate exam is 30 per cent). Unfortunately teachers in this group believe that there is no need to obtain pedagogical knowledge in order to become effective teachers. Rather, they believe that a good command of subject matter is enough. According to them, the constraints of the syllabus do not allow for the activities suggested by educational specialists. 'There is no time for group activity or inquiry based activity,' some teachers declared. They added that these activities are probably better for lower level classes.

In terms of their attitude towards inservice training, teachers could be classified into two subgroups. There were those with long years of teaching experience who were extremely comfortable with their practice, and who believed that knowledge of the subject matter area is all that they need. The second subgroup were novices who thought that they needed some guidance in classroom management but, like their colleagues in the other subgroup, viewed subject matter knowledge as a priority for inservice training programs. In fact, the results of a study carried out by the author in 1997 on ranking the qualifications of a good mathematics teacher showed that 80 per cent of teachers viewed subject matter knowledge as first rank.

One successful strategy used that appealed to both subgroups, and initiated them into reflection on their own practice, was to begin inservice sessions with tasks related to subject matter area which required the teachers either to solve non-standard problems or to answer in-depth questions on mathematical concepts. Such type of tasks put teachers in student-like situations and helped them realize the importance of pedagogical knowledge in teaching. Below are some examples of non-standard problems:

1. ABC is an acute triangle. On its sides draw equilateral triangles BCE, ACD and ABF. Show that DB = CF = AE.

Such a problem is at the level of 3rd intermediate, i.e., students aged 13–14, yet many teachers were unable to identify quickly the pair of congruent triangles with BD and CF as corresponding sides.

2. Given a triangle ABC with points P, Q, and R on sides AC, AB and BC such that these points are collinear, show that $(AQ\backslash QB)(BR\backslash RC)(CP\backslash PA) = 1$

In the above problem many teachers did not think to draw the auxiliary line BD parallel to AC.

As for understanding in such a way as to be able to teach the necessary basic features of a concept, one would expect a deficiency because teachers' knowledge of the mathematical concept was acquired through university study of mathematics which is not oriented towards the teaching of the concept. Hence, some aspects of the concept were not dealt with adequately. Presenting trainee teachers with in-depth questions about the mathematical concepts taught at the high school level always engaged the student teacher, and led to long and interesting discussions about methods of teaching the concept. Below are some examples:

1. Are all equations functions?

2. Are all functions equations?

3. Which of the following are transitive relations?

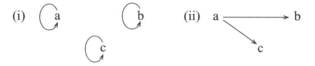

As I mentioned previously, high school teachers in general are not interested in training sessions about methodology. However, a strategy based on pedagogical knowledge was used successfully with several groups of these teachers. The strategy was based on student misconceptions of mathematical concepts. The training started with the work of the teachers' own pupils. Sources of pupils' misconceptions were identified by the teachers. In many cases the teachers realized that their teaching was a source of misconception. This in turn assisted in initiating teachers' reflections about their own practice. The following vignette provides a picture of how the inservice program took place.

The aim of the inservice program was to help teachers identify student difficulties in constructing proofs and to suggest ways that the difficulties might be remedied. The program took place over two days, with the first day focusing on sensitizing teachers to the difficulty in applying previous knowledge to new situations, i.e. to place them in a position much like that of their own students. The second day was devoted to having the teachers identify sources of difficulty in presenting proofs to their own students, aged 13–14. There were 25 teachers participating in the training program, and they taught at the grade 7–10 level. About half of them had teaching experience ranging between 15 and 20 years. Only 5 of the teachers had less than 5 years' teaching experience.

The first day began with a test of 12 items dealing with the four logical implications of $p \rightarrow q$. The items were given in 3 types of context: neutral, consistent and contrary to real life. An example of a neutral context is given below:

Premise 1: If the cup is blue, then the plate is white.

Premise 2: The plate is not white.

Question: Is the cup blue?

Possible Answers: Yes, No, Maybe Yes, Maybe No.

Most of the teachers were not able to answer correctly the converse and inverse items. After correcting their answers on the test items, each teacher was asked to write down one difficulty his/her students face in constructing proofs. Most of the teachers with long years of teaching experience claimed that their students did not have difficulty in constructing proofs. The newer teachers, however, admitted that students did find difficulty in planning a proof. 'They do not know where and how to start,' they said.

One teacher with 18 years' experience was asked to give an example of a geometry problem which students had not seen, and to explain how his students would go about constructing a proof for the problem. The teacher provided the following illustration. (The teacher knew that at this stage of the year students learn proofs about supplementary and complementary angles.)

> A, B, C, and D are four points on a line such that m AC = m DB. Show that AB & CD have the same midpoint.

The teacher gave the following proof. Suppose that I is the midpoint of AB, then

AI = IB
AC = DB
AI − AC = IB − DB
CI = DI
and hence I is the midpoint of CD

Below is the dialogue between the researcher (R) and the teacher (T).

R: If the student hasn't seen anything similar to this how would he think of making the supposition in the first place?
T: He would, there is no problem, he just looks at the figure.
R: How did the child think of subtracting?
T: I've told him: he looks at the figure.
R: Are you sure the student hasn't seen a similar problem before?
T: Yes.

Most experienced teachers agreed with their colleague. At this point, it was difficult to continue the discussion and the session, because though the teachers expressed interest in having new ideas for teaching, they considered that the discussion about proof was not worthwhile. A commitment was made by the researcher to present some ideas on teaching geometric locus the following day.

In an attempt to deal with the dilemma posed by the teachers wanting inservice, but not what was being presented, the researcher prepared four problems for the next day. The problems were at the age 14 level, and as far as could be ascertained none of them were in any textbooks used by or known to the teachers. The hope was that the problems would be new to them. Two of the problems follow:

1 Given a square with side 4 cm. A 3 cm line-segment moves inside the square so that its end points are always on the sides of the square. Construct the locus of the midpoint of the moving segment.
2 A goat is tied to a square shed of side 4m and height 3m with a rope 5m long. If the goat is tied at the middle of one side of the shed, what is the region over which the goat could move?

Editors' Comment

While the previous chapters focused on raising teachers' awareness of the processes involved in the formal activity of doing mathematics, and of students' informal methods, the next two chapters extend the discussion to address issues in teaching. In particular, these chapters begin to take into consideration the connection between teacher inservice education and change in practice.

Serrazina and Loureiro in Portugal focus on creating instructional activities involving manipulatives as a basis for teaching. After completing workshops in which teachers experienced using the innovative activities, they found few teachers using these activities in their classes. Investigating the classroom practice of two teachers who are successful in the use of manipulatives, they found teachers attempting to resolve new dilemmas created by the use of the innovative practices.

Markovits and Even in Israel elaborate on their attempts to develop teachers' pedagogical content knowledge of mathematics, using activities based on real or hypothetical classroom situations. By reflecting on such situations, teachers came to question their own practices, and to consider modifications to their practice.

These two chapters are the first in the series to grapple with the difficulties teachers face as they attempt to translate constructivist perspectives to their practice.

The teachers were extremely frustrated because none of them could easily solvs
problems. After giving them 10 minutes to think about each problem, hints
provided to assist in the solution of the problems. Finally, the teachers realizec
it is not easy for students to construct proofs if they haven't seen similar prot
before, or if they haven't been helped to develop strategies, or given guideline
might help them in constructing proofs. After this experience, the teachers
much more receptive to the training which had been planned for them. Indeed
teachers asked for more training sessions.

References

FARAH-SARKIS, F. (1997) *Teachers and Administrator Conceptions of Qualificati
    Good Teacher. Educational Research: Part 2*, Beirut, Lebanon: Institute for Ec
    Development.
PONTE, J.P. (1994) 'Mathematics teachers' professional knowledge', in PONTE
    MATOS, J.F. (eds) *Proceedings of the Eighteenth International Conference for ti
    logy of Mathematics Education*, Volume I, Lisbon, Portugal: PME, pp. 195-
YACKEL, E. (1994) 'School cultures and mathematics education reform', in PON1
    MATOS, J.F. (eds) *Proceedings of the Eighteenth International Conference for
    logy of Mathematics Education*, Volume IV (pp. 385–92), Lisbon, Portuga

6   Primary Teachers and the Using of Materials in Problem Solving in Portugal

Lurdes Serrazina and Cristina Loureiro, Portugal

Inservice Education for Primary Teachers in Portugal

The first cycle of basic education in Portugal, usually called primary school, includes grades 1–4 (children 6–10 years old). Primary teachers are global teachers; that is, they teach all the subjects. For most of them, their mathematics knowledge and their mathematics education are rather weak. Indeed a large number of these teachers did not have any mathematics education in their preservice courses. Only in 1976 was a new curriculum established in mainstream schools which included mathematics as a subject. So, a large percentage of present primary school teachers did not have any mathematics education in their preservice courses, and there has not been any systematic inservice education in recent years. Some studies suggest that a large number of primary school teachers teach in the same way as they were taught, with a great emphasis in paper and pencil computations (Fernandes, 1985).

There have been a few experiences that we think important to mention. Those experiences developed in the late 1980s and early 1990s and were influenced by several international documents such as the National Council of Teachers of Mathematics (NCTM) *Standards* in USA and the Cockcroft Report in England (Guimarães et al., 1993). In Portugal, the Association of Teachers of Mathematics (Associação de Professores de Mathématica or APM) carried out a seminar in 1988, about 'the renovation of the mathematics curriculum', from which a report was issued. The report included some guidelines about mathematics teaching, the APM's objectives and principles, and the role of technologies (APM, 1988).

Most teacher education in recent years has stressed the use of materials within a problem-solving approach. Usually, the tasks are solved in group work and discussed in a large group. Such tasks tend to be closely connected with the national mathematics curriculum, particularly after the curriculum revision of 1990. This methodology of work with teachers has been applied in several activities, namely in training sessions developed by PIPSE (Interministry Programme for Promoting School Success), the MINERVA Project, and APM.

PIPSE was developed throughout the country and aimed to: i) decrease the number of pupils who are not successful in primary school; and ii) to provide inservice teacher education opportunities to teachers. The MINERVA Project, run by the Minister of Education and higher education institutions from 1985–88, was concerned with the introduction of computers in pre-primary, primary and secondary schools.

It carried out teacher-training activities, but only a small number of primary schools were involved. Mathematics was given strong attention through the computer language, LOGO. The APM was founded in 1986. From the beginning it has been concerned with all school levels. There has been a group of primary teachers developing materials and working together. These teachers, sometimes with the collaboration of teacher educators, have carried out training sessions at regional meetings. Now, both the PIPSE programme and the MINERVA project have finished. APM continues to develop training activities for primary teachers with the outlined characteristics, but the number of primary teachers involved is still rather restricted.

The Project

In 1991, we started a project to foster the use of manipulative materials (such as Cuisenaire rods, geoboards, wooden cubes) in mathematics teaching. The project's work was based on the selection and development of problematic situations and related resource materials for 6- to 12-year-olds. We organized those situations into thematic units according to communication, organization, interpretation, understanding and reasoning issues. In order to assess the materials we carried out case studies which focused on teachers' attitudes to using the situations in the classroom.

Three main reasons led us to the development of this project. First, the lack of materials for mathematics teaching in the Portuguese language. Second, the use of materials and problem-solving was emphasized by the new curriculum. Third, in Portugal there were few research studies concerned with primary and middle school teachers and mathematics teaching.

The project team — three researchers and two teachers — worked together in order to prepare the materials. These consisted of sets of activities, usually formulated as problems. Each set was matched to a manipulative material or the calculator. The manipulative materials used were: Cuisenaire rods, geoboards, tangrams, multibase attribute blocks, wooden cubes, cube links, counting objects, tiles, polydrons, waste materials (boxes), measurement tools, dice and other random materials. One of our concerns was to use the same materials for different problems, and also to select problems which could be explored with different materials.

When we were selecting the problems, we wanted to focus on the kind of reasoning implicit in the situation, so we also decided to organize what we called 'teachers' notes', that is, suggestions of how the teachers could accomplish some aspects of the curriculum with those activities and how they could expand them. One group of materials was related to questions such as: What is a problem? Why should we solve problems? Which are the strategies to solve problems? We intended that the teachers should analyse and solve the problems in group work and discuss the answers to these questions.

To select teachers who would participate in the training sessions we asked for volunteers among members of the Association of Teachers of Mathematics. Thirty primary school teachers attended, but not all of them were members of APM. They carried out the activities with great enthusiasm during two days. They worked with manipulative materials and calculators, discussed with their colleagues and ana-lysed the 'teachers' notes'.

Three months later we sent out a questionnaire to the teachers. Our aim was to know how they were using the materials, to know if they were interested in a new teacher-training session, and to get an idea of future themes they would like to discuss. Visits and informal talks with primary school teachers complemented the responses from the questionnaire. With the data collected, we developed another group of materials. As a result of some suggestions from the teachers, the activities were organized around a theme of the national curriculum. Again, the activities were formulated as problems, dealing with measurements, data analysis, probability and statistics.

Another two-day session took place and once more the teachers participated with great enthusiasm. At this session, we were also able to evaluate how the teachers were using the first set of materials. We concluded that they were being used in different situations: some were using the materials with minor adaptations; others had picked up the ideas but, for several reasons, were working them in a different way; the majority had considered the activities very interesting but did not feel at ease to develop them in their classrooms.

During this process we chose a primary school to carry out a case study. This was a public school, from which two of the teachers had participated in the training programme. We already knew that these two teachers used manipulative materials in their classrooms, so the reasons why we decided to carry out the case study were: 1) to get more information about *how* they used the materials; 2) to understand how they adapted our proposals; and 3) to know how they managed their classrooms when they used manipulative materials. As we said earlier, there are few studies about Portuguese primary school teaching so we used this as an opportunity to gather some data about meaningful experiences of using manipulative materials in primary classrooms and some ideas to improve our proposals for use of materials and the way to disseminate them among primary Portuguese teachers.

The Case Study — School Context

The school we selected is a rural one located in the Lisbon district. It has five regular teachers and one support teacher. The school has 115 pupils divided among five classes, one of 1st grade (age 6), one of 2nd grade (age 7), two mixed 2nd/3rd grade (ages 7, 8) and one of 4th grade (age 9). A support teacher works with pupils with learning difficulties from all classes. In the Portuguese school system the same teacher teaches the same group of pupils from first to fourth grade, whenever possible. Sometimes, however, teachers are moved to other schools disturbing this process. As this school has five classes and only four rooms, two classes run in the same room, one in the morning and the other in the afternoon. Although the number of pupils has been decreasing every year, this is still a common situation in primary schools, whenever there are not enough rooms for all the classes.

The school is located in a small village. The teachers have a good relationship with parents and local authorities and there is collaboration among them. All the teachers are involved in school activities especially in extra-curricula activities, such as the kitchen garden, the traditional procession, out-of-school visits (zoo, museums, other cities in the country, etc.).

We observed the classes of the two teachers who participated in our study: Miguel who was teaching second grade and Rita third grade. Both were very enthusiastic about mathematics. Although in a different manner, they faced mathematics teaching in a holistic way as they used problematic situations and manipulative materials, had a good understanding of mathematics and tried to integrate arithmetic and geometry. In both classes, materials were used to solve problematic situations. At the end of each observed lesson the teachers were interviewed and documentation from their classrooms was collected.

Miguel

Miguel is an enthusiast of materials. He told us that when he sees 'materials' he becomes very excited. In fact, we observed that his classroom was equipped with many different materials. There we found counting objects (beads, straws, etc.), didactic games, measurement tools, geoboards, puzzles, computers, etc. and we could verify that everything was a meaningful part of the children's daily lives. Every day, usually in the afternoon, children developed their own activities where they needed to use manipulative materials, such as word problems, geometric problems, numerical problems and games. These were usually challenging for pupils, either due to their intrinsic interest, their relationship to out-of-school activities, or because they promoted pupils' own discovery. Sometimes Miguel proposed activities which required the pupils to interpret a representation on paper — for instance, a drawing of a classroom with representations of chairs and tables and a path which the children had to follow. Although Miguel recognizes that the geometry can provide good problems and uses them in his classroom, he seems to value problems with computations:

> The problems with computations allow us not only different strategies but also the use of different strategies of solution. In this kind of problem they can use algorithms, counting . . . while with geometric problems, for instance, problems with tangrams, they have to use the tangram. On the other hand the pupils have a great capacity for learning geometry.

Miguel thinks that problems are a good way to develop the pupil's reasoning, and believes that they can come through written text, orally, or rise spontaneously from a situation.

> I use problematic situations with pupils to develop their reasoning or as a way to practise computational skills.

He gave pupils time to think about the diversity of activities and encouraged them to work sometimes in small groups, at other times individually. Once the teacher had delivered the tasks, the pupils helped themselves to materials. All of them worked very well in spite of being just second grade pupils.

For Miguel, mathematics teaching and learning is inconceivable without the use of materials. He considers that materials allow a better conceptual understanding, they help construction of pupils' own reasoning, they lend physical support to explain how pupils are thinking, and help pupils develop greater autonomy. In his opinion: '. . . the pupil is not afraid of showing his/her work to the teacher and the materials are a good support to his/her reasoning'. In fact we observed his pupils working with great autonomy, interest, persistence and a sense of responsibility. In some situations they went to get materials when they felt they needed them, even when the teacher had not directed them to do so.

Miguel thinks that working with the support of manipulative materials allows him to observe individual differences about the way pupils understand the situation and think about the solution. For him,

> . . . materials are a physical support that help pupils to make explicit their reasonings. At this age level it is a fundamental pathway to the verbalization and the confidence that the pupils need to explain their work and what they have thought. Children can set up their individual reasonings . . . The way they arrange what they are doing shows how they are thinking and we are there watching their construction of strategies.

However, Miguel also mentions negative aspects to the use of manipulative materials in problem solving. The time consumed is much larger and positive outcomes only seem to appear when pupils use the materials systematically.

> The activities with materials, besides being more time consuming, also require special attention from the teacher in such a way that he can follow children's reasonings. The individual differences are more obvious and he has to be attentive to everybody. The teacher's attention has to be divided among all pupils. Furthermore the results are not shown immediately, it is necessary to wait.

Another problem is created if the teacher is not certain to continue with the same pupils the following year. The use of manipulative materials and a problem-solving approach do not have a great tradition in Portuguese primary teaching, which is usually focused on paper and pencil computations, so the methodology used by the other teachers may not be the same.

Rita

Rita affirms that she has always used manipulative materials in her classroom. Since she learnt to use materials during her preservice education, she considers it inconceivable to work on conceptual aspects of mathematics without their support. Despite being convinced that this is the only way for children to understand the concepts, Rita considers that the process is slow and that results are not as immediately observable as those evidenced through routine acquisitions:

> I have always worked with materials and it has always astonished me, for teachers who didn't work with materials, that their pupils seemed to know much more than mine.

However, Rita expresses some doubts about the 'pseudo-learning' that pupils seem to obtain when they have no support from materials. For her, what matters is that 'the pupils understand what they are doing' and for this they need to engage in material manipulation.

Although Rita expressed a great concern with the use of manipulative materials, the activities proposed by her, while problematic, are mostly geared towards the development of concepts. She also thinks that solving a problem should involve computational skills.

> I think that is natural that teachers emphasize computations. Indeed it is what we have done mostly in our schooling, in word problems. We did not do other kinds of problems. So we are not awakened to, for instance, geometric problems. So it is natural that my classes have rather more computation and computation problems than proper geometry.

Interestingly, we observed in her classes a number of problematic situations without computations. That leads us to think that for Rita the word 'problem' is related to situations where there is a written text with two or more questions and in which children need to do some computations.

In her classroom we also observed a concern to develop pupils' abilities for problem-solving, and attention is given to problem understanding. The problems included those with lack of data, data in excess, or the need to look for data, problems with open questions, or multiple choice. On the other hand, the problem context is carefully chosen bearing in mind the things that are happening in pupils' lives.

From time to time, Rita is concerned about the speed of her pupils' acquisitions. During these times she needs to speak with colleagues about her worries, experiences and concerns. She chooses colleagues usually with whom she feels some affinity and who can analyze her practices critically.

Teacher Education

Although there are some differences between them, these two teachers consider that the use of materials will produce greater achievement. It seems that Miguel deepens and tries to understand the reasons and effects of that use, questioning his work in a permanent reflection from which some doubts and anxieties result. Rita, on the other hand, seems to be confident, and does not express big doubts. Miguel seems to invest a lot in the search for activities and materials for his pupils, showing a greater concern with problem-solving, in providing diverse situations and materials, as well as the management of different mathematical curricular components. Rita is more concerned with the classroom context and with the relationship of her teaching to children's experiences, and she tries to connect that with mathematics learning.

These two teachers relate their interests in using manipulative materials to their own preservice and inservice education. Rita says that her experience with materials began in her preservice education where manipulative materials were used to introduce concepts. Later, she also had some very positive experiences using materials in problem-solving in the PIPSE program. From her previous experiences what seemed more remarkable is the sharing of experiences with colleagues and discussing their problems:

> How should I do it? Which type of things can I try? It is very important the existence of dialogue in the school, it is the exchange of experiences that is actually important.

Miguel, who was a support teacher in the PIPSE program, thinks teacher training must have a practical emphasis.

> When teachers come to the teacher-training sessions they want the practical sense of that training. They accept the theoretical part if it as a basis for the practice they are engaged in.

Rita thinks in the same way. She refers to her experience as trainee in PIPSE as very positive because

> . . . it was essentially practical, things that people had to think and to think how to do. I think that awakened the interest of many teachers to teach mathematics in other ways.

Miguel mentions that the use of materials in the classroom should be related to teacher education as a whole and specially to inservice education. For him, teacher education in mathematics passes through the manipulation of materials and problem-solving. The teachers should have their own experiences with manipulative materials in problem-solving in order to use them effectively in their classrooms. Nowadays, Miguel considers that mathematics learning is not conceivable without the support of materials.

> If the teacher training doesn't include materials manipulation by the teachers, it fails.

They do not reject the theoretical training, as they feel they have some need in that area, but they want that training closely related to the content knowledge they have to teach to their pupils, together with the matching methodologies.

Rita and Miguel feel that reflection about their work is a necessity. However, the way each one fulfils that need is different. Rita looks for a more immediate solution, asking her colleagues from the same school or from other schools if she considers them competent teachers:

> And does that work? — I will try it then . . . How do you do it here? Which other things did you do? — How shall I do it?

For her an open environment 'to dialogue' in the school 'is really the most important'. She likes to try 'new things'. If she listens to a report of an experience that she thinks has worked well, she becomes very interested and tries to concretize it. Miguel works in a more individual way, reflecting about and questioning his practice alone. He needs 'a basis' where he can support himself and, for that, he tries to keep up to date. He advocates informal, non-compulsory training, believing that it is in informal talks with other people, in teacher meetings, and in teacher training sessions that he keeps himself up to date.

For both Rita and Miguel, inservice training should have begun immediately after the preservice training. They both felt very solitary in their first year of teaching. They also think that training should 'be available' any time and that teachers should be able to access it whenever they want. They do not believe that small courses can contribute to awareness of 'new methodologies':

> To change, a person needs to be sure, and it is only possible to acquire security if there is continuous training.

Although they agree about the availability of the training, they have different ideas about the way the teacher training should be provided. Rita's idea relates to her way of solving day-to-day problems. She would like the training to be

> . . . a kind of resource centre . . . when I need something, I have someone to help me.

For Miguel, the teacher meetings and the teacher-training sessions can answer to his needs

> . . . in an informal level and with determined aims . . . when I go to the APM meeting or when I go to the meetings in Escola Superior de Educação, it is, in some way, that perspective.

Conclusions

These two teachers faced professional development in the sense expressed by Aichele and Castle (1994). True professional development, which results in meaningful and long-lasting qualitative change in a teacher's thinking and approaches to educating, is an autonomous activity chosen by the teacher and not externally mandated by the hierarchy or imposed by career progression. That development is constructed by each one through reflection on her/his practices and in the sharing of these among her/his colleagues.

On the other hand, research also suggests that teachers need to learn mathematics in a manner that is consistent with the way we expect them to teach (Cooney, 1994). The teachers with whom we worked were aware of that necessity and agreed with it. They considered that true training only exists when the sessions are meaningful and desired. For them, the teacher education sessions developed in our project were a stimulus and a reinforcement of the way they faced the use of materials in problem-solving:

> We could learn new ideas and new materials and could discuss with our colleagues other ways of working with them. We discovered new approaches to mathematics learning and teaching.

However we think that in order for teacher education sessions to become more meaningful for the teachers we should discuss with them some reports of experiences in the use of materials. Another aspect we need to discuss with teachers is pupil assessment when we are using a problem-solving approach to teaching.

Rita seems to live well with her doubts, but she is always alert and looking for new things. Miguel's anxieties and doubts were becoming stronger as the school year was nearly at the end and there were pupils who did not seem to have acquired the basic skills. This seemed to be increasing and he did not know if he could continue his work in the next school year. Miguel reflects much about his practice but as he reflects he becomes more anxious. In fact, and according to Garcia (1992), 'the reflection is a tool of development of thinking and of teacher action'. However, that reflection can create instability with which the teacher has to deal and that is not easy, particularly in mathematics teaching where the understanding/routine issue is clearly a critical aspect. Miguel challenged us many times with questions and insecurities for which we did not have answers which could satisfy him.

In relation to their professional knowledge these two teachers seem to have a pedagogical content knowledge much deeper and more developed than their content knowledge (as defined by Shulman, 1987). However we can say that they have developed their content knowledge along with their practical experience bearing in mind the curricula of their preservice courses. That professional knowledge has allowed these teachers to transform their own practices progressively and continually. These changes pass through the integration of new ideas about mathematics learning that they manage albeit with some concerns about the routines of computation. In their classrooms, problem-solving, discovery and investigative activities, and routine and mechanical exercises appear side by side. It is with this dialectic, which can seem contradictory for an outsider, that they work effectively within the system (involving parents, other teachers) and develop their epistemological beliefs about mathematics learning. In this context, progression can seem slow but it is firm. The teacher education role can be about providing elements for a better basis and promoting space for exchange and reflection.

Although we had observed, in Miguel's and Rita's classrooms, that the pupils solved challenging problems, did collaborative group work and participated in some interesting class discussions about their mathematical solutions, we agree with Wood (1993) that this was not in accord with the teaching tradition. This study shows us that even very interested teachers still need great support to accomplish the new mathematics teaching that is being established in the new Portuguese curriculum. We need to carry out more research studies in primary education in order to have a more complete picture about what happens in our primary classrooms and in mathematics classes. At the same time we should develop a coherent mathematics education support system in our primary education.

Note

This work is sponsored in part by the JNICT (Junta Nacional de Investigação Científica e Tecnológica). The authors would like to thank João Ponte for his helpful comments on an earlier version of this article.

References

AICHELE, D.B. and CASTLE, K. (1994) 'Professional development and teacher autonomy', in AICHELE, D.B. and COXFORD, A.F. (eds) *Professional Development for Teachers of Mathematics* (pp. 1–8), Reston, VA: National Council of Teachers of Mathematics.

APM (1988) *Renovação do Currículo de Matemática*, Lisboa: Associação de Professores de Matemática.

COONEY, T.J. (1994) 'Teacher education as an exercise in adaptation', in AICHELE, D.B. and COXFORD, A.F. (eds) *Professional Development for Teachers of Mathematics* (pp. 9–22), Reston, VA: National Council of Teachers of Mathematics.

FERNANDES, D. (1985) 'A mathematics needs assessment study of the elementary school teachers of Viana do Castelo', Unpublished master thesis, Boston, MA: Boston University.

GARCIA, C.M. (1992) 'A formação de professores: Novas perspectivas baseadas na investigação sobre o pensamento do professor', *Os Professores e a Sua Formação*, coord. por António Nóvoa. Publicações Dom Quixote, Instituto de Inovação Educacional, Lisboa.

SHULMAN, L.S. (1987) 'Knowledge and teaching: Foundations of the new reform', *Harvard Educational Review*, **57**, pp. 1–22.

WOOD, T. (1993) 'Creating an environment for learning mathematics: Social interaction perspective', in WOOD, T., COBB, P., YACKEL, E. and DILLON, D.R. (eds) *Rethinking Elementary School Mathematics: Insights and Issues*, Journal for Research in Mathematics Education Monograph Number 6, Reston, VA: National Council of Teachers of Mathematics.

7 Mathematics Classroom Situations: An Inservice Course for Elementary School Teachers

Zvia Markovits and Ruhama Even, Israel

Background

This chapter describes a course for inservice Israeli elementary school teachers that aims to improve their pedagogical content knowledge of mathematics. The recognition that pedagogical content knowledge is an important characteristic of teacher knowledge is growing fast. Shulman (1986) describes this kind of knowledge as: knowing the ways of representing and formulating the subject matter that makes it comprehensible to others; understanding what makes the learning of specific topics easy or difficult; and knowing the conceptions and preconceptions that students of different ages and backgrounds bring with them to the learning situation.

The course focuses on the interrelationship between teaching and learning. It has grown out of research in which we designed, conducted, and studied three-hour workshops for junior high school teachers, which dealt with students' ways of thinking when they work on the function concept, and with characteristics of teachers' responses to students' questions or ideas (Even and Markovits, 1993). Such short activities could not, of course, change drastically teachers' pedagogical content knowledge, but they raised teachers' awareness of students' ways of thinking and characteristics of teachers' responses. Based on what we learned from these workshops, we designed a longer and more comprehensive course for teachers, this time concentrating on elementary school teachers.

The Course: Mathematics Classroom Situations

Twenty elementary school teachers participated in the course. These teachers were participants in a two-year program that prepared mentors for elementary school teachers; the program was held in a teacher college. As mentors their task is to help teachers from their own school and from several neighboring schools in teaching mathematics. The participants in the program were chosen from a large number of candidates, selection being based on their reputation as successful teachers with the potential to become good mentors. As is usually the case in Israel, the teachers were general teachers, teaching all elementary school subjects, not only mathematics. However, almost all have participated in inservice courses on mathematics teaching;

59

some completed a two-year course for elementary school mathematics coordinators. Most of the teachers had at least 10 years' experience teaching in elementary school, usually in the upper grades (grades 4–6 (ages 9–11)). It can be said that their background in teaching mathematics was somewhat better than the average elementary school teacher.

The course 'Mathematics Classroom Situations' was held in the second semester of the first year and consisted of 15 two-hour meetings. It was team-taught by one of the authors and another teacher. The classroom was structured as a community of learners. The instructors did not give the final verification that the ideas put forward were the 'correct' ones. Instead, the instructors' role was to pose interesting tasks for the participants to consider and work on individually, in small groups, and as a whole class; and to encourage maximum interaction and exchange of ideas among the participants. The following is a description of three of the main components of the course.

Analysis of Situations

A major part of the course was devoted to work on mathematics classroom situations (as is reflected in the course's title). We use the term 'mathematics classroom situations' to describe real or hypothetical classroom situations involving mathematics, in which the teacher has to respond to a student's question or idea. The situations chosen highlighted students' ways of thinking and misconceptions as known from research and personal experience (e.g. Markovits, 1989). The following are examples of such situations.

- *Height*
A student was asked the following question: 'The height of a 10-year-old boy is 1.5 m. What do you think his height will be when he is 20?'

The student answered: 'In mathematics it will be 3 m, because $1.5 \times 2 = 3$, and in everyday life it will be about 1.80 m.'

How would you respond?

- *Division by 0*
A student comes to you and says that he checked several division exercises using a calculator. When he divided 72 by 0, 1459 by 0 or 8 by 0, the calculator showed 'Error'. But when he divided 0 by 72, 0 by 1459 or 0 by 8, it showed 0. The student asks why it happens.

How would you respond?

- *Decimal Point*
A student was told that $15.24 \times 4.5 = 6858$, and was asked to locate the decimal point. The student said that the answer is 6.858 because there are two

places after the decimal point in 15.24 and one place after the decimal point in 4.5. Together it makes three places after the point in the answer.

How would you respond?

Teachers' Own Responses

The teachers were first introduced to the situations a few months before the course — at the beginning of the first semester. They were given a questionnaire that included eight situations (three of which are listed above) and were asked to answer the open-ended questions at home and to return the questionnaire a week later.

The first course meetings focused on analysis of mathematics classroom situations, some of which were part of the questionnaire tasks while some were new to them. They analyzed the situations and talked about the ways they had responded to the questionnaire tasks or suggested and discussed ways of response to the new tasks. For example, when discussing the 'Height' situation, the teachers debated the relationships between mathematics and reality. Some assumed, like the child, that there is a difference between answers in mathematics and answers in everyday life, as if answers in mathematics imply that one has to do some operation with the given numbers:

T1: I think it is a wonderful answer, that he is able to separate mathematics and reality. His answer 'about 1.80' is nice.

T2: I feel uncomfortable because of the separation of math from everyday life, like they are two things without any connection. I liked the answer [that another teacher gave] that the child knows when to pay attention to rules and how to use them in everyday life. But he should not say that in math it is so and so and in everyday life it is so and so.

T1: What I said is that he knows how to correctly separate math and everyday life in this situation. Every problem should be answered according to the situation involved.

Some of the teachers felt uncomfortable about putting the child in a situation of having to answer what they considered to be a 'trick question':

T1: It is like the teacher tries to play the wise guy. [The student would say:] 'He gave me twice the age, so what does he want? — to make twice the height.'

T2: It is like forcing the math on something that is not true in reality.

T1: The child thinks, 'you tried to mislead me, but look, it is not true in reality.'

T2: There are so many problems you can give in math that are correct, and here I feel we forced the mathematics. I wouldn't give a problem like this.

T3: When a teacher gives a problem like this in a math class, she has a reason for doing so. So if she gives such a problem but actually knows that we should not give such a problem, what exactly does she want to do here? What is the point?

The same issue of 'misleading' the child came across when discussing the 'Decimal Point' situation:

> *T*: He was misled from the beginning. They took off the zero . . . Because if the zero was there, the whole story would have ended differently . . . He knows the rule, but he was misled from the beginning, because we always say it is 68580, the zero is important in multiplication. He didn't use estimation, he was told that this is the answer and was asked to locate the decimal point, so he went ahead and used the rule.

Teachers' analysis of some of the situations centered almost entirely on the situation characteristics and did not reach the stage of analysis of responses to the student. When it did, teachers suggested various responses. For example, a common suggestion to the 'Decimal Point' situation was to use estimation as a response to the student. The extensive use of estimation might be explained by the fact that the teachers had attended a course on estimation and number sense during the first semester, at the same time they were given the questionnaire. Other teachers based their response on the standard multiplication algorithm, showing that actually there are five and not four digits in the final answer. An interesting characteristic of many of the teachers' responses was the inclusion of some positive statements about the child, something that can make him or her feel good although his or her answer was incorrect. For example, 'I understand that you remember the rule, and it is very good to remember the rule. But . . .' This kind of behaviour which extends the mathematical context and takes the child's feelings into account was not in evidence in our previous study (Even and Markovits, 1993).

Reactions to Other Teachers' Responses

After responding to several situations, the teachers were presented with responses that were given by other teachers to the same situations, and were asked to react to these responses. Some of the responses were based on real teacher responses while others were made up with the purpose of representing different approaches and highlighting various aspects of teaching and learning. For example, the following responses were presented for the 'Decimal Point' situation:

1. I would tell the child: You located the decimal point correctly and also explained it correctly.
2. I would ask the child to find two whole numbers that are close to the given numbers and to multiply them. I would then ask him to look at his exercise and the given exercise and to check what is going on.
3. I would tell the child that the multiplication of the integer parts alone (15×4) is 60. So we get more than 60. That's why the answer should be 68.58. In addition, I would write down the exercise, and ask the child to multiply. The answer would be 68.580 and I will explain that 68.580 equals 68.58.

4. The child does not understand how to multiply decimal numbers. I would give him several exercises and ask him to solve them using the standard algorithm.
5. I would tell the child: You stated a correct rule but your answer is incorrect, because when you multiply 4 and 5 the answer has a 0 at the end. 0 is not shown in your answer, and that's why you made a mistake in locating the decimal point. The answer is 68.580.

In their reactions to these responses, the teachers did not notice the difference between responses that put the student in the center, suggesting to him or her activities that have the potential for helping him or her construct a solution by and for him or herself, and responses that put the teacher in the center, telling the student how to reach the correct solution (e.g. responses 2 and 3 above).

After reacting freely to other teachers' responses for several situations, the teachers were asked to analyze the responses according to the following criteria:

- Does the teacher understand what the student does not understand?
- Does the teacher's response concentrate on the student's misconception?
- Does the teacher's response emphasize rituals? Does it pertain to meaning?
- Is the response teacher-centered? student-centered?
- Is there any problem regarding content knowledge?

Not all teacher responses can be analyzed according to all criteria. More than that, for each situation some criteria are more relevant than others. For example, the issue of ritual versus meaningful response was in evidence in most of the responses that were presented for the 'Decimal Point' and 'Division by 0' situations while less in responses to other situations such as the 'Height' situation.

Acquaintance with Research on Student Learning of Mathematics

The second part of the course concentrated on understanding better how students learn. Several research studies and articles on student learning and ways of thinking in mathematics were presented and discussed with the teachers. (Language difficulties prevented us from assigning actual reading of articles in English to the teachers.) The articles centered on two interrelated issues. One was to do with students' misconceptions and difficulties in elementary mathematics topics, especially in fractions and decimals (e.g. Bright, Behr, Post and Wachsmuts, 1988; Markovits and Sowder, 1991; Nesher and Peled, 1986; Vinner and Hershkowitz, 1980). Possible sources for those difficulties were discussed, and various ways for dealing with them were suggested. The other issue has to do with how students learn. Special attention was given to the conception of learning as construction of knowledge by the student as opposed to the transfer of knowledge from the teacher to the student (e.g. Blais, 1988; Confrey, 1990). Different styles of learning and different styles of teaching were also discussed, highlighting their potential contribution to student reasoning and justification (e.g. Garofalo, 1989; Schwartz, 1992).

The presentation of the articles took several forms. Sometimes, the teachers worked on assignments that were based on the research findings. For example, they were presented with student work on ordering decimals (taken from Nesher and Peled, 1986) and were asked to describe the rules used by the students. At other times, a specific teaching style was presented. For example, a 'silent teacher' lesson (Schwartz, 1992) was described to the teachers. In this lesson, almost all the talking is done by the students while the teacher remains silent most of the time. The discussion that followed this description centered first on the teacher's goals and then on the implications of such behavior on students' learning. At some point, the participants changed the focus of the discussion from a general theoretical point of view to more personal practical considerations, debating if it is possible to do this under their actual working conditions:

> *T1*: You [the instructor] are saying that you bring us things from the field, but I work in the real world out there and there are many difficult situations. This kind of lesson is very nice, but in my class only 3 children will talk, and 25 will not. So what would I achieve?
>
> *T2*: With time some more children will join in.
>
> *Instructor*: It takes time to reach the situation described in the article. Education takes time.
>
> *T3*: Education is a process and it takes time. I don't think it is easy to do it.
>
> *T4*: I'm not saying it is not a nice idea.
>
> *T1*: [Cynically] The school I am working in . . .
>
> *T5*: But you should not give up.

At this point of the discussion, some of the teachers broadened the issue and described changes that had occurred in their awareness of students and in their own teaching styles as a consequence of their participation in the course. The first excerpt is taken from a teacher talking about the importance of asking children questions and listening to them in order to understand their ways of thinking, and the difficulties she encounters when trying to do so. The other excerpt describes a change that another teacher made in her teaching which took time for the pupils to adjust. Both teachers emphasized to their classmates that making such changes, while neither an easy nor a quick task either for the teacher or for the students, is still possible:

> *T6*: This is not a question of time. It has nothing to do with the curriculum. Because what you are doing here is taking a different look at teaching. Even when there are 50 students in my class [classes in Israel usually have 30–40 students] and a student gives me an answer and I think that he has a mistake, I can ask him at that moment: How did you think? And by listening to his answer I know what his mistake was . . . Now, all this method of asking questions — I came to you [to the instructor] this morning and I told you that I interviewed two students [part of the course assignments] and I decided to erase the tape. Because when interviewing them I got so excited that I talked for at least half of the time. There are things we have to pay attention to. It is not that we were born with them. These are new techniques that you learn and you have to use them and to understand them and to let them incubate for a while, and it takes time.

T3: I think it is difficult for us to change attitudes. In the first year only a few [pupils] will go with us. In the second year, more pupils will go with us. I told you [the instructor] this morning that following your course on number sense [at the beginning of the program], I start every lesson with a mathematical puzzle problem, and now I cannot come to school on Tuesdays without a puzzle, because the pupils will ask me: 'Isn't there any puzzle today?' When I started to use puzzles not all the students were with me on this. But now it is beginning to work, they even ask me for puzzles. So you have to start trying.

Student Interviews

As part of the final assignment for the course the teachers were asked to explore students' ways of thinking about mathematical situations and teachers' explanations. To do that, each teacher interviewed a pair of sixth-grade students. They presented three situations to the students (the 'Height', 'Decimal Point' and 'Division by 0' situations) and asked the students to respond. Then they presented the students with teachers' responses to these situations (the same responses that were used in the course) and again asked the students to react.

When asked to interview students the teachers were told that the objective of this task was to explore students' ways of thinking. To do so they needed to ask students to explain and clarify their thinking. Besides their free, voluntary explanations, the students needed also to be probed to clarify ambiguities. Some of the teachers used neutral probes such as 'Why?' 'What do you mean by that?' This kind of probing encourages students' own thinking without specific direction from the teacher and at the same time helps the teacher-interviewer to understand better the students' thinking. Even though it was tempting at times to 'teach' the students 'the material' during the interview, some managed to avoid it. For example, one teacher, whose students did not use estimation for the 'Decimal Point' task, did not mention it to them during the interview. In her report she wrote that she had realized that there was a need to teach this to the children and therefore taught it in her class in subsequent lessons.

Other teachers were more occupied either with directing the students to what the teachers thought students' ways of thinking were or with straightforward teaching of the material. The following example illustrates the first approach, which can be characterized as use of 'negative' probes. One teacher presented the students with the exercise $15.24 \times 4.5 = 6858$ and asked them to locate the decimal point. Then, instead of letting them decide, she turned to one of the students and directed her to use the rule of counting places after the decimal point (a method which leads to wrong results in this case): 'What do you say? Where would you locate the decimal point? Do you remember the rules for decimal fractions? How do we locate the point? What do we do in order to locate the point after we multiply [decimal] fractions?' The child replied: 'We count the number of digits after the point.' The teacher continued in this direction: 'So, where would you put it?' The child: 'After the 6.' Such interviewing does not really help the teacher explore students' ways of thinking. Instead, it 'helps' the students guess what the teacher has in mind.

Some teachers felt that they had to 'teach (without probe)' the students the correct answer or the 'correct' way of thinking during the interview. For example, after the students had decided where to locate the decimal point, one teacher comprehensively discussed with them the difference between the 'rule method' and the method of estimation. She discussed the issue from many angles and only then asked the students to react to the teachers' responses. By doing that, the teacher directed the students to what she considered to be the correct choice. This teacher kept correcting mistakes that the students made. She also told the students at times whether she agreed with their answers. While some of the teachers who 'talked too much' during the interview referred to this issue in their report, claiming that they had directed the students too often, this teacher wrote that there was a need to direct the students so that they would not get confused.

Conclusion

This chapter is intended to give a picture of the kinds of experiences that the course offered the participants. What the teachers learned from these experiences was greatly influenced by their previous experiences, their knowledge of and about mathematics, their beliefs about mathematics learning processes, and their beliefs about mathematics teaching. It was also influenced by their communication and interaction with each other and with the instructors. Therefore, when asked at the end of the course what is it that they learned, each participant concentrated on aspects that were relevant to him or her. Following are representative responses.

- 'I learned not to talk so much, but really listen to my pupils.'
- 'To think what goes on in the pupil's head. Where is he now? What does he think? What is his knowledge structure? How can I connect to it?'
- 'Before the course, if I saw a mistake I would have waited half a second and immediately said what is wrong and explained how to solve it. Today, I am much more aware of that . . . Give time, Time is very important. The pupil needs to think by himself, to find the mistake by himself and correct his work.'

This last remark about the importance of time in the process of student learning can be extended to the context of our course. The participant teachers did learn, in the course, more than they would have learned from just one short workshop. Still, at the end of the course, we felt that the teachers needed time to think about the ideas that were introduced in the course and to explore their application in real teaching. They needed time to make those ideas a functional part of their pedagogical content knowledge. The need for time, indeed, was raised by many of the teachers in an interview that took place after finishing the course, as illustrated by the following quotation:

In most courses that I take, when I receive an interesting worksheet, I immediately use it in my class. Here some time had to pass for the ideas to sink in. Only when I felt that I can make the 'switch' in my thinking I started to use those ideas. It took time for things to sink in. It took time to 'filter' them my own way before I really started to work with them.

References

BLAIS, D.M. (1988) 'Constructivism — a theoretical revolution for algebra', *Mathematics Teacher*, **81**, pp. 624–31.

BRIGHT, G.W., BEHR, M.J., POST, T.R. and WACHSMUTS, I. (1988) 'Identifying fractions on the number line', *Journal for Research in Mathematics Education*, **19**, pp. 215–32.

CONFREY, J. (1990) 'What constructivism implies for teaching', in DAVIS, R.B., MAHER, C.A. and NODDINGS, N. (eds) *Constructivist Views on the Teaching and Learning of Mathematics* (pp. 107–22), Journal for Research in Mathematics Education Monograph Number 4, Reston, VA: National Council of Teachers of Mathematics.

GAROFALO, J. (1989) 'Beliefs, responses and mathematics education: Observations from the back of the classroom', *School, Science and Mathematics*, **89**, pp. 451–5.

EVEN, R. and MARKOVITS, Z. (1993) 'Teachers' pedagogical content knowledge of functions: Characterization and applications', *Journal of Structural Learning*, **12**, pp. 35–51.

MARKOVITS, Z. (1989) 'Reactions to the number sense conference', in SOWDER, J.T. and SCHAPPELE, B.P. (eds) *Establishing Foundations for Research on Number Sense and Related Topics: Report of a Conference*, San Diego, CA: Center for Research in Mathematics and Science Education, San Diego State University.

MARKOVITS, Z. and SOWDER, J. (1991) 'Students' understanding of the relationship between fractions and decimals', *Focus on Learning Problems in Mathematics*, **13**, pp. 3–11.

NESHER, P. and PELED, I. (1986) 'Shifts in reasoning', *Educational Studies in Mathematics*, **17**, pp. 67–79.

SCHWARTZ, J.E. (1992) ' "Silent teacher" and mathematics as reasoning', *Arithmetic Teacher*, **40**, pp. 122–4.

SHULMAN, L.S. (1986) 'Those who understand: Knowledge growth in teaching', *Educational Researcher*, **15**, pp. 4–14.

VINNER, S. and HERSHKOWITZ, R. (1980) 'Concept images and common cognitive paths in the development of some simple geometric concepts', in KARPLUS, R. (ed.) *Proceedings of the 4th International Conference for the PME* (pp. 177–84), Berkeley, CA.

Editors' Comment

The next two chapters continue the discussion by presenting the dilemmas that teachers faced as they began to put new visions of mathematics learning and teaching into practice in their classrooms. Both Carter and Richards in the USA and Goldstein, Mnisi and Rodwell in South Africa reveal the difficulties teacher educators face as they follow up the teachers into the classroom. Both express a sense of external pressure to hurry the process of transformation and the ensuing frustration of knowing the impossibility of such expectations and demands. Further, both are contending with the dilemmas of change within society which include demands for improving the quality of mathematics education and stipulations for improving social inequity, both of which create tensions between innovation and tradition.

8   Dilemmas of Constructivist Mathematics Teaching: Instances from Classroom Practice[1]

Richard Carter and John Richards, USA

The National Council of Teachers of Mathematics (NCTM) Curriculum and Professional Standards (NCTM, 1989, 1991) and the California Framework (California Department of Education, 1991) lay out a vision of how mathematics learning and teaching should happen. This vision is in strong contrast to what one finds in the vast majority of standard classrooms. This new vision is becoming common in the mathematics education community. Researchers have written about their own attempts to transform the classrooms they work in and the difficulties they have encountered (Lampert, 1990; Ball, 1990; Cobb, Wood and Yackel, 1991). The NCTM's *Professional Standards* (1991) are full of classroom vignettes, and there are even some videotapes that show exemplary practices. Yet, there has been little written about what it means for regular classroom teachers to try to make the transition from traditional mathematics teaching to the vision of inquiry learning articulated in these documents. In this paper we present some of our own efforts to help classroom teachers make this transition and some of the enduring dilemmas these teachers have encountered.

Over the past several years at Bolt Beranek and Newman, we have been working with middle school math teachers in a series of teacher enhancement projects[2]. The format of the work begins with an intensive workshop or course in which we support teachers in exploring some mathematical topics. When possible this has been followed by classroom visits and follow up meetings. The accounts that follow are drawn from some of these visits and from journals we asked the teachers to keep. In the workshops the teachers typically work in groups and use technology. In the activities we try to model what we have come to call an 'inquiry' approach to teaching and learning: putting teachers in a situation where they generate data; look for patterns; make hypotheses or conjectures; share and discuss their ideas with their peers; and then test, revise and extend those ideas. An important element of this process is what we call mathematical discussion situations (Richards, 1991) where students or teachers discuss or argue about mathematical ideas. We do not use the term 'constructivist' with the teachers because it may be off-putting, but our inquiry approach is framed in a constructivist epistemology. There is a constant focus on individual sense-making, building up one's own ideas, understanding how different people approach problems in different ways, and exploring how sharing and reflecting on these differences can help deepen one's own understanding. The teachers find that articulating their understandings and having to defend their ideas forces them to grapple with what it means to really understand something. This approach is based on the belief that unless teachers directly experience inquiry learning for themselves it is quite unlikely that they will be able to implement it in their classrooms.

Although teachers are almost universally excited about the chance to explore mathematical ideas with their peers, and to experience a different way of learning, they often find that translating these experiences back into their classrooms is not an easy task. There are a number of common dilemmas they seem to face. In this paper we will share three dilemmas that many of our teachers have described when they talk about trying to recreate with their students the experiences they have had in our workshops. The first involves making decisions about what ideas to pursue; the second involves when to tell an answer and when to push students to work things out for themselves; and the third, which we believe is a fundamental under-lying theme, is about time.

Which Ideas Should I Pursue? What Should I Teach?

The first example is from a 6th (age 11–12) grade class. Joan, the teacher, starts the class with the following problem: 'Can anyone see any mathematical relationships in the date 6/15/90?' Joan poses this problem as a warm up at the start of her class. She hopes it will lead to work on the idea of inverse operations. One student suggests: $6 * 15 = 90$. Joan puts it up on the board and asks for others. Another student suggests: $6 + 9 = 15 + 0$. Joan challenges: 'Do you think we can we find ten different true mathematical statements?' The students come up with several more and then one student suggests: $90 = 6 \times 15$. Another says: 'No, that's the same as one we already have . . .'

Joan reported afterward that when she heard this she envisioned the possibility of a long discussion about issues of likeness and difference, degrees of likeness, arbitrariness, and the need for the community to decide on some issues such as what they want to count as 'the same'. She felt these were important issues, but this was not the direction she had planned. This activity was just supposed to be a 'warm up'. She had planned some serious review work to help her students prepare for a test. Joan was also under pressure from her supervisor to cover material in the textbook. She felt in conflict and did not know what she wanted to do. Having students invent multiple solutions often put her in a position of having to decide between competing demands and she said it drove her crazy.

This was Joan's first dilemma. At a later point in the date problem she ran into another dilemma. One student suggested: 6 divided by 90 equals 15. She assumed that he had simply reversed the 6 and the 90 and tried to correct him with what she assumed would be a brief aside. But he maintained his answer even when she wrote $6/90 = 15$ on the board. She reported that she couldn't make sense out of how he was thinking about it. She considered opening this up to the class, but she was also hesitant because she was concerned about making this student feel stupid by publicly discussing his answer. She believed that discussion among students is an important part of inquiry learning, but she was also grappling with what kinds of responses can be turned back to the class for productive discussion. At first she had just thought this student's response was a careless reversal, but when the student stuck to his original answer she was perplexed about what to do. She says she has found there are so many opportunities for turning ideas back to the class, and there are so many issues about how safe the students feel, it was often hard to decide when to try to open up and pursue a student's seemingly wrong answer. (Note: one thing she did not do was to do the mathematics and see that 6/90 = 1/15.)

After working through the example of 6/15/90 she closed up the activity with the following question: 'Can anyone think of a date in 1991 that would have interesting mathematical relationships?' (She later reported that she was hoping that this would provide a meaningful situation where they could discover and use the idea of 91 being a prime number.) The students explored for a couple of minutes. Many of them tried dividing different numbers into 91 and kept getting remainders. Then one student said: 'July 24 1991, that is 7/24/1991.' Once again the answer made no sense to her, and when she asked him how it worked, he said, '91/24 gets 3 with a remainder of 19 and 19 is 7'. She still was not clear and probed further, eventually she found out he was talking about hours (19 hours into a day is 7 PM). Everyone else had been stuck on the problem of remainders and he had the idea of using the remainder as a number of hours. She was in conflict once again because some of the students had decided there was no answer and were moving toward the idea of 91 being prime, yet this student's turning the remainder into hours was an innovative idea and there was potential for some interesting mathematics

The idea of inquiry learning had opened up this teacher's view of mathematics learning and expanded her view of worthwhile activities immensely, but now she found she continually ran up against difficult decisions about what to pursue.

Another variation of this problem of deciding what to pursue is reflected in a journal entry by a 6th grade teacher in another school. Shirley had just been doing some work with palindromes with her class. They had become fascinated with the idea that you could start with any number and turn it into a palindrome by reversing it and adding the two numbers repeatedly, e.g. start with 168:

```
    168
 +  861   reverse and add
   1029   not a palindrome yet
 + 9201   reverse and add
  10230   not a palindrome yet
 + 03201  reverse and add
  13431   voila, a palindrome
```

She had had a very exciting class on palindromes which grew out of some kids posing a challenge to the class about finding the number that took the most additions to turn it into a palindrome. In the next class the students moved from the conjecture that longer numbers would take longer to some speculation about the relationship between 'carrying' and the number of steps. At the end of the class she asked them to explore just three digit numbers to find out which ones took more or less steps. In her journal, under the heading 'Curriculum', she wrote:

> As the students were leaving I was feeling quite smug until Kristin asked, 'Why are we doing this anyway?' I suddenly felt like I was crashing, I think I gave Kristin an answer but inside I was thinking, 'Why *are* we doing this?' Its not enough to ask the questions anymore. I need answers. Answers about the curriculum. What's important to learn? Its ridiculous to talk big ideas with the textbook topics and objectives. The NCTM standards are helpful but seemingly vague for my purposes. What about standard algorithms and accountability? Am I the only one with such nightmares about these issues? I'm floundering because I can't decide what's important I can't decide how long to stick with something (the old rule of thumb was 80–85% mastery of a skill area by the class). What is mastery anymore? What is a skill? I think that perhaps I am closer than ever to being an inquiry teacher, I mean it actually seems within my reach for the first time but I have no content. In years past 'How do I teach?' was an issue. Now it is what do I teach and, even more puzzling, why teach that?

Once again an introduction to inquiry opens up new possibilities and expands a teacher's view of mathematics, but it can also be overwhelming and filled with dilemmas about what to teach.

To Tell or Not to Tell

Gina who taught an 8th grade algebra class wanted to use algebra tiles to introduce the idea of adding polynomials (e.g. $2x^2 + 3x + 4 + x^2 + 2x - 3$). Algebra tiles use a black square to represent x^2, a bar the same length as the side of the square to represent x and small squares to represent 1s. Gina wanted to start by engaging them in constructing the meaning of the tiles. She decided to introduce her students to the tiles by simply giving them out and asking them to use them to represent $2x^2 + 2x + 2$. The students worked in groups and, to her surprise, came up with things like:

Figure 8.1   Using algebra tiles to represent $2x^2 + 2x + 2(1)$

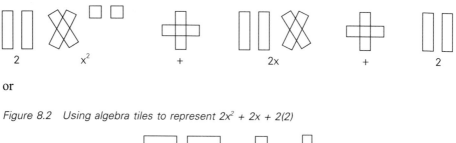

or

Figure 8.2   Using algebra tiles to represent $2x^2 + 2x + 2(2)$

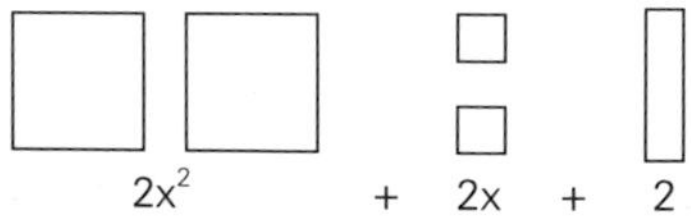

In the first case they tried to use the rods to make a direct representation of the symbolic notation (some variation on this was, in fact, the most common response), and in the second they made what seemed like arbitrary choices about what to use for x and 2.

For Gina (and for us as observers), this was completely unexpected and it ended up taking over the whole class. As the class went on it became clear to her that a number of the students were having a very difficult time understanding why the square piece should represent x^2. Needless to say, she never got to adding polynomials. She wondered whether it would have been better to just tell them what the representation was so they could use it as a tool to do the addition of polynomials. Her question was, 'What do you tell and what do you try to have them construct? If for each topic I have to go back to something like the formula for the area of a square I'll never get anywhere in my algebra text.' Opening up her class to allow students to reveal their intuitive responses led to a wide range of unexpected responses, revealed a confusion for which she was not ready, and left her confused about what ideas and tools students should develop for themselves and what she should tell them. She was led into issues of representation (How do you talk about one representation being better than another?) and what it means to understand (To understand x^2 do students have to be able to map it onto the area of a square?). She was not ready to deal with these topics. This teacher had done some wonderful work with her students trying to invent rules for finding lowest common multiples, and where the students had come up with ideas and presented them to the class. But in this situation she felt perplexed by their confusion and was unsure what to do.

Time

A final universal issue/dilemma is time. In fact, we believe that one of the underlying issues in dilemmas of 'What to pursue?' and 'What to tell?' has to do with time and the teachers' belief that if they do not spend their time 'covering' the 'curriculum' they will be damaging the students. Through the workshops teachers do come to believe that exploring, inquiring, discussing, trying things out for yourself, and asking students to explain their ideas are important, but they also find these activities all take a lot of time and they cannot 'cover' the number of topics they are used to covering. The difficulty is well articulated in the following 6th grade teacher's journal entries.

Angela had been experimenting since the beginning of September with her students working in groups:

Friday September 13th
I was real excited today to see how the groups would work. They all worked well together. I walked around and listened. Their assignment was to go over their weekly problems. They were to check papers and come to an agreement. They were to appoint one student to summarize what took place in the group.

Problem there was not enough time. Only one group out of four corrected their papers and was able to report to the rest of the group. It was real frustrating to have to stop, especially since the weekend was involved and it would be hard to follow up.

Friday September 20th
When we corrected word problems I notice that is seems important for the students to tell me their way of arriving at the answer. At first I sort of answered that as long as they got the right answer it wasn't important how they got the answer, but then I realized it was important for them to show me so I had them come up and put answers on the board. The trouble is it takes too long . . . I just don't think I can do it all the time.

The Source of the Dilemmas

From our work we have a great deal of data which suggests that teachers who explore an inquiry approach to teaching invariably run into a series of difficult dilemmas as they try to change their practice. Three common dilemmas are deciding what to pursue, figuring out what to tell students directly and what to push them to figure out on their own, and resolving the conflict between their commitment to student exploration and their felt need to cover material. Why is it that these teachers, inspired by a new vision of learning mathematics and determined to explore new ways of teaching, are having so much difficulty?

The problem, as we have come to see it, is that the vision of teaching and learning mathematics outlined in the NCTM standards is not just a reform of old practices, or a shift to new topics, it is really a new world view in which the very words we use take on new meanings. Let us take as an example the idea of coverage. In a traditional math classroom, coverage means getting through the 170-odd textbook or scope and sequence activities in the 180-day school year. Coverage in an inquiry-based classroom means a deep engagement with a much smaller set of fundamental themes. There is a delightful metaphor used by a staff developer we know. She says that in a traditional math classroom when you 'cover' the material, you often 'cover it up' and make the underlying mathematical ideas less accessible to students. Our goal should be, she suggests, to 'uncover' the material so that students' own ideas can interact with it. In our experience, resolving the dilemmas of time and coverage demand that teachers change from a one-sided definition of coverage that focuses on presenting a set of topics to a definition that involves an ongoing dialogue between the students' own ideas and a smaller number of large curricular themes. In this view the very meaning of 'coverage' changes.

Resolving Dilemmas

For some teachers, the dilemmas described above become overwhelming and defeat their attempts to explore new practices; for others, struggling with the dilemmas over time leads to a strong cohesive sense about what they are doing and why. How do teachers who are successful at making this transition manage it? This is an area we are just beginning to explore. Some common themes are beginning to emerge in the stories told by teachers who have reached a sense of resolution about some of these dilemmas. The following two vignettes are representative of reports from teachers who have become committed to devoting extended periods of time to mathematical investigations and a process of inquiry.

The first is from an experienced 5th grade teacher named Evelyn who had spent most of each Spring teaching first multi-digit multiplication and then multi-digit (long) division. As she began to explore a constructivist perspective she became less and less satisfied with teaching her students a mechanical set of procedures for each of these operations. She felt her students never learned it very well and made lots of careless mechanical errors. One year Evelyn decided to have the students explore their own ways of doing and representing multi-digit multiplication. She posed real world problems and had her students work in groups to solve them. They could use concrete materials and she asked them to invent their own ways of representing what they were doing. As a class they collected and named the methods that the students invented. She also asked them to try to explain why the methods they came up with worked. Evelyn reported that it went well, in fact it was very exciting, but it felt like it was taking forever.

As the Spring wore on, she got more and more concerned that she would never have time to teach them how to do long division. When she finally decided that most of her students had made sense out of multi-digit multiplication, she moved on to division and she discovered that the students brought many of the ideas they had developed about doing multiplication to the problems she posed that involved division. As a result they moved through mastering long division more quickly than any class had done before. She ended the year at the same place in the curriculum, but her students' mastery of long division convinced her that the students had developed a powerful set of ideas from spending the extra time on their own exploration of multiplication. For this teacher it was the success of her own students that made her willing to spend the time necessary to support students developing their own ideas. In addition, Evelyn and her students seem to have experienced Sizer's principle of less is more (Sizer, 1984), as her fear of not covering enough material turned into a realization that opening up to the possibility of covering less led to learning more.

A second teacher's story also reflects the power of a teacher discovering unexpected things about her students as she opens up time to allow students to explore ideas. Susan, a 6th grade teacher, decided she wanted to do a unit on surface area with her students. She began with an activity titled Space Food Packages from the *Mouse and Elephant* book in the *Middle Grades Mathematics Project* series (Shroyer and Fitzgerald, 1986). The activity begins exploring surface area by getting students to cut out patterns from graph paper to wrap cubes. Susan's students began with this, but quickly got involved in exploring how the surface area changed for the different arrangements that could be built with a given number of cubes. This was not the direction that Susan had planned to go, but she decided to follow their interest. She and they got interested in questions of maximum and minimum surface area

Figure 8.3   *Keeping surface area the same*

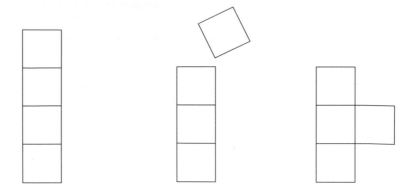

of a given number of cubes as they are placed in different arrangements. This investigation went into the next day. At one point a student said that a tall stack of cubes placed end to end would always give you the largest surface area no matter how many cubes you had. Another student responded that there were lots of other arrangements that were the same and she could prove it. She held up a stack (see Figure 8.3) and took off the last cube and said, 'I am now uncovering two sides'. She then took the cube she had taken off the stack and placed it on the side of the stack to make a different arrangement, but she noted that she had now covered up two sides and that canceled out the two she had just uncovered. She argued that any arrangement that could be seen as a stack with one taken off and put back on someplace else would have the same surface area. The students then began to look at the various arrangements of blocks in terms of transformations (not the term they used) that left the same number of sides covered up.

Susan was, to use her own words, 'blown away'. It had never occurred to her that her students could think in that way and spontaneously initiate that kind of argument. She said that it was experiences like these that have led her to regularly try to transform standard textbook activities into situations that are complex enough for students to do their own thinking. She also notes that she is convinced now that giving them time to explore an idea is a necessary ingredient in this process. Susan also reports that when her students are given a challenge that makes them grapple with an idea, as opposed to simply being shown how to do something, they seem to learn it more thoroughly.

In both of the above instances, instead of the standard practice of telling students how to do something these teachers challenged their students to figure things out for themselves in rich interactive environments and in both cases they were happily surprised by the results. This theme of 'discovering something in your students that you did not know was there' is common in reports from teachers who feel they have at least begun to overcome the dilemma of time and curriculum coverage.

It should also be noted that both of these teachers emphasized the importance of talking with colleagues and the support of a professional development staff in helping them think about and reflect on what they were doing in their classrooms.

The importance of getting ideas, perspectives, and encouragement from other teachers and staff developers who know them and their classrooms is a second common theme among teachers who have reported some success resolving the dilemmas that arise as they try to change their approach to teaching mathematics.

Notes

1   This work was supported in part by a grant from the National Science Foundation (Grant No. TPE-9153760). The opinions expressed herein are the authors' and do not reflect the position, policy, or endorsement of the Foundation.
2   Two NSF projects: Mathematics Computer Curriculum (TPE-8751765), and Empowering Teachers—Mathematical Inquiry Through Technology (TPE-9153760), and one grant from the US Department of Education: Training Teacher Trainers (R215A93025).

References

BALL, D. (1990) 'With an eye on the mathematical horizon: Dilemmas of teaching', Paper presented at the annual meeting of the American Educational Research Association, Boston, MA.

CALIFORNIA STATE DEPARTMENT OF EDUCATION (1991) *Mathematics Framework for California Public Schools Kindergarten Through Grade Twelve*, Sacramento: California State Department of Education.

COBB, P., WOOD, T. and YACKEL, E. (1991) 'A constructivist approach to second grade mathematics', in VON GLASERSFELD, F. (ed.) *Radical Constructivism in Mathematics Education* (pp. 157–76), Dordrecht: Kluwer Academic Publishers.

LAMPERT, M. (1990) 'When the problem is not the question and the solution is not the answer: Mathematical knowing and teaching', *American Educational Research Journal*, **27**, pp. 29–63.

NATIONAL COUNCIL OF TEACHERS OF MATHEMATICS (1989) *Curriculum and Evaluation Standards for School Mathematics*, Reston, VA: NCTM.

NATIONAL COUNCIL OF TEACHERS OF MATHEMATICS (1991) *Professional Standards for Teaching Mathematics*, Reston, VA: NCTM.

RICHARDS, J. (1991) 'Mathematical discussions', in VON GLASERSFELD, E. (ed.) *Radical Constructivism in Mathematics Education* (pp. 13–52), Dordrecht: Kluwer Academic Publishers.

SHROYER, J. and FITZGERALD, W. (1986) *Mouse and Elephant: Measuring Growth*, Menlo Park, CA: Addison Wesley.

SIZER, T. (1984) *Horace's Compromise: The Dilemma of the American High School*, Boston: Houghton Mifflin.

9   Changing Teaching in a Changing Society[1]

*Colleen Goldstein, Phillip Mnisi and
Pam Rodwell, South Africa*

South Africa, in transforming to a more just society, stands at a critical crossroads: changes can be controlled by the existing power structures or they can be directed by the needs of those teachers whose lives will be affected. This paper outlines a mathematics research programme, which sought to develop a participatory model for curriculum and professional development that is feasible and sustainable within prevailing South African conditions. The project supported junior primary teachers in moving to teaching practices which enable teachers and pupils to construct their own knowledge. Action research guided all levels of the programme, ranging from macro concerns regarding the direction of the development of the project as a whole, to micro concerns such as the nature of classroom interventions.

Introduction

In the past, attitudes to curriculum policy in South Africa have been dominated by rationalist, linear approaches (Samuel and Naidoo, 1992) where policy emanated from elite experts (government agencies or universities). They researched, evaluated and developed curricula, and expected unquestioned implementation by teachers. It is argued here that such approaches are not appropriate or effective, particularly within the current South African situation. Support for this conclusion centres around three broad areas.

Socio-political Concerns: Need for Redress

Top–down structures function to create and maintain hegemony for the dominant group (Fasheh, 1990). This has been particularly evident in South Africa where apartheid education was explicitly engineered to create minority control and provide inferior education for the majority in order to sustain their position of social, political and economic subjugation. Different sections of the South African community have been exposed to vastly different educational experiences, particularly in terms of access to resources.

> The debacle of Bantu Education has left a legacy of overcrowded, under-equipped classes; teachers whose education, training and confidence has been undermined;

and children who have been denied the opportunity to develop their full potential. These conditions combine with rigid, authoritarian teaching methods to produce a double depression of achievement levels in Department of Education and Training (DET)[²] schools. (Goldstein, James and Rodwell, 1991, p. W17)

Mathematics and science have been particularly negatively affected. In 1991, of the 290,918 pupils who wrote DET school-leaving examinations, only 392 passed maths at the higher grade with a C and better. In classrooms across the country, in both townships and rural areas, maths and science are viewed as foreign constructs and as integral parts of the structure of oppression. They have been identified as clear markers of the elitist society and the province of the culturally and academically advantaged.

Many South African teachers and parents in disadvantaged groups see the solution in terms of redressing the imbalance. They enshrine the authority of the existing dominant culture and attempt to appropriate it. Simply put, they believe that if they were afforded the same facilities as in the white schools, all would be well. In South Africa, this means a call for good, transmission teaching in well-resourced classrooms, conforming to the demands of authoritarian, top–down structures and syllabi. One symptom of this belief is the fact that, since restrictions on racial enrollment in schools have been removed, township children are flocking to the white and Asian schools which are perceived to be well resourced. Pressing needs to fulfill immediate educational or career needs leads to acceptance of such 'band-aid' solutions. However, there is much evidence in Africa that merely increasing educational budgets does not, in itself, improve the education of previously deprived groups (Putsoa, unpublished Address, SA Association for Research in Maths and Science Education, 1993).

Educational Concerns

Even within the most advantaged sections of the community, there is a great deal of dissatisfaction with the limited educational outcomes of 'expert designed' curricula and teaching practices, particularly in science and mathematics. Within marginalized communities, failure in these subjects is endemic and they have been 'identified as clear markers of the elitist society and the province of the culturally and academically advantaged' (Goldstein, Mnisi and Tshongwe, 1993, p. 233)

A major concern has been that top–down curricula centre around the interests of universities and, to some extent, industry. They do not address the circumstances and needs of learners. The exact direction that future practices should take is under debate, but various methodologies based on constructivist thought are gaining increasing support because they hold promise for developing flexible, reflective learners better able to meet the challenges of a changing society.

Since constructivist theory holds that individuals construct their own knowledge, it supports practices which locate responsibility for a great deal of what and how children learn firmly within the classroom itself. This is not to suggest that outside researchers should be excluded but rather that researchers and teachers should become interdependent and link their expertise. Elmore and Sykes (1992) point out:

> ... policy is reasonably effective in determining the broad content of the school curriculum. But as the aims of policy become more ambitious — to introduce new conceptions of content, to jointly influence curriculum and instruction, to change what teachers and students know, believe, and choose to work on together — then the limits of policy emerge. (p. 202)

Teacher Development Concerns

Bureaucratic curricula which dictate to teachers disempower them since they generate a 'culture of non-participation' (Samuel and Naidoo, 1992) in curriculum development. This in turn strongly militates against the implementation of change. Once again this is particularly evident in South Africa. Discussions with local teachers have highlighted pervasive beliefs which serve as strong barriers to implementation of curriculum change. These include beliefs that within the constraints of their authoritarian work structure, their under-resourced classrooms, and their poor educational background they are ill-equipped to effect change.

Classroom observations of local teachers indicate that these attitudinal barriers lead them to filter the mandated curriculum through the sieve of their established practices and attitudes: unless teachers understand and support proposed changes they, consciously or unconsciously, remould them to fit established practices. For example, teachers expressed great enthusiasm when first introduced to mathematical games and equipment. However, when observed during their initial classroom implementation, they rigidly structured children's interaction with the equipment, so that it had merely become a medium for new rote practices.

Moving Towards Change

Government

In 1978, of the 14,389 lower primary teachers working for the DET (Department of Education and Training, responsible for so-called 'black' education under the Apartheid Government) only 207 had at least matriculation plus a teaching qualification. As the world's attention focused on such statistics, a major government response was to pressure teachers to upgrade their paper qualifications.

> The feverish academic paper chase which resulted may have more negative than positive outcomes. Courses remove teachers from their classrooms and deprive them of thinking and preparation time. Teachers popularly choose 'soft option' subjects which bear no relation to classroom practice. (Goldstein and Rodwell, 1993, p. 10)

Gordon, Goldstein and Rodwell (1989) point out that this strategy raises many queries concerning the relationship between qualifications and competence, particularly for experienced teachers who are now considered to be 'unqualified' in terms of promotion and wage increases. Hartshorne (1992) sums up this kind of government inservice endeavour and concludes that it is doubtful that such centralized, top–down, efficiency approaches contribute to positive changes in classroom practice.

Other Agencies

The violent explosions of disaffection since 1976 have brought an increasing number of players into the field. A ground swell of non-government educational organizations have (NGEOs) sprung up. The challenge for these NGEOs has been to counter the negative effects of the paper chase. They have sought ways to effect and sustain meaningful change in classroom practice, in the face of limited resources as well as their lack of authority to institutionalize their work in recognized educational frameworks.

A further limitation has been that many agencies come to schools with their own agenda and usually with pre-packaged solutions. Teachers have been overwhelmed, confused and frustrated by this myriad of conflicting interventions which, therefore, do not have grass roots support. Meso (1993) describes how teachers' perceptions and belief systems impact negatively on their identification with programmes. She reports that most teachers participate under false pretences, and for wrong reasons: they take part on instruction from above, to gain access to the materials offered, or out of courtesy. They identify the projects with the existing power structures and perceive them as businesses which come into schools either to make money or to conduct research for their own purposes.

Particularly relevant to the South African situation is Gordon's (1993) examination and critique of the aims and practices of selected (international) mathematics programmes working within the constructivist paradigm. She states:

> . . . practices underwritten by certain of the programmes support narrowly defined educational agendas. In the main, political aims remain hidden as programmes are silent on the success of their strategies to reduce class, race and gender inequities in access and achievement. It therefore appears that few constructivist programmes have the potential to radically transform classroom practice, at least in the domain of redressing current inequities regarding race and gender. (pp. 182–3)

An alternative view to finding solutions calls for a total restructuring of society to create an environment which will enable people to develop structures to meet their needs. In a country whose economy has been ravaged by greed and self-interest, the implications of such restructuring are overwhelming. In 1993, Naidoo and Golombik pointed out that a future democratic South Africa would not have sufficient resources to meet all its pressing developmental needs. The driving question, therefore, becomes how best to utilize our available resources.

In order to find a way forward for mathematics education in South Africa, work needs to advance on four fronts: first, finding a new and enabling way of teaching maths; second, making it work within the realities of the prevailing South African context; third, helping teachers to make the cognitive and attitudinal shifts necessary to embrace new practices thereby assuming ownership; and fourth, redressing inequalities.

The remainder of this chapter describes the attempt by the Maths Centre for Primary Teachers (MCPT) to develop an alternative inservice model, taking the above considerations into account, and linking practitioner and researcher in curriculum development. We argue that for change in classroom practice to be meaningful and sustained, programmes should be built up in an integrative and participatory manner in order to locate ownership within the community of educators. Centre personnel did not want to tell teachers how to teach maths. The Centre rather attempted to find ways to expose teachers to alternative methodology that they could evaluate for themselves and then decide whether they wished to adopt it or not. Together with teachers, the Centre tried to develop a 'home-grown' set of teaching practices, based on constructivist thought, which gives broad access within current conditions.

The Maths Centre for Primary Teachers (MCPT)

The MCPT seeks to help junior primary teachers from under-resourced communities to improve their own maths competence and teaching practice. Between 1985 and 1995, the project made three major changes in its intervention model based on action research which was an integral aspect of the programme. The progression from one model to the next has, therefore, not been arbitrary, but was informed by observation, reflection and critical analysis on the part of both the MCPT staff and participating teachers: 'each new conceptualisation has added another dimension to the approach' (Volmink, 1993, p. 2).

The initial computer-based tutorial model, intended to improve teachers' mathematics, was soon abandoned when it became apparent that it could not deal with teachers' conceptual difficulties, with respect to both mathematics and teaching methods. On the contrary, the drill-and-practice programmes fed into old didactic approaches.

The Centre changed to using modelling strategies which mirrored targeted classroom changes. During workshops, in small collaborative groups, teachers were encouraged to grapple with mathematical problems and investigations, and devise and practise methods of dealing with them in the classroom. MCPT staff modelled facilitation strategies which helped teachers reconstruct their ideas about mathematics and how to teach it.

In terms of personal development this was effective. Teachers were excited about their growing mathematical empowerment. They became progressively more able to extract and reflect on teaching implications, such as the need to replace 'telling' practices with 'questioning' practices; to set up appropriate problem-solving opportunities; use concrete materials; value individual problem-solving strategies; harness the power of collaborative work and critical exchange of ideas; change classroom organization; and deal constructively with pupils' misconceptions.

However, we observed that these selfsame teachers regressed to established patterns at the chalk front. They could not visualize how to bridge the gap between their workshop insights and their classroom practices; they lacked the confidence to challenge existing structures; they feared that the new methods were overly time-consuming and would prevent them from completing the overloaded syllabus. It became apparent that more direct intervention was necessary to carry the changes through to the children. We would have to take the approach into the classrooms to prove to ourselves and the teachers that it could be effective in spite of prevailing conditions.

> We needed to work alongside the teachers in their classroom, face the problems together and find local solutions. We used the investigative approach itself to surmount difficulties. In this way, we, with the teachers, arrived at solutions and ways of working investigatively. (Goldstein, James and Rodwell, 1991, p. W21)

From reflections on classroom experiences, the MCPT created a model which involves participants simultaneously in personal development and in the growth of a different culture and practice of teaching and learning. The model is conceptualized in four broad stages (which overlap considerably in practice).

Model for School-based Approach

Phase 1: Information Phase (usually about 2–4 weeks)

Aim:

- To sensitize teachers to the need for change in learning and teaching styles.
- To expose teachers to inquiry-driven methods as possible alternatives to current methods.
- To initiate the establishment of intra-school structures to sustain new practices once the project has withdrawn.

Methods used:

- Modelling, through demonstration lessons to groups of teachers; incorporates alternative methods such as investigations, questioning techniques, group work; uses simple, available equipment; supports individual problem-solving strategies.
- Initiating reflective practices, through introducing teachers to: the concept of the action cycle; collaborative reflection on class experiences; journal writing.

83

- Initiating collaboration between teachers, through sharing of experiences and expertise during discussion and video workshops.

Phase 2: Classroom Practice Phase (about 3 months)

Aim:

To provide teachers with specific, intensive, practical experiences of investigative work in their own classes in order to:

- Facilitate the creation of the necessary classroom ethos to enable children to construct knowledge.
- Facilitate teachers in evaluating how their own class explores and develops a single mathematics concept/topic.
- Enable teachers to take ownership of the changes.

Methods used:

- This phase grows out of phase 1 and the methods are similar except that the initiative is progressively shifted to the teacher who ultimately directs classroom activities. Collaborative work among teachers is strongly supported.

Phase 3: Gradual Withdrawal Stage (length of time varies)

Aim:

To hand over the project to the school, which has access to the MCPT as required.

Methods used:

- Gradual, negotiated withdrawal: joint decision between teacher and MCPT about nature and extent of future support.
- Strengthening of intra-school structures by continuing workshops, but handing over organizational responsibilities to the teachers.

Phase 4: Building a Local Educative Community

Aim:

- To draw together local schools in an educative community which will independently sustain and spread change in its area.
- To offer the MCPT's expertise to the community as teachers feel further need to develop their own maths and teaching skills.

Methods used:

- Complete withdrawal from classrooms unless invited to deal with particular concerns.
- MCPT initiates and supports continued contact between clusters of local schools.
- Joint organization (MCPT and community) of local workshops dealing with mathematical content, or pertinent issue such as evaluation.
- MCPT available to assist with maths days, maths competitions, etc.

This classroom-based approach is a powerful way of assisting individual teachers to become reflective practitioners. In her journal, a staff member points out that 'Teachers move from a fascination with keeping up-to-date with the syllabus, to a realization of the need for more time to be spent on concept development' (Volmink, 1993, p. 11). Speaking of change in one teacher, the staff member comments, 'She moved from being bored and authoritarian to being capable of organizing group work and asking open questions' (p. 11). One teacher expressed the realization that she and her children were as capable as any of their more advantaged peers as follows: 'I never knew my children could be so clever. They don't need to go to white schools. We are better' (Goldstein, Mnisi and Tshongwe, 1993, p. 238). Referring to the progress of a group of first grade children (ages 6–7) previously identified as non-achievers, another Centre staff member says:

> Both teacher X and I have been amazed at how much the children have extracted from the workcards, and how much independence they have developed. The fact that they are coping with the task and understanding its demands seems to have given them a great deal of confidence. (Volmink, 1993, p. 11)

Phases 1 and 2 served as a research base for developing principles of effective implementation, but they were very cost and labour intensive. We realize that to become an agent for substantial change within the country, we have to find ways to provide broader access to the Centre's work. The community building phase is embryonic, having been conceived towards the end of 1993 and having been introduced in only two schools. However, it is already showing promise of helping to meet the great challenge of sustaining and spreading our work. One of the teachers in these schools informed his colleagues, 'This [experience] has changed my way of teaching all subjects. I will never go back to my old ways. I will try and help others to change.'

Our other vehicles for replication have proved to be extremely effective, not only in spreading our work but in giving teachers a vision of how they can become active stakeholders and participants in curriculum transformation. Teachers' and children's ideas are depicted in a series of text booklets developed by the MCPT. Classroom experiences are also shared through our newsletter which is broadly disseminated. Appropriate, cost-effective equipment, devised and tested in conjunction with teachers, is also available from the MCPT.

We have argued that for strategies to be effective they should exemplify the constructivist message, both in the way they are made and the way they are used (Goldstein et al., 1993). Videos seemed an obvious way to disseminate our work and are probably our most powerful tool. At first the Centre used programmes developed by the Open University in the United Kingdom. These videos had been highly effective when used within their target group. However, experience soon taught us that they served to increase rather than decrease feelings of alienation in our teachers. At best they elicited comments such as, 'Mm, very interesting'. More characteristically they served to reinforce teachers' beliefs about their own power-lessness. Comments which reflected these views were as follows:

> Just look at her beautiful classroom; she's got so much equipment; she has had proper training; look at her small groups; I could never do that in my class, there are too many children and too many problems; my children are not so clever; my children could not be so independent; my principal would never allow me to do that: we would never finish the syllabus; what would the inspectors say?

It became evident that for the videos to be effective they should provide teachers with a multiple vision: a vision of the activities, strategies, and skills teachers like themselves and their pupils are struggling to develop to implement the methodology; a vision of the huge educational gains which are emerging; a vision of how this can genuinely be achieved despite present physical limitations. Such videos should be directly contextualized within local teachers' circumstances and reality. We therefore sought to develop participatory structures to supplant the 'expert teacher' model with one which makes spectator-learners active and reflective participants of the entire process.

The process of video-making evolved through experience. First, a team, consisting of 2 or 3 Centre staff members together with a volunteer teacher, reflected on how to present a particular part of the syllabus within the paradigm. They developed a series of activities and low-cost supporting material which they thought might be effective. They also discussed appropriate organization for implementing their ideas in her large, under-resourced classroom. The teacher piloted these ideas in her class for about a week in order to test their feasibility and familiarize herself and the children with processes. This preparation time was not a rehearsal. It was the beginning of a new learning cycle. Shooting took place on one day and was the next day's progression in the teaching. It showed an actual teaching and learning situation and not an artificially pre-scripted scenario.

The proposed activities were introduced, modified and developed as needs became apparent. In trying to ensure teacher identification, we deliberately started the videos from 'where the teachers were' and moved to depict acceptable changes. For example, we moved away from initial activities which were highly teacher directed to those which handed more and more control of learning processes and strategies to the children. A reflection of this mechanism is that the videos started with whole class teaching and moved to small group investigations.

The team identified relevant teaching issues which emerged in the rushes. The material was then broken into short excerpts and the voice over was written in such a way as to direct viewers' attention to these issues. The voice over also posed open-ended questions and problems regarding both the content and the processes within the video. After each excerpt there is time for discussion and reflection which is usually introduced by questions in the voice over or in the accompanying booklet. For example, the introductory voice over to one video says:

> My Standard 1 class and I are discovering about adding and subtracting. We are all very new at working this way. We are also new at doing maths in English. I spend a long time helping the children build up their counting skills. I am finding that when children discover the patterns in numbers, it helps them in many ways. As you watch, try and work out all the different patterns and skills the children are developing. How will this help them with adding and subtracting?

The videos provide teacher-viewers with a window into the actual implementation experiences of a colleague and her pupils within the complex environment of an authentic class. This means that teachers can be led to interact with the videos on many different levels and to consider the complex interrelationships and dependencies. The richness of such exposure stands in stark contrast to those instructional programmes which attempt to develop concepts by focusing only on critical features and break learning material into small component parts which are then systematically presented to the learner.

   We have gathered considerable ethnographic data which show that this identification is at last beginning to translate into action (Goldstein et al., 1993). More importantly, the teachers in our project, as well as a wide variety of outside teachers and teacher trainers, are also beginning to assume ownership of the material and are beginning to use it independently in discussion groups and workshops. A teacher, Lizzie, wrote this about developments in her school:

> When we were invited to watch a video presentation, we expected that it would involve white teachers and white pupils in the suburbs. To our GREAT SURPRISE the video was in North Sotho, and had been done in one of the Black Schools. That made the difference.

> Maria taught 47 pupils successfully. If she could do this, why can't we do the same? This was a challenge. We were impressed by Maria's 'How do you know?' questions. Most teachers do not ask such questions.

> We discussed the video presentation the following day. Some thought it was a success while others expressed no opinion. Someone said: 'Ja! It had to be a success, after all whites have everything, equipment and the lot. The equipment used in the video was expensive.'

> But, when we discussed the video critically, we realised that in fact, Maria used inexpensive material. Then I realised that I have the same materials, such as pegs, matchsticks and cards . . . together with the pupils, we collected acorns in the school yard for counting.

Our videos (five are now available) are, therefore, produced collaboratively by volunteer teachers and small MCPT teams. Together they construct an approach to an aspect of the syllabus. No script is written. Rather, the video sets out to capture the teacher's genuine attempt to implement the approach within the constraints of a large class. Since the videos emanate from familiar and relevant contexts, teachers identify more strongly with them. Volmink (1993), in his evaluation of the MCPT's work, states, 'The MCPT videos are amongst the best documentation on participatory curriculum development available in the country' (p. 12).

Conclusion

Our experiences during the past 10 years have led us to a participatory model of professional and curriculum development which we believe to be pertinent, feasible and sustainable in present South African conditions. We also believe that the model has relevance for other countries, particularly developing countries. The challenge for 1995 is to convince a new government that this — rather than old, familiar and seemingly more simple top–down practices — will form an effective basis for educational upliftment in a democratic society.

Postscript

Since this chapter was written, our new democratically elected government has announced fundamental changes which will affect all aspects of life in South Africa. The key principles which will inform these changes, particularly as they relate to education, are redress of past inequalities and access to quality lifelong education for all citizens. Specifically the government has announced that from January 1998 a new outcomes-based curriculum framework will be phased in. The national overarching 'critical outcomes' and the 'specific learning area outcomes', which stakeholder committees have already produced, support a shift from knowledge transmission and drill-and-practice to an emphasis on critical and creative interpretation, evaluation and application of knowledge.

While many educators support the new policies in principle, there is wide concern that the proposed hasty implementation of as yet locally untested and unadapted ideas is being driven more by political imperatives than by sound educational considerations. There is concern that the hasty imposition of such committee-developed outcomes will negate the experience of community-based organizations, as described in this chapter, that unless a participatory model of curriculum development is adopted, teachers will be marginalized and real change in the classroom will not occur.

Notes

1   This paper draws heavily on two earlier papers co-authored by Goldstein and marked with an asterisk (*) in the list of references.

2 Department of Education and Training was responsible for so-called 'black' education under the Apartheid Government.

References

ELMORE, R. and SYKES, G. (1982) 'Curriculum policy', in JACKSON, P.W. (ed.) *Handbook of Research Curriculum* (pp. 185–215), New York: Macmillan.

FASHEH, M. (1990) 'Community education', *Harvard Educational Review*, **60**, pp. 19–36.

GOLDSTEIN, C., JAMES, N. and RODWELL, P. (1991) 'I'm a culprit because I'm a victim', *Proceedings of the 14th National Convention on Mathematics and Natural Science Education* (pp. 17–26), Cape Town, South Africa.

GOLDSTEIN, C., MNISI, P. and RODWELL, P.* (1994) 'Working together for change', in PONTE J. and MATOS, J. (eds) *Proceedings of the Eighteenth International Conference for the Psychology of Mathematics Education Vol. 2* (pp. 9–16), Lisbon: University of Lisbon.

GOLDSTEIN, C., MNISI, P. and TSHONGWE, T.* (1993) 'Medium and message', in JULIE, C., ANGELIS, D. and DAVIS Z. (eds) *Political Dimensions of Mathematics Education*, **2**, pp. 232–9.

GOLDSTEIN, C. and RODWELL, P. (1993) 'Empowering mathematics teachers', *Financial Mail Education Supplement*, **2**, 10, Johannesburg, SA: Venture Publishing (Pty) Ltd.

GORDON, A. (1993) 'Constructivism and politics of pedagogy', in JULIE, C., ANGELIS, D. and DAVIS, Z. (eds) *Political Dimensions of Mathematics Education*, **2**, pp. 175–84.

GORDON, A., GOLDSTEIN, C. and RODWELL, P. (1989) 'Technology and pedagogy in mathematics', *The Proceedings of the 3rd International Conference: Children in the Information Age*, pp. 327–41.

HARTSHORNE, K. (1992) *Crises and Challenge: Black Education 1910–1990*, Cape Town, SA: Oxford University Press.

MESO, M. (1993) 'Creating positive entry points to sensitise teachers to change', Unpublished Facilitator's Reports on Action Research, Auckland Park, S.A.: Maths Centre for Primary Teachers.

NAIDOO, K. and GOLOMBIK, N. (1993) 'Key issues facing the democratic movement with regard to electronic media in education', Unpublished paper at Electronic Media Education Workshop, Johannesburg, SA.

SAMUEL, M. and NAIDOO, P. (1992) *Paradigm Shift: From Teacher Non-participation to Teacher Participation in Curriculum Development: A Case Study in South African Science Education*, Durban, SA: University of Durban Westville.

VOLMINK, J. (1993) '*Maths Centre for Primary Teachers*', Unpublished evaluation report, Auckland Park, SA: Maths Centre for Primary Teachers.

Editors' Comment

The next two chapters address issues in teaching development when teachers start to undertake research in their classrooms into aspects of their own practice.

Irwin and Britt in New Zealand highlight the continuing differences between the goals and purposes of intermediate education and those of secondary education and their impact on teaching development.

The paper by Krainer in Austria charts the movement from teacher to teacher-as-researcher in the classroom and casts the role of the teacher educator as collaborator in improving mathematics education.

10 Teachers' Knowledge of Mathematics and Reflective Professional Development

Kathryn C. Irwin and Murray S. Britt, New Zealand

> When I went through school, I did subtraction using equal additions . . . But I
> didn't understand what I was doing . . . I just knew I had borrowed ten and I had
> paid it back. But I could do subtraction and I always got it right and I felt good
> about that. (Emily, May 1992)

> My confidence as a teacher was heavily undermined due to the project . . . From
> the project itself I got the impression that I was not working enough on maths or
> had the right emphasis on maths even though there was not enough time to do this
> with maths as well as teach everything else. (Emily, November 1992)

These quotations come from one teacher who was involved in a two-year professional development project entitled Teachers Raising Achievement in Mathematics (TRAM). She was not typical of the other teachers in the project. However, her difficulties appeared to be similar to other teachers whom such professional development programmes hope to help. In this chapter we look at what our professional development project did for Emily, and what she taught us.

Background

Most professional development programmes for New Zealand teachers are of short duration. They may last for one afternoon, a whole day, or for 10 days spread over 10 weeks. The TRAM project was developed in the belief that teachers would be more likely to change their practice if they concentrated on this change for a longer period and if they themselves initiated change in response to needs that they identified in their own classrooms. Some studies of teacher development programmes (e.g. Simon and Schifter, 1991; Cobb, Wood, Yackel, Nicholls, Wheatley, Trigatti and Perlwitz, 1991) have suggested that if teachers were to develop a new teaching methodology compatible with a constructivist view of learning, the professional development itself should be constructivist in nature, and would necessarily be of a longer duration.

To test this belief in a New Zealand setting, 18 teachers were recruited for an experimental two-year professional development project. They came from four intermediate schools and four secondary schools. These schools were selected from an initial pool of 25 schools, on the basis of the interest of school principals and teachers in this project, pairing of intermediate schools with secondary schools in the same area, and geographical spread across the city. Two or three teachers participated from each of the schools. The eight intermediate school teachers taught all subjects to students aged 11 or 12 but concentrated on their teaching of mathematics for the purposes of this study. The 10 secondary school teachers taught only mathematics to students from 13 to 17, but focused on their youngest class for this study.

The focus of the project was what teachers wanted to do in their own classrooms. The authors visited each classroom a number of times, giving the teachers notes on what they observed. Teachers audiotaped and videotaped their own classes for their own analysis as well as for the authors. The teachers and authors met together in individual schools to clarify the teachers' goals and suggest ways of testing how these goals could be met.

Sessions were held with the whole group on a regular basis over the two years. These whole group sessions often started with a novel mathematical activity, and then moved to a discussion of what the teachers had been doing, common discoveries or problems. New Zealand's new mathematics curriculum (Ministry of Education, 1992) was introduced to the group early on, as one of the authors was instrumental in its development. Some whole day workshops were held in which the teachers developed plans for helping students learn the concepts suggested in this curriculum and then reported back on the implementation of these innovations.

The combination of both intermediate and secondary school teachers in the project was intentional if somewhat unusual. Both groups of teachers were concerned about the difficulty that students had in moving between the two levels of schooling. They thought that by working together they could help their students with this transition. The authors also saw the two groups of teachers as having different strengths to offer each other. The intermediate school teachers brought expertise in teaching other subject areas in an investigative manner. The secondary school teachers came with greater knowledge of mathematics which helped them to see the big ideas in mathematics that their teaching aimed toward.

Most measures used indicated that the project was an effective method of professional development. These measures included students' performance, teachers' responses to questionnaires and interviews, classroom observations, entries in journals kept by the teachers, students' appraisals, and intermediate and longer term appraisal of the project by the teachers themselves. A full report on this project can be found in the *Teachers Raising Achievement in Mathematics: Final Report* (Britt, Irwin, Ellis and Ritchie, 1993).

In a session held nine months after the project finished, teachers made evaluative statements that captured the nature of the project for them. Some of these were:

> At first I was frustrated with the project because I expected to be given something. Then it dawned on me that if I was going to change, I had to be the one to do it. The project has given me the courage to try new teaching approaches and where they don't work to try a different tack.

I am more willing to take risks in my classroom.

It empowered me to have a greater input into decisions affecting the directions for mathematics education. I learned that anything I tried in my classroom had validity. It made me more tolerant of myself, of the students, and of other teachers.

I have realized the value to me of writing things down, and then sharing what I have written with others.

The project enabled me to talk about the new curriculum and about constructivism. As a consequence I am more positive about the curriculum, encouraging teachers to try suggested approaches.

I now constantly ask the question, 'What is the mathematics in this activity?'

I now see that there is little value in one-day teacher development programmes. Even in our 10-week teacher development contract teachers may not progress for the first eight weeks (or 10 in some cases). Teacher development takes time, and it is essential to have more than one person per school.

Differences in Effect of the Project for Different Teachers

Some teachers indicated that they had made major changes while others thought that there had been only minor changes in their teaching. In response to a questionnaire in which teachers reported on their own change in teaching and beliefs on a number of measures, change was rated (by an outside assessor) as in line with, or in opposition to, a constructivist view of learning. Responses from secondary school teachers indicated that they had changed more than the intermediate school teachers, and teachers with more experience had changed more than teachers who were relatively new to the classroom. Other differences between intermediate school and secondary school teachers were shown in their choice of objectives, with intermediate school teachers favouring 'developing an awareness of the importance of mathematics in everyday life' and secondary school teachers favouring 'developing an attitude of inquiry' (items from the SIMS questionnaire, Binns, Carpenter, Elliffe, Irving and McBride, 1987).

Case studies based on all the material available on individual teachers showed that the nature of experimentation and reflection done by the two groups of teachers was different. A reflection by an intermediate school teacher which indicated change was, 'I now constantly ask the question "What is the mathematics in this activity?" ' Secondary school teachers, on the other hand, reflected on their increased ability to watch and help their students, their interest and ability to influence their colleagues and to influence the wider educational system.

Notes made at the whole group sessions show that teachers from the two levels of schools responded differently to novel mathematical tasks. The secondary school teachers were generally eager to try out ideas on these tasks, while the intermediate school teachers participated less. Some of these teachers commented that they felt inhibited by the presence of the secondary school teachers. However, when a special session was held with only the intermediate school teachers, it was apparent that some of the intermediate school teachers were unwilling to take the risk of trying out ideas in a mathematical context, even without the presence of secondary school teachers.

This drew our attention to looking for reasons why some teachers were more willing than others to investigate mathematical ideas. We noted that the teachers who were least willing to experiment tended to be those with the lowest level of training and confidence in mathematics. As pointed out by Glaser (1984), there is evidence to suggest that both reasoning and learning are knowledge driven. Those who are knowledge-rich reason more profoundly: knowledge thus begets knowledge. This may have been a factor inhibiting some of the teachers from exploring mathematical ideas or trying new classroom procedures.

Relationship of Confidence, Competence, and Professional Development in the Project

It was possible to categorize teachers by their previous formal and informal training in mathematics; their confidence in the classroom, based on observations, journals and responses to interviews and questionnaires; and their degree of change during the project, using their own assessment together with that of the authors. Table 10.1 shows the relationship among these factors. Only the teachers who were in the project for the full two years are included.

For the secondary school teachers the relationship is clear. Those teachers with a high level of mathematics and a high level of confidence judged that they had changed considerably. If either the level of mathematics or confidence as a teacher was relatively low, change was less extensive.

More explanation is needed for the intermediate school teachers. The teacher who was rated as having a high level of mathematics and a high level of confidence

Table 10.1 Number of project teachers with high or low levels of mathematics, high or low levels of confidence in the classroom, and reported benefit from the project (N for Secondary teachers = 10, Intermediate school teachers = 5)

Mathematics Level*	Classroom Confidence	Change in the Project
Secondary - high - 6	high - 6	high - 6
Secondary - high - 1	low - 1	medium - 1
Secondary - low - 3	high - 2, low - 1	medium - 1, low - 2
Intermediate - high - 1	high - 1	medium - 1
Intermediate - low - 2	high - 2	medium - 1, delayed - 1
Intermediate - low - 2	low - 2	low - 2

* Mathematics level is high or low for school level taught. For secondary school teachers high is 3 or 4 years of university mathematics, and low is 1 or 2 years of university mathematics. For intermediate school teachers, all had stopped formal mathematics in 5th or 6th form, but one had continued to learn informally, in a family of engineers and scientists.

in the classroom was already a very innovative and reflective teacher. Her teaching at the end of the project was exemplary, but there had only been a moderate amount of change in her practice. The pair of teachers rated as having a low level of mathematical knowledge but high classroom confidence both commented that they felt good about their teaching in language areas but less confident in mathematics. They were confident enough to ask basic questions about mathematical procedures during the project. One of them said: 'I have to remind myself that I may not be a good mathematician, but I am a good teacher.' The other commented at the end of the project that she had not changed, but a year later phoned the authors to change her appraisal and tell them how much her teaching had changed as a result of the project.

Of the two teachers in the bottom category, one was a novice teacher, aware of his weaknesses, and although eager to get help still had other difficulties common to novice teachers. The other was a more experienced teacher, and is the subject of this chapter. They both could be described as having a low level of pedagogical content knowledge (Shulman, 1987).

Other differences appeared in the goals set by different groups of teachers. The secondary school teachers with advanced mathematics and considerable classroom experience all emphasized problem-solving for the construction of mathematical understanding, while the least mathematically competent intermediate school teachers favoured learning mathematical facts.

Mathematical Knowledge and Professional Development Programmes

There has been considerable interest in the mathematical knowledge needed by pre-service and serving teachers (e.g. Ball and McDiarmid, 1990; Ball, 1993; Putnam, Heaton, Prawat and Remillard, 1992). Putnam et al. discuss teachers' knowledge and beliefs about learning, teachers' knowledge of mathematics, and teachers' knowledge and beliefs about mathematics. Ball (1993) cites Schoenfeld as arguing that

> ... learning to think mathematically means (a) developing a mathematical point of view valuing the process of mathematization and abstraction and having the predilection to apply them, and (b) developing competence with the tools of the trade, and using those tools in the service of the goal of understanding structure — mathematical sense-making. (p. 376)

Our findings and concerns are in agreement with those of these writers. We argue that teachers who have a broad and integrated knowledge of mathematics in advance of the mathematics that they teach are also more likely to have a perception of the nature of mathematics as 'fallible, changing, and like any other body of knowledge, the product of human invention' (Ernest, 1991, p. xi). We argue further that such teachers are more likely to be able to use teaching approaches that emphasize problem-solving so that students can construct appropriate knowledge, and be able to articulate for themselves a set of values related to mathematics and mathematics teaching which reflect this view of mathematics. Supporting evidence for these claims can be found in the teachers' judgments about the nature of mathematics and emphasis on what was to be taught. The two examples given below, from intermediate school teachers, show the difference that these factors can make when teachers attempt to improve their practice. Pseudonyms are used.

A Teacher with an Adequate Mathematical Background Who Was Able to Reflect on Her Teaching

One of these teachers was Jennifer. She was a teacher who had had a year of university mathematics, unusual among intermediate school teachers. She left the project after the first year so is not included in the final data, but her experiences in the first year were of interest. If she had been rated by the criteria used for the other teachers, she would have rated as high in mathematical ability, moderate in classroom confidence, and high in change within the project. She had been teaching for three years in a traditional manner, with tightly structured lessons which included a quick quiz, a teacher-directed session, a worksheet to complete, and similar work for homework. Her impetus for change came from a comment of her 15-year-old daughter, who complained, 'Why don't they ask us in exams what they have taught us, and not put it in a different way?' She realized that her daughter was learning about procedures, and had difficulty transferring this knowledge to novel problems.

In her own class she wanted to try encouraging students to develop their own problems to help them see the generality and applicability of what they were learning. She asked the pupils in her class write their own problems for fractions, using situations from outside school, and discovered that this was not something that her pupils could do immediately. She therefore asked the students to write a problem in groups, then put these problems on the board to see if others in the class could understand them. This helped to sort out what information a problem needed to contain if it were to be solved, and helped students to rewrite the problem so that it could be solved by others in the class. Students then wrote problems individually, from their home experience, and these problems were used in class as the basis of future lessons.

This teacher's comments in her journal describe both her feelings about this innovation, and the students' response:

> 22.7.91 Feel as if I have made a breakthrough here. The 40-minute period was spent totally covering around 6 of the problems created by the children. I was surprised at the number of skills we covered by dealing with these problems. The class was very attentive and good discussion took place. Children who gave problems felt a great sense of importance. . . .

> I feel excited about outcomes today. I discussed with the class how they felt. I firstly asked whether they enjoyed the lesson. Overwhelming 'Yes'. They certainly appeared highly motivated. Secondly I asked whether they learnt more this way, and I wanted honest answers. They felt they had learnt many different skills and that they understood the use of fractions. . . .

> I felt quite anxious at the beginning of the lesson as I did not have my normal mental, reinforcement, followed by teaching of a new skill, then a worksheet. I actually had nothing prepared. The children gave me what I needed and took greater responsibility for their learning. I feel their self esteem has improved through sharing their ideas.

Jennifer could teach this lesson entirely from student prompts (despite her anxiety) because of her firm conceptual and relational knowledge of the mathematics involved. She could see the potential relationships between the knowledge that her students had, and that which they needed in order to solve what were originally ill-structured problems (Resnick, 1988). In reflecting on the lesson, she looked at what had happened in relation to values that matched what she valued about mathematics and mathematics learning. These included: students talking and writing mathematics; students understanding mathematics; students taking greater responsibility for their learning; and students reflecting on their learning.

A Teacher Whose Limited Mathematical Knowledge Restricted Her Ability to Reflect on Her Teaching

Emily, the teacher quoted at the start of the chapter, had a limited mathematical background. She said that although she learned from participating in the TRAM project, she never felt comfortable in it, especially not in the presence of the secondary school teachers. This teacher also ran tightly structured classes. These began with a skills test and were followed by work in ability groups, working on exercises, word problems, or with Emily on number concepts. Her lessons were heavily procedural. She saw herself mostly as the 'explainer'. However, in observed classes she let some serious misconceptions pass unchecked. For example, for much of the first year of the project she placed emphasis on learning to name place value. In an observed lesson on writing expanded numerals, she asked for the expanded version of 25002.2. A student wrote $200000 + 50000 + 2 + .2$, and was commended for her effort before being asked to clean the board. It seemed that Emily's own limited knowledge of place value prevented her from recognizing that the student's answer represented either a careless error or a serious misconception.

Although she reported in an interview that she did quite a lot of problem-solving, she used a book as the source of problems, and appeared not to be able to solve some of these problems herself. The confused and tentative nature of some responses that she gave did not stimulate the class discussion and investigation that might have led students to adjust their understanding. She found that a group of students was having difficulty with the problem: 'Mary is 6 years older than Jean. The sum of their ages is 20. How old is Mary?' Two students had written as their answers, '20 and 26'. She did not ask whether or not this answer fitted the constraints of the problem, or give the students help, for example, by offering the hint 'suppose the girls were the same ages, what would their ages be?' Instead she only said, 'Put your thinking caps on.' She did not ask students who had successfully solved the problem to discuss their reasoning. There were few in-built ways for students to check their mathematics, as it was rarely tied to situations of importance to them.

During the period of the project she reported a growing commitment to incorporating everyday contexts and more games in her mathematics programme. Nevertheless, despite some minor observed shifts, Emily herself maintained that she had changed 'very little'. She believed strongly that learning tables and procedures came first, and that, for many students, there was little time for conceptual understanding. She suggested that, for her, there was a conflict between changes to a less structured style of teaching suggested by other project teachers and the new mathematics curriculum, and the culture of the school which had a strong focus on testing. She felt that the students liked her tightly structured lesson format and that pressure for increased testing from the school administration had prevented her from moving away from her current approach. She commented:

> . . . if you wait for understanding, sometimes you could be working at a very basic level, and I know understanding is important. When I went through school, I did subtraction using equal additions . . . But I didn't understand what I was doing. I had no idea where this ten came from or where I was giving it back to. I just knew I had borrowed ten and I had paid it back. But I could do subtraction and I always got it right and I felt good about that. (May 1992)

When interviewed about any changes she had made as a result of her participation in the project, Emily made the following comments:

> I thought that I would get guidance but the project has actually wanted me to find out, me to do. And there's nothing wrong with that but . . . ideas don't just come. It needs to be a sharing. So I was sort of hoping that I would come back from there motivated to do, whereas that hasn't actually been the case.

> . . . If the project is going to move from here into helping teachers, there's got to be an awareness of all that (fund raising, the need for school promotion resulting from the removal of school zones) because those are the realities of school, particularly at this level, more so than at high school where teachers get their (free) period most weeks.

This comment about high school teachers was added to in an evaluation that she completed at the end of the project.

> My confidence as a teacher was heavily undermined due to the project. I was given the impression by the high school teachers that we did no work and taught nothing and were particularly looked down on. From the project itself I got the impression that I was not working enough on maths or had the right emphasis on maths even though there was not enough time to do this with maths as well as teach everything else. (November 1992)

The most obvious effect of this professional development project on Emily was to arouse her old anxiety about mathematics. The demands of the new curriculum, that she teach mathematics in a different way, aroused emotional responses that had only just been kept in control in her role of teacher-as-explainer. She repeatedly objected to the presence of secondary school teachers, who made her feel 'dumb'. She used diversionary tactics to avoid doing mathematics in group sessions or being observed in her own classroom, possibly to save her self-respect. Her behaviour fits Mandler's view (cited in McLeod, 1992) that the emotion aroused by her uncertainty about mathematics was stronger than her memory for the mathematics she may have learned.

> ... when I went through teachers college, they were right into the new maths and I cried a year through college ... A year of maths at college put me right off maths and it's taken me a long time to sort of say it's okay, I can cope again.

Emily's own anxieties and lack of confidence were reflected in her goals for the project. She wanted to have her students enjoy mathematics and she wanted them to know the basics so that they could have a sense of achievement. But she also wanted them to see the relevance of what they were doing and to develop an understanding of the processes.

Her class did appear to be a happy place overall. However her happy class made very little progress. On the Chelsea Diagnostic Test of Place-value and Decimals (Hart, Brown, Kerslake, Kuchemann and Ruddock, 1985), given at the beginning and at the end of the school year, 37 per cent of the class increased one level or more, 44 per cent stayed on the same level, and 19 per cent scored at a lower level at the end of the year than at the beginning. The average rate of progress for the class was the lowest of any of the classes in the project, and considerably lower than the rate of progress shown by a large sample of English children (Hart, 1981).

The report on this project (Britt et al., 1993) concluded that teachers' reflections lay at the heart of a successful professional development project. The teachers who made important changes in their practice did so by reflecting on their pedagogy against a background of mathematical understanding and a set of values. This enabled them to see if their pedagogy was in fact enabling their students to construct a more complete understanding of mathematics. Without an understanding of mathematics, and a set of values against which these reflections could be judged, teachers like Emily could only reflect against that aspect of mathematics that was most important in her own learning, that of her negative feelings about the subject.

What Emily Taught Us

Emily taught us that however much we tried to let the participating teachers set the focus of the project, there were unspoken messages that Emily was more aware of than we were. These messages valued reflection on the mathematics of a task, and having a set of values about the nature of mathematics against which teachers' experiences could be reflected. Emily wanted to be told how to be a better mathematics teacher, and we didn't tell her. We thought that she would find out in a way meaningful to her, but her need to protect her thin layer of self-respect in this area was too great to allow her to experiment.

What could we have done to be more helpful to Emily? There are several possibilities, some of which we have tried with other teachers. Instead of a project which she found to be destructive, she needed to feel empowered from the start to choose or design the type of inservice project that would be helpful to her. Because she wanted ideas for what to do, it might have been possible to start with ideas which were close to her current teaching, rather than the challenging investigations presented at the joint meetings. Then, with a group of teachers with a similar level of skills, she could be encouraged to draw the mathematics out of the activities, similar to the problems that she set as challenges for her own class.

We discovered that, rather than volunteering for the project, Emily had been asked to come by her principal in a manner which made it difficult to refuse. Perhaps she should not have been involved in any programme until she saw the need, as two other teachers did who knew that they were good in teaching literacy but unsure of their mathematics teaching or their own mathematics. She may have needed to acknowledge her anxiety about mathematics early in the project and see that it could be overcome when she understood some mathematical concepts.

Both of the authors are involved in preservice and other post-service teacher training programmes. One of these programmes is a longer period of inservice training which can be taken at a pace allowed by the teacher's available time. In this programme, teachers take some specially designed courses in classroom teaching, some courses which introduce them to studies of the effect of different teaching methods and other relevant literature, and some mathematics courses at a level appropriate for them. If Emily had enrolled in this programme, she might have taken the ideas that she wanted from the classroom-oriented papers first, and when successful in using these, move on to an appropriate mathematics paper.

One author has been involved in designing a novel university mathematics course for both pre-service and inservice teachers. It is intended for teachers who have had as little mathematics as Emily. Its emphasis is to enable students to gain confidence in operating mathematically, especially in seeing the relationships between different mathematical procedures. If students do not understand how to find 2/3 of a number (which is not uncommon) there is adequate tutorial time and inclination to discuss fractions as divisions by the bottom number, then multiplied by the number of parts. This course has received considerable acclaim from the students who have completed it.

What is certain is that we need to do something to acknowledge and help the 'Emilys' among our teachers. They need greater mathematical knowledge, together with confidence in classroom organization, if they are to reflect on their own teaching in a way that is likely to improve it. It is unrealistic to expect them to do this, or to teach their students to reflect on mathematical ideas and processes flexibly unless they themselves can do so.

References

BALL, D.L. (1993) 'With an eye on the mathematical horizon: Dilemmas of teaching elementary school mathematics', *The Elementary School Teacher*, **93**, pp. 373–442.

BALL, D.L. and MCDIARMID, G.W. (1990) 'The subject-matter preparation of teachers', in HOUSTON, W.R. (ed.) *Handbook of Research on Teacher Education* (pp. 437–449), New York: Macmillan.

BINNS, A., CARPENTER, R., ELLIFFE, R., IRVING, J., and MCBRIDE, N. (eds) (1987) *Mathematics Achievement in New Zealand Secondary Schools. A report on the conduct in New Zealand of the Second International Mathematics Study within the International Association for the Evaluation of Educational Achievement*, Wellington: Department of Education.

BRITT, M.S., IRWIN, K.C., ELLIS, J. and RITCHIE, G. (1993) *Teachers Raising Achievement in Mathematics: Final Report to the Ministry of Education*, Auckland NZ: Centre for Mathematics Education, Auckland College of Education.

COBB, P., WOOD, T., YACKEL, E., NICHOLLS, J., WHEATLEY, G., TRIGATTI, B. and PERLWITZ, M. (1991) 'Assessment of a problem-centered second-grade mathematics project', *Journal for Research in Mathematics Education*, **22**, pp. 3–29.

ERNEST, P. (1991) *The Philosophy of Mathematics*, London: Falmer Press.

GLASER, R. (1984) 'Education and thinking', *American Psychologist*, **39**, pp. 93–104.

HART, K. (ed.) (1981) *Children's Understanding of Mathematics: 11–16*, Newcastle-on-Tyne: John Murray.

HART, K., BROWN, M., KERSLAKE, D., KUCHEMANN, D. and RUDDOCK, G. (1985) *Chelsea Diagnostic Tests*, Windsor: NFER-Nelson.

MANDLER, G. (1984) *Mind and Body: Psychology of Emotion*, New York: Norton.

MCLEOD, D.B. (1992) 'Research on affect in mathematics education: A reconceptualization', in GROUWS, D.A. (ed.) *Handbook of Research on Mathematics Teaching and Learning*, New York: MacMillan.

MINISTRY OF EDUCATION (1992) *Mathematics in the New Zealand Curriculum*, Wellington: Learning Media.

PUTNAM, R.T., HEATON, R.M., PRAWAT, R.S. and REMILLARD, J. (1992) 'Teaching mathematics for understanding: Discussing case studies of four fifth-grade teachers', *The Elementary School Teacher*, **93**, pp. 213–29.

RESNICK, L.B. (1988) 'Teaching mathematics as an ill-structured discipline', in CHARLES, R.I. and SILVER, E.A. (eds) *The Teaching and Assessing of Mathematical Problem Solving* (pp. 32–60), Hillsdale, N.J.: Erlbaum.

SHULMAN, L.S. (1987) 'Knowledge and teaching: Foundations of the new reform', *Harvard Educational Review*, **57**, pp. 1–22.

SIMON, M. and SCHIFTER, D. (1991) 'Towards a constructivist perspective: An intervention study of mathematics teacher development', *Educational Studies in Mathematics*, **22**, pp. 309–31.

11 PFL-Mathematics: Improving Professional Practice in Mathematics Teaching

Konrad Krainer, Austria

Background to the PFL Programme

In the 1970s more and more high school teachers in Austria felt that, in addition to their competence in two subjects (e.g. mathematics and geography), further development of their pedagogical and didactic competence would be required for coping successfully with the complexities of teaching and learning. In awareness of this need, an interdisciplinary team of researchers from the University of Klagenfurt began to plan the teacher inservice courses PFL in several subjects, of which mathematics is one. PFL is an abbreviation for 'pedagogy and subject-specific methodology for teachers'. Since 1982, four PFL-mathematics and two PFL-science courses, each attended by about 30 participants, have taken place. Each course lasts for four semesters and consists of a variety of formats, in particular three one-week seminars, five one-and-a-half-day regional group meetings, and individual practical work. The teachers are required to write case studies on innovations introduced in their schools. After the conclusion of the course, participants receive a university certificate with a description of their achievements during the course.

Most PFL courses are led by a team of 5–6 members (educationalists, subject-matter specialists, practitioners) who are responsible for the preparation and realization of the course and for follow-up activities (e.g. evaluation, publication). All in all, this involves three years of intensive theoretical and practical work. The activities of the team members are seen not only as a contribution to the further education of teachers but also as an experience in interdisciplinary cooperation.

Guiding Principles of the Programme

One of the most important principles is stressing the importance and interconnectedness of pedagogical and didactic aspects of teaching and learning. Above all, it is realized that the complexity of the teacher's task cannot be reduced to content-related considerations. For example, the teaching of topics such as 'proof' must consider student motivation, the use of different heuristic strategies, engaging students in reflections on the nature of proof, and discussions on pupils' understanding of proofs.

Engaging the *interest* of teachers is an important starting point for work within a course — emphasizing the practical experiences of the participants in order to begin from 'where they are', and to improve their teaching by identifying strengths rather than weaknesses. Action research, which is understood as the systematic reflection of practitioners on action (Stenhouse, 1975; Schön, 1983; Elliott, 1991; Altrichter, Posch and Somekh, 1993), is used as a framework to achieve a broader situative understanding and to improve the quality of teaching.

Appreciation of teachers' work is seen as a second key factor. Teachers are regarded as professionals who systematically try to develop further their competence in, and attitude towards, the different dimensions of professional practice. One main aim of the programme is to encourage teachers to do research work related to their own practice. Another is to motivate and qualify them to organize further professional development for themselves and for other teachers after the conclusion of the course.

A third key factor is *open-mindedness*. A basic question within the courses is 'What can teachers learn from (other) learners?', whereby learners can be students in a teacher's own school as well as fellow students on the course. Promoting active learning processes and reflecting on them is a basic strategy in a dual sense. Firstly, with regard to an epistemological understanding of learning which sees the learner as an active producer of knowledge rather than a consumer. Secondly, with regard to the conviction that transfer from the course to the classroom — where students also should be seen as producers — is more successful if the participants learn such processes through their own experience.

Communication among teachers often happens 'in passing' and is often felt to be unsatisfactory. In the programme, an attempt is made to find useful ways in which teachers can engage in professional exchange of knowledge, making their innovative work accessible to others, and thus promoting a culture of communication on educational issues. If countless good ideas exist only in teachers' minds, they cannot be accessible to others. It is an important intention of the programme to help teachers find ways to make their private ideas public.

Such communication and cooperation among teachers is increasingly seen as an important element of teachers' work. Opportunities are provided, within the programme, to connect individual and social learning experiences. The open atmosphere of the courses is used as a basis for initiating and organizing communication and cooperation with colleagues. This is something which is in many cases difficult to achieve in a teacher's own school. The regional groups become small 'professional communities' in which mutual understanding and constructive criticism are conducive processes.

In order to promote the further integration of theory and practice, a close cooperation between team members and participants is sought by the former involving themselves in concrete and specific situations of the teachers' practical work, and the latter involving themselves in theoretical and general considerations. For this purpose it is an advantage if people come from different systems, namely 'school' and 'university', and are able to overcome their 'restricted' perspectives.

One aim of the programme is to motivate and qualify the participants to organize further inservice education for themselves and for other teachers after conclusion of the course. Thus it is important that the participants are actively involved in the planning and realization of the course, and increasingly take charge of their own education within (and later outside) the course. Therefore the role of the team of university educators is to provide input and structure (to initiate teachers' activities) in order to organize communication among the teachers and for them to view themselves as experts. The course aims to contribute to each of the factors outlined above, however, its strengths lie in its whole composition which is decisively influenced by the people working in it — the university team members as well as the teachers.

Within the limits of this chapter, it is only possible to sketch some of the selected activities of teachers within and after the course. This will be done by considering four dimensions of teachers' professional practice: action, reflection, autonomy, and networking. Altrichter and Krainer (1996 p. 34) describe these dimensions as follows:

- Attitude towards and competence in experimental, constructive and goal-directed work (action).
- Attitude towards, and competence in, reflective, (self)-critical and systematically based work (reflection).
- Attitude towards, and competence in, autonomous, self-initiative and self-determined work (autonomy).
- Attitude towards and competence in communicative and cooperative work with increasing public relevance (networking).
(translated from the German by KRAINER)

The following two examples provide insight into these four dimensions of professional practice (see also Krainer, in press). The first example, a teacher's case study of her students' errors in algebra, provides evidence of the importance of systematic reflection by teachers on their own practice, thus interconnecting action and reflection. The second consists of teacher comments on a follow-up activity by a self-organized group of teachers to illustrate autonomy and networking. A more detailed description of activities within PFL-mathematics is given in Fischer et al. (1985), Krainer (1994) and Krainer and Posch (1996).

Action and Reflection: A Teacher's Efforts to Improve Her Knowledge about Her Students' Understanding

In the first seminar, the aims, ideas and methods of action research are introduced, along with some practical activities in the use of these methods (e.g. analytic discourse, interview techniques). After this seminar, participants select an issue in which they have a professional interest and begin to collect data for their first case study. In the regional group meetings (partial) results of these case studies are discussed; some participants present their research at the next seminar.

One teacher's case study (Mayer, 1992) concentrated on her students' errors in algebra. It was the teacher's goal to learn more about her students' misconceptions and errors in learning algebra as a way to improve her teaching. She tried to find new strategies in order to help students avoid some errors or to find a constructive way of handling their misconceptions. A quotation from her case study provides an insight into the manner in which errors seem to have an essential influence on her actions and reflections concerning mathematics instruction:

> After several years of work as a mathematics teacher one almost gets the feeling that most of the time, instead of explaining, one has to deal with errors.

The teacher studied articles about error analysis in mathematics education and finally began to investigate misconceptions and errors of students from her own classes (15–18-year-old girls). She collected different kinds of data including diary notes, interviews with students and 'error-books'. Referring to 'error books' she writes:

> The students had to keep a so-called 'error-book' which included an identical reproduction of the error, a verbal formulation, if possible a statement about the reason for the error and an exact correction. Thus the students had, for the first time, to think about their errors, which for many was a totally new and unusual experience, and in particular the verbal formulation was especially problematic. In this context the students discovered numerous systematic errors.

One important aim of the teacher's analysis was to work out 'error frames'. She finally identified about 50 types. Here are two of them (the students' explanations are in parentheses):

$1/6 > 1/5$ (6 is bigger than 5)

$x^2 - 2x = x^2 + 2x \Rightarrow x^2 = x^2$ (+2x and –2x cancel each other out)

In the concluding chapter of her study she writes:

> Only during such investigations does the teacher realize again, how important it is to scrutinize from time to time one's own teaching and to draw consequences. All too easily one falls back into daily routines.

The teacher continues her case study by sketching a range of general and concrete improvements in her own teaching. For example, she says,

> The students must be given enough time to understand mathematical strategies (the student's learning pace should not be overestimated). As a result of teaching the same subject matter frequently, the teacher tends to increase the working pace or to choose trickier tasks each time. Side-calculations should not be 'hidden' (removed by an ink-eradicator) because these enable the teacher to recognize students' strategies and above all they should not be assessed negatively.

In her concluding remarks the teacher sums up:

> The appreciation of an achievement from the mathematical point of view — being true or false — and the teacher's interest in investigating the thinking behind the work which leads to a right or wrong result, are important factors for student motivation in also tackling difficult calculations.

This was the teacher's first confrontation with systematic reflection on her own teaching in which writing down her experiences was a crucial element.

Of course, many of her results sketched above are well known, investigated and published — but this is not the point! She constructed her knowledge herself; she started at a point which was of real interest to her; she looked for — and partially found — answers relating to her individual situation; and she produced meaningful 'local knowledge' which simply cannot be replaced by reading the research results of others. Systematic reflection by teachers on their own practice — here with regard to student understanding (see Krainer, 1993b) — can contribute to an improvement of mathematics instruction in many respects. Teachers' interest in how students understand a mathematical topic gives students the feeling that they are really taken seriously. This makes it easier for students to experiment with ideas and actions, and thus improves the teacher's opportunity to gain further insights into students' understanding.

Attempts by teachers to replace assessments like 'the student does not understand' with a search for meaningful explanations (even for so-called misconceptions and errors) can be seen as part of a general attitude of orienting teaching towards students' strengths and not towards weaknesses. This makes it easier for situations previously regarded as instances of 'not-understanding' by students to be viewed as opportunities for learning not only for students but for teachers as well.

For teachers to realize that they can learn from learners positively influences the relationship between teachers and students. Efforts to analyse and to discuss so-called 'errors', helps teachers to gain insights which are normally not available to them — strangely enough, precisely because of their expertise. Trying to take the student's point of view is an opportunity for teachers, partly, to overcome the constraints on their own way of thinking and to become aware of 'blind spots' caused by their specific involvement in 'the system of' mathematics instruction. Having the flexibility to change one's point of view promotes a better understanding of the ideas and thought processes of students. Efforts by teachers to make the thought processes of students visible, and to reflect on their meaning, increase the opportunities for students to reflect on their own learning process and promote self-evaluation and self-organization. These abilities, then, make it easier to discuss consciously the different meanings of a mathematical concept and differences in student intuitions, and therefore to increase student understanding.

The activities in which teachers acquire knowledge about their students' understanding, and in which systematic reflection on their own investigation is provided, contribute to the improvement of their ability to assess student understanding. In addition, teachers' own experiences of investigating student understanding increases their understanding of results from other research which further provides teachers with new ideas for their own investigations. Moreover, the efforts of teachers to increase their competence with regard to student understanding promotes self-critical and profound discussion with colleagues and researchers on the course, thus improving the culture of communication about educational issues.

These issues show that the interplay between action and reflection is of great importance. This interplay is an essential characteristic of action research and it is also regarded as an important aspect in the teacher's decision-making processes (Cooney, 1988), the student's generalization processes (Dörfler, 1991), or the student's problem-solving processes (Krainer, 1993a).

Autonomy and Networking — Teachers Organize Further Inservice Education

Fostering autonomous and self-initiative work by teachers and encouraging professional communication and cooperation among them is an important aim of the programme. The participants are invited increasingly to take charge of their own learning process within the course both as individuals and as a group. A participant after a course commented,

> I slowly realized that this course cannot be restricted to 'taking'; but also not to an oral 'giving' of a few personal ideas. The 'giving' should become very concrete, in the form of two case studies. This was connected with a very painful process . . .

This comment shows that the transition from viewing learning as consumption of knowledge to viewing learning as production of knowledge is not an easy one. To be able to mediate, and to 'live', such an understanding in the classroom, it seems absolutely necessary to experience this transition directly. Referring to the last seminar — where participants organized different workshops — a teacher wrote:

> . . . formerly I was mostly a consumer of various seminars, not trying to make my own suggestions — concerning organization or content. In this respect I have become more self-confident. Above all I have found it very good that the third seminar has been designed to a large extent by the participants themselves . . .

Feedback from former PFL participants shows that they have involved themselves in a number of individual and joint activities which contribute to pedagogical and didactic innovation in classrooms and schools, for example:

> I have also become braver and take more initiative concerning my relations with colleagues. Small contributions at staff meetings, even organizing parts of a staff meeting with colleagues, preparing and carrying out projects together are activities I tackle because I have observed, seen and learned a lot . . .

Many of these participants act as 'agents of change' in their region. They may be engaged in teacher inservice courses, in teacher education, or they may actively participate in conferences in which they present the innovative work they are doing in their classrooms (e.g. Krainer, 1994; Kern and Kröpfl, 1996).

Of course, not all participants change their teaching in this fundamental way, but it was my intention to show here what is possible. Indeed, this is one of the main ideas of the PFL programme: to show teachers (and other interested people) that things can be done within the existing general conditions or after successfully fighting for their change; and to make the good work of teachers visible and available for discussion. More than 130 studies written by German, English, mathematics and science teachers within the framework of PFL courses, which have since been bought by teachers, researchers, schools, etc., demonstrate its value.

The teachers' systematic reflections on their own practice may not only improve their own teaching but may also have consequences for the further development of teacher education (see, for example, Krainer and Posch, 1996), for mathematics education (see, for example, Fischer and Malle, 1985) or for the personal and professional development of team members (see, for example, a mathematics educator's reflective paper on his activities within the course; Peschek, 1996).

The fact that writing case studies causes some problems for both the teachers, and the teacher educators supporting them, should not be withheld. In writing case studies, teachers have to do at least three things which are rather unusual in their normal practice:

- they have to gather data and to reflect on them systematically (and not only take action);
- they have to write down their findings (and not just communicate them orally); and
- they have to formulate these results for other people (and not just practise something within their own classrooms).

That this is more difficult for teachers than for teacher educators and researchers — living in a 'culture of publishing' — should be taken into consideration. Nevertheless, it seems to be worth promoting teachers' investigations for at least four reasons: systematic reflection on their own work creates new knowledge which in turn positively influences their teaching; writing down is an additional opportunity to learn; writing a study (to be read by others) increases the opportunities for communicating and cooperating with interested people (teachers, theoreticians, administrators); and finally, it gives us an additional opportunity to learn from them.

Continuous Work with Groups of Mathematics Teachers Based on the PFL Philosophy

Programmes like PFL give teachers a good opportunity for initiating and organizing communication and cooperation with colleagues in an open atmosphere —, a fact which, in many cases, is not so easy to achieve in a teacher's own school. On the other hand, inservice teacher education which depends on voluntary participation is sometimes confronted by problems of realization and dissemination. For example, given a good seminar or course, the motivation to change one's mathematics teaching might be high and many participants might try out new things and might apply learned methods and ideas. However, the participants may find: that few colleagues really want to join in their efforts; that their motivation and the perseverance to realize changes are (in the long run) not high enough; that innovative things at schools are often regarded rather critically and cause (open or hidden) resistance or opposition; that the participants on seminars are 'always the same' and those who really would need some improvement do not come; and that links between different subjects are used too rarely. Although the experience with PFL shows that participants' engagement in long-term teacher education — which places an emphasis on professional communication among teachers — efficiently supports teachers' efforts to bring about change, it is worth investigating the question whether continuous work with groups of mathematics teachers — based on the PFL philosophy — could be a promising approach to promoting teachers' professional work.

Therefore, parallel to the PFL programme, we initiated a pilot project where a university team collaborated with the two groups of mathematics teachers from two Austrian high schools. It is too early to draw conclusions but it seems that working continuously with such a group yields some important advantages:

- It is possible to take the 'culture' of the school (the context in which the teachers live and work and which is a decisive general condition of what is possible or not) into consideration.
- Collaboration among individuals might develop towards the establishment of a group.
- Teachers might have the encouragement of others (who work next door to them) or even colleagues who were ready to join their efforts to improve their mathematics teaching.
- Innovations would be more likely to become a relevant component of mathematics teaching (or even of the whole school).
- Mathematics teaching could be more visible and could play a greater role at the school.

Let me sketch some 'miniatures' which show steps towards developments mentioned above:

- A young teacher, being positively surprised by the efforts of more experienced colleagues who also critically reflected their teaching and strove for new ideas, highlighted: 'Even older colleagues try out new things.'
- A mathematics education journal from which different volumes were analysed by different teachers during a part of a seminar was subscribed to after the principal was persuaded by some representatives of the group that this would contribute to the further development of mathematics at this school.
- Based on the group's interest the researcher team organized a unit dealing with alternative assessment. Some of the teachers took some concrete steps in their teaching towards this direction. One team member was invited to lead a seminar on alternative assessment for all teachers of the school.

- A conflict between two teachers arose: one of them became the successor of the other's mathematics class and argued that this class would be the worst he ever had. The other members of the group and the university team planned, carried out and interpreted interviews with pupils of this class. This helped them get a deeper understanding of the situation and to find a better way to cope with the challenge. The teachers concluded that the group can even be successful in dealing with such bigger challenges.
- The analysis of the teaching of one member of the university team led to a vivid discussion about the importance of comparing one's own approach to teaching with other approaches in order to get a feeling of one's own beliefs and strengths, with possible realistic steps of change.

Summary and Outlook

The PFL programme and related projects aim at *promoting teachers' action, reflection, autonomy and networking*. In general, these dimensions seem to be an important challenge for teachers' professional development. In particular, designers of inservice courses should ask themselves questions, such as: To what extent do we succeed in motivating the participants to reflect (self-)critically on their own activities and the collaborative work on the seminar and on using it as an opportunity for corresponding learning processes? To what extent do we succeed in promoting deeper communication and collaboration among the participants and in linking individual and social learning experiences meaningfully?

Questions like these show an understanding of inservice education which sees teachers not as receivers of prefabricated knowledge and complete solutions but as reflective practitioners who develop their own knowledge and solutions, and fit them into the context in which they work. Building on teachers' self-critical investigations into their own work does not decrease the importance of research in mathematics education, rather, more research is needed, in particular on teachers' professional development. But we need to find *new ways* of mediating between theory and practice; of collaborating with teachers on different levels; of taking into consideration the culture in which they live and work; of (re)constructing our beliefs on teacher education while at the same time questioning them thoroughly; and of (re)defining teacher change and teacher education as an inevitable part of professional practice.

Note

The PFL Project is organized by the Center for Interdisciplinary Research and Development of Austrian Universities (IFF). It is primarily funded by the Federal Ministry for Education and Cultural Affairs (ZI 15.615/10–I/12/93) and the Ministry of Science and Transport (GZ.72.000/13–I/A/4/94) in Austria. A smaller part of the budget comes from fees of the participants themselves.

References

ALTRICHTER, H. and KRAINER, K. (1996) 'Wandel von lehrerarbeit und lehrerfortbildung', in KRAINER, K. and POSCH, P. (eds) *Lehrerfortbildung zwischen Prozessen und Produkten* (pp. 33–51), Bad Heilbrunn: Klinkhardt.

ALTRICHTER, H., POSCH P. and SOMEKH, B. (1993) *Teachers Investigate Their Work: An Introduction to the Methods of Action Research*, London: Routledge.

COONEY, T.J. (1988) 'Teachers' decision making', in PIMM, D. (ed.) *Mathematics, Teachers and Children* (pp. 273–86), London: Open University, Hodder and Stoughton.

DÖRFLER, W. (1991) 'Forms and means of generalization in mathematics', in BISHOP, A., MELLIN-OLSEN, S. and VAN DORMOLEN, J. (eds) *Mathematical Knowledge: Its Growth through Teaching.* (pp. 63–85), Dordrecht: Kluwer.

ELLIOTT, J. (1991) *Action Research for Educational Change*, Milton Keynes: Open University.

FISCHER, R. and MALLE, G. (1985) *Mensch und Mathematik. Eine Einführung in didaktisches Denken und Handeln*, Mannheim-Wien-Zürich: Bibliographisches Institut.

FISCHER, R., RAINER, K., MALLE, G., POSCH, P., ZENKL, M. et al. (eds) (1985) *Pädagogik und Fachdidaktik für Mathematiklehrer*, Stuttgart: Hölder-Pichler-Tempsky, Wien und Teubner.

KERN, A. and KRÖPFL, B. (1996) 'Von PFL zu AFL — oder: Am Weg zur selbstorganisierten Gruppe Aktion forschende LehrerInnen', in KRAINER, K. and POSCH, P. (eds) *Lehrerfortbildung zwischen Prozessen und Produkten*, (pp. 111–24) Bad Heilbrunn: Klinkhardt.

KRAINER, K. (1993a) 'Powerful tasks: A contribution to a high level of acting and reflecting in mathematics instruction', *Educational Studies in Mathematics*, **24**, 1, pp. 1–29.

KRAINER, K. (1993b) 'Understanding students' understanding: On the importance of co-operation between teachers and researchers', in BERO, P. (ed.) *Proceedings of the 3rd Bratislava International Symposium on Mathematical Education* (pp. 1–22), Bratislava: Comenius University.

KRAINER, K. (1994) 'PFL-Mathematics: A teacher inservice education course as a contribution to the improvement of professional practice in mathematics instruction', in PONTE, J. and MATOS, I. (eds) *Proceedings of the 18th Psychology in Mathematics Annual Meeting Vol. III* (pp. 104–11), Lisboa: University of Lisboa.

KRAINER, K. (in press) 'Dimensions of teachers' professional practice: Action, reflection, autonomy and networking', in *Proceedings of Norma 98*, Norway: Kristiansand.

KRAINER, K. and POSCH, P. (eds) (1996) *Lehrerfortbildung zwischen Prozessen und Produkten*, Bad Heilbrunn: Klinkhardt (See review in *Journal of Mathematics Teacher Education*, **1**, pp. 113–16, 1998).

MAYER, C. (1992) 'Unpublished case study of PFL-mathematics 1991–93', Klagenfurt: University of Klagenfurt/ IFF.

PESCHEK, W. (1996) 'PFL — Eine wissenschaftliche wie auch persönliche Herausforderung', in KRAINER, K. and POSCH, P. (eds) *Lehrerfortbildung zwischen Prozessen und Produkten*. (pp. 167–80) Bad Heilbrunn: Klinkhardt.

SCHÖN, D. (1983) *The Reflective Practitioner: How Professionals Think in Action*, New York: Basic Books.

STENHOUSE, L. (1975) *An Introduction to Curriculum Research and Development*, London: Heinemann.

Editors' Comment

The final chapter in this section, from Chris Breen in South Africa, takes a rather more critical perspective than the earlier papers. Here Chris Breen examines his particular philosophy for teacher education and recognizes some of the problems it raises for teachers when they begin to practise their teaching in South African schools. This leads to a critical review of issues of teacher change in a climate of national need and vested interests, and the roles of teacher and teacher educator within this panorama.

12   Circling the Square: Issues and Dilemmas Concerning Teacher Transformation

Chris Breen, South Africa

Introduction

This chapter is located within the specific context of the South African education system at a time of general optimism following sweeping political and social change in the country. It is based on a paper given in 1994 to the first national conference of the newly formed Association for Mathematics Education in South Africa (AMESA). The previous occasion at which I had presented a paper at a national conference of South African teachers of mathematics had been in 1986 against the background of a very different and contested political context[1]. On that occasion there were two specific issues that I tried to address. My first area of concern centred around the absence of public critical voices in mathematics education in a societal and school context of enormous political conflict. I attempted to begin an examination of some of the ways that 'alternative mathematics programmes' might be conceived, including the introduction of a non-Eurocentric historical perspective, as well as the challenging of the myths of South African society with a different reality (Breen, 1986a). In my second paper at the 1986 conference, I explored some different teaching possibilities under the headings of investigations, do-talk-and-record activities, and 'deeper structures' (Breen, 1986b). In terms of methodology both papers were making a strong appeal to move away from harsh authoritarian teaching methods in the classroom and to move towards a far more exploratory learning-centred approach to teaching.

A New Context

The South African context has certainly changed considerably in the intervening eight years[2]. There has been a dramatic and irreversible shift in the political situation in the country since 1986 and the inequities of the previous apartheid system of education are beginning to be redressed. The teaching of mathematics in primary schools has been seriously challenged and changed through the enthusiastic and committed work of groups of dedicated mathematics educators (lecturers, project members and teachers) in different sites throughout the country. The changing focus to a learner-centred approach has been dramatic as has been the way in which constructivist theory (in different forms) has taken a central position on the stage to

113

motivate these changes. There is a general feeling of optimism for this 'new maths' and a new kind of classroom folklore has begun to emerge. An oversimplified version of this story runs along these lines. Classes are presented with problems or investigations which allow them to explore the topic and develop their own understandings and algorithms. The teacher's role becomes one of facilitation rather than of direction to allow each different method to emerge and be valued, so that learners can build up their own self-concept and facility with their own methods. Learners act as their own peer-tutors and help each other through group work.

The mood and discourse of aspects of the national reality is reflected in these activities of the mathematics education community. There is a valuing of this group process as one which affirms the principle of democracy in the classroom and allows the voice of the learner to be heard, and for issues and meanings to be negotiated. Learners are being enskilled to participate in group situations which will strengthen their abilities to function actively and critically in society. No longer are learners seen as empty vessels that need to be filled, and Freire's banking metaphor is seriously challenged. This mood of optimism impinges on the teachers as they become regarded as the tools for the transformation of the education system and selected individuals are invited to become 'change agents' in their school and community. The focus is on change, participation and self-expression.

These developments in the teaching of mathematics in schools in South Africa offer a seductive vibrancy and enthusiasm which is hard to resist. However, I have been feeling a growing sense of disquiet and hesitancy about the process and believe that it is an appropriate time to raise these new concerns[3].

Alias Smith and Jones

Before I can start to explore these concerns, I need to retreat briefly into my own biography in order to continue to locate myself firmly within this movement for a change in teaching methodology in schools. This will hopefully make it clear that my concerns come from within rather than from a sceptic vantage point outside the arena.

My vision of how mathematics might be taught in a different way was initially formed at Exeter University in 1974 where I was inducted into the ideas of Caleb Gattegno (see, for example, Gattegno, 1988). It was a period of extreme personal intellectual confusion where I was soon made to realize that very little of the mathematical knowledge I thought I had was available to me in a connected and accessible way. This was a horrifying realization. What exactly is algebra to you? What do you think? My securities were taken away from me by the lecturer's provocative teaching style which reflected the responsibility for learning back to his students.

On returning to South Africa after the course, I spent six years attempting to put some of these ideas into practice in my different school teaching situations. I immediately faced a resistance to new methods. It was only when 'my' school-leaving class obtained better end-of-year examination results than those of the other teachers that I was allowed the freedom to introduce new methods with classes in the lower standards. The irony was that these 'good' results were obtained using traditional conservative teaching methods. Gattegno writes that any new method must demonstrate that it can provide at least as good results as those being obtained through existing methods before it will be seriously considered (Gattegno, 1970).

At university, one of the mechanisms that I have used to try to highlight different teaching methodological options is to create a few teaching personae using some drama in education ideas (Breen, 1992). The first creation was that of Mr Smith[4]. He is a caricature of the authoritarian teacher and is a bully and intimidates his pupils through abuse. One of the surprises from his appearances in my class was that he was apparently not nearly as uncommon as I had thought, particularly in DET schools[5] where I was told he would more commonly be found carrying a cane or hosepipe. In trying to move a bit closer to a different classroom persona, Mr Jones, came into being. He is a serious type who teaches for results. He does this by presenting the work from the textbook without frills and generally without humour. He is all professional as students have to do their homework to pass the regular tests. He is firm with his punishment, patient with his explanations, certain about life and the rewards for those who achieve what he wants them to achieve. Finally I created a third persona and tried to act authentically to demonstrate this teacher in practice. This person (call him Chris) held a very different vision of how mathematics learning could take place[6]. His classes became ones of self-discovery where the teacher provided no answers and students were faced with the challenge of having to get deep into their relationship with themselves and mathematics. This teacher valued students and was prepared to listen to their issues and there was a great deal of group work . . . and fun.

In the protected university environment the choice is simple. No-one wants to be a Mr Smith so he is easily rejected. Mr Jones is much more difficult to deal with initially. He is everything that students believed they wanted to be, but by the end of the course, they have generally been convinced that Chris's approach is the best of the three, and the majority of students have decided to go out into schools measuring their success and effectiveness against this new standard.

The problems then started occurring. On beginning their teaching careers, most first year teachers received the message: 'forget that idealistic nonsense you learnt at university, it doesn't work in practice.' Some reported that they felt guilty because they believed I'd be disappointed to see how they were actually teaching in their classroom. Some left teaching after becoming disillusioned — how much did the process of opening the student to new possibilities add to a sense of not belonging[7]? There is also the story of Dennis who enthusiastically tried to introduce changes into his school, initially met with some success followed by growing resistance from his colleagues, and then found himself suspended at the end of his first year when the supportive headmaster was transferred[8].

Why, Then, My Concern?

This brief background has been intended to signal an ongoing personal involvement in the process of attempting to introduce different teaching possibilities to teachers and student-teachers and a growing awareness of some of the complexities of the issue — particularly for those who are left with the responsibility of reconstructing and implementing others' ideas in different contexts. The rest of this paper will be an attempt to use this base to highlight issues and to ask questions about certain apparent features of the present national situation.

My starting point is the incredible pressure for change. A powerful image of schooling as a social institution has been described by Stafford Beer (Beer, 1975) as being like an esoteric box that has an equilibrium-seeking character. Using Le Chatelier's principle from physical chemistry, he describes how the box will react to any outside prodding, not by fighting back, but by moving its point of equilibrium along the scale so as exactly to counterbalance the effect of the prod. The combination of the dimensions of the widespread crisis in education and the sweeping euphoria of the dramatic political changes in South Africa have given rise to an expectation that revolutionary change in this esoteric box of schooling is possible and needs to happen immediately. My sense is that this view does not originate from those in the field but rather from those who have a major investment in being seen to have successfully brokered the reconstruction of this esoteric box — the funding agencies and the politicians. And we should be aware that world events of the past five years have certainly encouraged this view of the possibilities for radical change, although Beer warns of changes in government resulting in changes of faces but also in life remaining the same.

The arguments to become involved in this pressure for change so as to address the obvious deficiencies in the education system in South Africa are very seductive, so those running programmes or projects[9] find themselves having to draw up mission statements of the definite product that they aim to deliver, to demonstrate that their project has a large scale impact, is cost effective, and is sustainable. These demands are very rational but they also frame and constrain the field of operation. If a programme is to have demonstrable impact, and more importantly continue to survive by getting funding in a time of shrinking financial support for NGOs, its promised product will have to be radical and very different from what exists at present. The powerful movements of changing practice in South African primary mathematics classrooms have taken the position that lessons must be pupil-centred (as opposed to traditional teacher-centred lessons) and that the theoretical base for this change stems from constructivist theories. The pressures for large-scale impact have been such that concepts such as 'teachers-as-change-agents' and 'multiplier effects' have become common, and departments of education have co-opted some of this work by issuing edicts which force teachers to implement these ideas in their classrooms. We have become what David Pimm (1993) calls the 'change merchants', and it has become one of our major tasks to convince others of the quality of our own particular merchandise.

To do this effectively we have to employ many of the tricks of the advertising trade so that we direct the customers' attention to those aspects with which we feel most secure and away from our insecurities — and in doing this we run the risk of creating a fictional reality that becomes taken seriously as a literal reality. In effect we are forced to cut corners. An exaggerated caricature of the results of such a sales pitch might be the following. The new product is packaged and a set of hand-outs drawn up together with special workshops designed to demonstrate the new model. Selective quotations from overseas experts are used to encourage the teacher-consumer to back this product. It is important for this product to succeed so popular workshops are repeated. A sample package with limited focus that can travel well and is sufficiently context-free to be effective in different environments is generated. Customers are assured that this product has been successfully used in many different settings and that it will be easy for them to extend it and use it in their own particular classroom setting irrespective of the number of learners in their classroom or of the resources at their disposal. It is important for us to impress in our workshops, so we develop a repertoire of sure-fire crowd pleasers. We introduce apparatus and people activities. In trying to put across a single message to a large group, we minimize the tensions and simplify the message. So we give out a set of rules for teachers to follow — external criteria that rely on an outside judge. We project ourselves as being kind of square, reasonable people.

The degree of cynicism involved in this account can be contested. However, I believe that very few reformers give teachers a true account of the complex and problematic nature of the task we are setting them. We are asking teachers to follow our example and to radically alter their teaching patterns without giving them a picture of what we have gone through in the process. If we look at our own practice and reflect on the degree to which we have been able to integrate our theories of student-centred activities and our classroom practice, I would suspect that there will be a considerable degree to which Mr Smith and Mr Jones creep into our own personal practice. Would we honestly adopt a single methodology and expect it to cover all eventualities as well as the needs of all learners? What do we do with our own personal voices of discomfort? To what extent have we engaged in systemic change in our own institution. Would we be prepared to sacrifice our job for our belief? Is the image we project authentic or is it one that has been compromised by external forces and demands?

The passing on of methodology does not happen by osmosis. It needs to be made explicit and even here Mason's formulation of Brousseau's didactic tension (Mason, 1988) shows the possibility that this very explicitness is likely to lead to the form being taken on without the security offered by the substance of the accompanying understanding. An example of this is the way our simplified workshop presentations can come back to haunt us. There is a temptation for imitators to take on the more visible aspects of our presentation, such as the icebreakers, the apparatus and the group work. What is often left behind are the crucial invisible and complex features underpinning the activity. In particular, it is often hard to find the mathematical base of some activities which claim to be improvements. It is as though the mathematics is somewhere off-stage waiting desperately for a cue or invitation to participate. Is our emphasis on changing methodology occurring at the expense of the mathematical imperatives of our teaching? Are we paying attention to the improvement of the mathematical skills of the teachers we are working with — skills that are essential for recognizing the differing mathematical potential of responses from the class?

There are considerable difficulties involved in introducing change into a school. Most of us involved in the process work with isolated teachers or with groups of teachers in a subject department. Very little attention has been paid to large-scale systemic change. If we are successful in our intervention with teachers, there will presumably be a change in their practice. The more successful the innovation by the teachers, the more likely their teaching will disrupt the school because they will be undermining the status quo — and the system will move to restore its equilibrium. The next step may be for these teachers to be marginalized. How do these 'change-agents' withstand this pressure? They will need to be so secure in themselves and their own beliefs that they can withstand their own inner doubts as well as such outer attacks from others. There is no room for uncertainty and their message must be unequivocal and unshaking. How does one prepare a teacher to be a change agent? Should a course in salesmanship and public relations form an integral part of the course? The concept of change agent also has dimensions of revolution contained within it. Are these change agents to run clandestine cells or are they to be publicly identified? How can we put an effective and appropriate support system into place for these teachers if we are not involved with the whole school and in understanding

Becoming change agents will necessitate that teachers contemplate a large shift in their own perceptions. If this is to be a real and integrated move away from authoritarian teaching methods to more pupil-centred methods, there will also have to be fundamental personal shifts in their own belief systems that will have serious repercussions in their own lives. If they are to be authentic in introducing these new beliefs of learner-centredness, they will have to face the degree to which they are empowered in their own interactions within their family and in society in general. We value the developmental stages of children as learners, but what about the different developmental stages of adults? Are there times when adults are more ready for change than at others? What is viewed solely as a movement to improve the teaching of mathematics in schools has a hidden demand that teachers get involved in personal change. Pimm (1993) cautions: 'I believe it is dangerous to lose sight of how difficult personal change can be — and we should not talk lightly or glibly about it, let alone expect or demand it' (p. 31).

My own experiences with student-teachers strongly support this view. It is not coincidental that much of the rhetoric of transformation is to be found in the field of psychotherapy — a discipline that is concerned with personal change. In particular, process-oriented psychology focuses on awarenesses and changes caused by being on the edge. Change doesn't just happen in a vacuum. Hillman and Ventura (1992) emphasize how the problems of personal change magnify if there is a definite direction in which you are supposed to change. In our case, we are asking teachers to transform their teaching practice. Transformation means turning something deficient into something good. We have decided that teachers' present practice is not good enough and we can project a clear image of what should be regarded as the good practice teachers should strive to demonstrate. It is of course a perfect image that no-one will ever be able to reach, which means we have built in an inevitable result of failure. In order to keep the movement going, will there be a set of rewards for those who partially succeed and punishments for those who fail? To exacerbate matters, in presenting this model our well-intentioned intervention has placed the expertise in our hands at the teachers' expense. We have negated the teachers' existing experience of other methods and, in doing so, have taken away their security in established forms of teaching and classroom organization.

This leads on to a sense of a missing sensitivity to context in this drive for reform in teaching methodology. Socio-political considerations seem to have taken a back seat — although the lonely voices of the critical maths pedagogists are still occasionally heard. To what extent do the new methods encourage all members of the population to become better mathematicians? Will teachers who have relied solely on authoritarian teaching methods be more disadvantaged in introducing new learner-centred methods than those who have taught in more open environments? What of those who have relied on corporal punishment as a means of maintaining classroom organization? Will the introduction of these new methods exacerbate the enormous divide in achievement in mathematics between the previously privileged and disenfranchised sections of the South African community?

What Can We Do About It?

There are many complex issues that have been raised in the previous section, and competing voices and priorities are present in each. In trying to move this paper beyond one of pure critique, I have tried to suggest a few possibilities for action.

The first centres around the mathematics educators driving the reform programmes and revisits some of the thoughts of Stafford Beer (1975). In the opening chapter of his book, *Platform for Change*, he describes different players by Latin nomenclature:

> The difficulty is how to replace Homo Faber with a new kind of man[10]. He will not be man the maker any longer. He will be the steersman — of large complex, interactive systems. I call him Homo Gubernator . . . He is around, but not in office . . . He spoils his case with the people by failing to offer pat solutions off the top of his head. He wants to investigate first . . . But people prefer to hear slogans, and asseverations of intent, from men who know all the answers in advance. It does not matter if their policies are internally inconsistent; it does not matter if they are repetitions of policies known to have failed over and over again in the past. They are selling the stereotype, which is alone acceptable. I fear that the revolution will be formulated by just such men, successors to Homo Faber true — but not Gubernator at all. We must choose to become Gubernator ourselves, while there is time. (pp. 36–7)

This task of becoming Gubernators ourselves, I believe, is our first priority. Accepting this task means challenging inappropriate external priorities forced upon us, whatever their source. If political quick-fix solutions have deficiencies, they need to be challenged; and the danger of quick-responses becoming entrenched because of the personal investment that has been placed in them also needs to be highlighted.

However, just as important, is the need to investigate our own practice and this means allowing the full story to be told — the one which also allows the focus to be put on those areas we have kept in the shadows. The fear of letting light into the problem areas of our work is part of the ideology that rewards right answers and punishes incorrect responses. Bly (1988) has powerful comments to make on the rewards of valuing the shadow. For me, acting as Gubernator means insisting that more than lip-service is paid to the importance of research — and this includes research that questions the value of the activity rather than just research which measures its degree of success.

If we are to advocate that others change their practice, we ourselves need to show in our own work that we are willing to accept similar challenges. For example, if we want teachers to challenge unfair practices in schools, we must experience what it is like attempting to do so in our own sites of learning. We should be working on this process of change informed by the literature of systemic and personal change. The affective needs to be an integral part of our workshops. The Gubernator will realize this and will include these areas in the investigation — an investigation of continuous responsibility in action, rather than one of delay or control.

Another aspect that needs to be addressed is the power base of teachers. If we want teachers to be the fulcrum of any change process we cannot deprive them of their confidence in their own skills. We do this when we suddenly label their present practice as 'bad'. Teachers need to feel confident that the framework for good teaching lies within themselves and their own particular context. We cannot set up a trivialized image of an ideal lesson because the context in which the lesson takes place is essential and brings into play the skills and resources of the particular teacher and the school and the community. The existence of a correct model sets all teachers up for failure and we start the concept of transformation off on a deficit model. The process seems to be much more about allowing teachers to explore the boundaries of their own learning to increase their possibilities of action. I have expanded on this theme of 'holding the tension of the opposites' in another article (Breen, 1993) and it links to the reality of the different persona that each of us can call on in our teaching as well as to the importance of the concept of 'appropriateness' rather than 'correctness'. It values expository teaching as well as other forms of traditional teaching where appropriate. Once we have assisted teachers in expanding their possibilities in any situation, we can turn our attention to developing criteria to evaluate the comparative appropriateness of a set of options in a particular context. This problem of creating different possibilities obviously forces us to focus on the previously underdeveloped options of learner-centred teaching and to develop the appropriate skills and experiences to push this opposite out further. It's a lifelong journey and we have no established way to set up such an experience for teachers. It's not a journey where one suddenly sees the light. Nobody is square — we all have a corner knocked off.

Finally, what do teachers think of this pressure to change? Pimm (1993) is unequivocal in his views: 'Their change is not our business; how, when and if they change is surely their concern alone' (p. 31). It seems as if national and societal needs are in competition with those of individual teachers. Where is the appropriate forum for the voice of the teacher to be raised and heard? It would seem to be essential that mathematics teacher associations such as AMESA take a lead in providing such a forum and that they ensure that their structures are driven by teachers at the receiving end rather than by those who are driving the change. The question of support structures for change has also been raised in this paper. Surely it is the teachers themselves who are in the best position to determine and manage appropriate support structures?

Conclusion

A danger in writing a paper such as this at a time of great national optimism (May, 1994) is that it might appear to be a condemnation of learner-centred approaches. My aim has certainly not been to do that, but I have attempted to reintroduce a critical voice into the debate so that we do not merely follow the inevitable progress of all passing fads. The move towards the inclusion of more pupil-centred methodologies is to be welcomed, but I believe we deceive ourselves and do education a disservice if we underestimate the multi-dimensional nature of the challenge we set teachers. This paper has attempted to highlight some of these issues.

Postscript

It is now October 1998 and over four years have passed since the chapter was written. Much of the initial optimism of radical change has been replaced by sombre realization of the magnitude of the task. In education, a radical new programme named Curriculum 2005 is already beginning to be introduced on a national basis. Curriculum 2005 uses an Outcomes Based Approach which divides the curriculum into Learning Areas and specifies Outcomes and Skills which have to be attained. The effect of this programme increases rather than decreases the concerns and issues expressed in this chapter. The need and demand for inservice work has increased but now on a wider scale — the previous focus on "problem-centred mathematics' has become one of 'OBE Learning Areas'. The task ahead is correspondingly more serious.

Notes

1 For an example of the effects of the crisis in schools in the Western Cape, see Breen (1985).
2 I have kept to the original use of the present tense in the paper to maintain the intended sense of immediacy and urgency.
3 The theme of the conference was redress, action and success.
4 The role-play is fully described in Breen (1991).
5 There were 19 different education departments in apartheid South Africa set up on regional and racial bases responsible for education in schools. DET refers to the Department of Education and Training which was responsible for the administration of African schools.

6 This vision is more fully described in Breen (1991).
7 One such story is related in Breen (1987).
8 Dennis's story is told in Breen (1994).
9 The crisis in education in schools caused by the perceived illegitimacy of the previous apartheid government in South Africa led to the creation of a plethora of Non-Governmental Organisations (NGOs) which ran projects which effectively provided services that would normally have been provided by the State. In general these NGOs ran programmes or projects that were funded by industry within South Africa or by international governments or funding agencies.
10 The original quotation is left unedited and is assumed to use the generic 'man' to include both genders.

References

BEER, S. (1975) *Platform for Change* (pp. 137–8), New York: Wiley.

BLY, R. (1988) *A Little Book on the Human Shadow*, New York: Harper and Row.

BREEN, C. (1986a) 'Alternative mathematics programmes', *Proceedings of the 8th National Mathematical Association of South Africa Conference* (pp. 178–88), Stellenbosch, 1–4 July.

BREEN, C. (1986b) 'Pupil-centred activities in primary mathematics', *Proceedings of the 8th National Mathematical Association of South Africa Conference* (pp. 151–8), Stellenbosch, 1–4 July.

BREEN, C. (1987) 'Catriona's letter', *Mathematics Teaching*, **121**, p. 45.

BREEN, C. (1988) 'Policing exams: The impact on teachers and students in Western Cape schools, 1985', *Perspectives in Education*, **10**, 1, pp. 4–11.

BREEN, C. (1990) 'A cautionary tale about rabbits, moles and choices', *Pythagoras*, **23**, pp. 20–2.

BREEN, C. (1991) 'Concerning Mr. Smith and his (very brief?) reign of terror', *Pythagoras*, **25**, pp. 31–7.

BREEN, C. (1992) 'Teacher education and mathematics: Confronting preconceptions', *Perspectives in Education*, **13**, 1, pp. 33–44.

BREEN, C. (1993) 'Holding the tension of the opposites', *For the Learning of Mathematics*, **13**, 1, pp. 6–10.

BREEN, C. (1994) 'An investigation into the longer term effects of a preservice mathematics method course', *Proceedings of the 18th International Conference for the Psychology of Mathematics Education Vol. 2* (pp. 136–43), Portugal, July.

GATTEGNO, C. (1970) *What We Owe Children*, London: Routledge and Kegan Paul.

GATTEGNO, C. (1988) *The Science of Education: Part 2B — The Awareness of Mathematization*, New York: Educational Solutions.

HILLMAN, J. and VENTURA, M. (1992) *We've Had a Hundred Years of Psychotherapy — and the World's Getting Worse*, New York: Harper Collins.

MASON, J. (1988) 'What to do when you are stuck (Unit 3)', *ME234 Using Mathematical Thinking*, Milton Keynes: Open University.

PIMM, D. (1993) 'From should to could: Reflections on possibilities of mathematics teacher education', *For the Learning of Mathematics*, **13**, 2, pp. 27–32.

Section Three

Critical Perspectives Linking Theory and Practice in Mathematics Teacher Education

Section Two of this book has consisted of a collection of papers from mathematics teacher educators in a number of countries represented in the PME Working Group, focusing on the inservice education of mathematics teachers. These papers reflect what became clear in our years of working together in the PME group: that, despite our national differences, we had much in common in terms of our aims, practices and the issues we faced. The papers are all written by teacher educators — teachers of teachers — who are also researchers. They bring expertise in conceptualizing teaching, both in theory and in practice, and in exploring issues through research. The programmes described are ones in which teacher educators work with teachers, in a variety of contexts both in and out of school, to develop and improve mathematics teaching.

Section Three contains four chapters. It begins with Chapter 13 which draws out themes which have emerged from the chapters in Section Two and addresses issues which seem central to an international perspective on mathematics teaching development. In particular it starts to address the underlying theoretical and philosophical bases of the programmes and relates them to prevailing social, political and economic conditions in a rapidly changing world.

This section continues with three further chapters, one from each of the three editors of this book. As noted in the Introduction, we, as editors, debated long and hard about our own contribution(s) — mainly, should we try to write *jointly* and address, together, the theoretical perspectives we each felt central to mathematics teacher education, or should we write separately? In discussing our various theoretical positions it became clear that these are diverse, not only in their particularities but in the nature of what we count as theory. There was, nevertheless, commonality and overlap in what we perceived and believed. We settled finally on three chapters, one from each of us. Our purpose was to offer personal perspectives which are related to our own current work in teacher education, and to try to indicate, critically, the theoretical perspectives on which we have drawn. We have attempted to take a rather wider, and more critical, perspective on theoretical issues than had been appropriate in the contributions in Section Two.

In Chapter 14, Sandy Dawson introduces us to the *enactivist* perspective on teaching and teacher education, giving some of the historical and theoretical background to this evolving world view. He draws on the work of Kieren and others to illustrate how the enactivist orientation can be used to analyse teaching practice. Finally, he describes one recent and one ongoing inservice programme which display enactivist roots and routes.

In Chapter 15, Terry Wood describes her current work that has grown out of a research programme which she carried out with Paul Cobb and Erna Yackel. She offers us an approach to inservice teacher development in which the goals are to provide educational opportunities for all teachers and yet meet the demands for reform which are so prevalent currently in the USA, and which are being made manifest world-wide. Wood's approach, while influenced by theories of learning, draws on empirical findings from reform-oriented teaching. She argues for the necessity to develop an understanding of teaching beyond the level of description and personal insight, to create theoretical constructs of pedagogy. Wood contends that is accomplished through a process that is grounded in findings from empirical data gathered in classrooms, to the formation of descriptive categories for the empirical work, and finally to the generation of theoretical constructs in the formulations of teaching.

The final chapter, by Barbara Jaworski, draws on a number of theoretical positions concerning learning and the growth of knowledge, and models and perspectives of teaching development, to address the complexities of development for mathematics teachers and teaching. It takes as examples two research projects into teaching development to highlight relationships between theory and practice, and to suggest that a perspective of 'plurality' is neither simplistic nor far-fetched. Within the three major sections of the paper, Jaworski deals with issues of the nature of knowledge and its growth in mathematics teaching, and the relationship of knowledge to the theory–practice dialectic in mathematics teaching and teacher education.

13 Themes and Issues in Inservice Programmes

Barbara Jaworski, UK and Terry Wood, USA

I thought and thought right through the evening and almost couldn't sleep last night. I have learnt the one thing I think is the most important thing I have learnt as a teacher; that is, that if you show somebody how to do a problem you stop him thinking. This is what happened to my mathematics. (Marilyn, quoted in Murray et al., this volume, Chapter 4, p. 40)

It is not enough to ask questions any more. I need answers. Answers about the curriculum. What's important to learn? The NCTM standards are helpful but seemingly vague for my purposes. What about standard algorithms and accountability? Am I the only one with such nightmares about these issues? I'm floundering. I can't decide what's important. I can't decide how long to stick with something (the old rule of thumb was 80–85 per cent mastery of a skill area by the class). What's mastery anymore? What is a skill? I think that perhaps I am closer than ever to being an inquiry teacher, I mean, it actually seems within my reach for the first time, but I have no content. In years past 'How do I teach?' was an issue. Now it is what do I teach, and even more puzzling, why teach that? (Shirley, quoted in Carter and Richards, this volume, Chapter 8, p. 72)

Only during such investigations does the teacher realize again, how important it is to scrutinize from time to time one's own teaching and to draw consequences. All too easily one falls back on daily routines. (Mayer, quoted in Krainer, this volume, Chapter 11, p. 105)

I now see that there is little value in one-day teacher development programmes. Even in our ten-week teacher development contract teachers may not progress for the first eight weeks. (Quoted in Irwin and Britt, this volume, Chapter 10, p. 93)

Introduction

- *What are the prevailing themes in mathematics teacher inservice education internationally?*
- *What issues are consequent on these themes?*

Themes emerging from the collection of papers in Section Two of this book can be seen to be of two sorts: those relating to the form, or methodology, of inservice practice (to *ways of working* with teachers); and those relating to the content or focus of a programme (to *what is being worked on*). So, for example, methodologies include short courses for teachers outside of the school context, classroom-based activities, modelling processes and teacher research projects. Content or focus of inservice activities include mathematical problem-solving, the use of manipulatives in mathematics learning, the implementation of problem-solving and inquiry methods in the classroom, the fostering of reflective practices, and the development of practices in classroom research. Methodology and content are, of course, closely related, and issues arise from the complexity of their interrelationship.

It is important to recognize differences arising from the diverse national contexts in which mathematics teachers and educators work. For example, issues in teacher education in an emergent South Africa have a political dimension very different to those in some other parts of the world. One example of this is the need for programmes which affect vast numbers of teachers, and whose very scale is a conditioning factor in what is possible. Educators from countries such as Austria or New Zealand report smaller scale projects with greater flexibility; where emphasis can be placed on finer details which have their own associated issues. In all countries, the experience, societal circumstances and previous education of teachers is a principle factor motivating what is and can be done. However, despite very obvious cultural, economic and political differences, there is considerable similarity in educational questions and concerns, seen for example in issues reported here from contexts in South Africa and the United States. Thus, this chapter has two main purposes:

1. To draw out the common themes which we see pervading the programmes described in Section Two, while recognizing particular national characteristics;
2. To highlight issues which emerge, for the development of mathematics teaching and begin to address these in a spirit of critical inquiry.

A Prevailing Tradition and a Need for Change

The motivation for many of the inservice programmes described in Section Two is the perceived status-quo or 'tradition' of classroom mathematics teaching. Despite examples of innovative teaching approaches which have been acknowledged internationally (Lampert, 1990; Ball, 1993; Jaworski, 1994; Stigler and Hiebert, 1997), it seems that the widely prevailing model of mathematics teaching is still one of knowledge transmission. Weinzweig (this volume) expresses this as follows:

> [Teachers'] major experience of a classroom . . . is that of a transmission line where the teacher is center, the source of knowledge which is to be transmitted to the students, and the students are passive receivers. Communication is vertical and usually one-directional, from the teacher to the students . . . In spite of the lip-service paid to teaching for understanding, emphasizing problem-solving, and moving from the concrete to the abstract, the mathematics courses to which they [students] are subjected reflect none of these characteristics. (p. 26)

A similar perspective is reflected in many of the other chapters in Section Two. All the programmes, therefore, set out to raise teachers' awareness of alternative ways of thinking about mathematics and students' learning of mathematics along with associated classroom practices in mathematics teaching. Some go further in this pursuit to engage teachers, over considerable time periods, in rethinking and reformulating their approaches to teaching.

It seems to be taken for granted that teachers' thinking and practice needs to change. The desired change is seen ultimately in terms of better or more effective learning environments for students of mathematics. The success of the teacher education programmes is measured in terms of the changes taking place. In some cases it is change manifested in teachers' awareness; in others, it is change demonstrated in their working with students. Murray et al. (this volume) suggest that inservice programmes should address at least two main issues: firstly teachers' perceptions (beliefs and attitudes) and secondly teachers' skills that are needed for day to day classroom activities.

Most chapters make reference to a reform movement and/or a constructivist view of learning and teaching, and to theories of learning which centralize the needs of students rather than those of teachers. It must be recognized that these chapters reflect programmes which have developed during the later 1980s and early 1990s as a result of 1980's thinking. During the later 1980s, constructivism in mathematics education has been seriously influential both in theoretical and practical terms for mathematics teaching and its development (see, for example, von Glasersfeld, 1987; Cobb, Wood and Yackel, 1990; Davis, Maher and Noddings, 1990). There has been wide concern to explore implications of a constructivist perspective for mathematics teaching. Simultaneously, the importance of communication and language in mathematics education, of cooperative learning environments, collaborative practices and the influence of culture and context has been acknowledged (see, for example, Bishop, 1987; Pimm, 1988; Cooney, 1994a; Lerman, 1996). Mathematics teacher educators are mainly in touch with this literature and debate while teachers, mainly, are not. It is therefore unsurprising that educators' own practice is motivated by these perspectives, although the nature of influence varies across programmes.

Thus, on the one hand, change in practice, philosophy, and beliefs of teachers underly the work of all the chapters. On the other hand, however, ways in which new thinking and practices might develop and become the reality of students' experiences in mathematics lessons are neither agreed upon, nor, possibly yet, well understood. At its simplest level, there is considerable common theory about the direction of change in teaching mathematics, but it is in the complex practical manifesting of this theory where issues arise. These issues lead to a necessary questioning of the associated theory.

One purpose of this book is to reveal and to make problematic the spectrum of inservice practice and current philosophy in mathematics teacher education in seeking development and change. Our starting point will be the themes arising from papers in Section Two. The following broad themes will be discussed:

1. Teachers doing mathematics themselves.
2. Out-of-school versus in-school contexts for developing teaching.
3. Aspects of changing practice for teachers in classrooms.
4. Teachers as researchers of their own teaching.
5. Learning as teacher educators in developing professional practice.

Themes and Issues

Teachers Working on Mathematics *in Inservice Programmes*

In teacher education, many issues of concern transcend subject boundaries — for example, issues of knowledge (such as, pedagogical versus disciplinary knowledge), the particular needs of girls and boys or of different social and cultural groups, educational organization, management and funding. These are issues for teachers of *all* subjects. Cooney (1994b) writes:

> It is striking that pedagogic concerns seem to be driven by forces outside the field of mathematics per se [communication, group dynamics and cooperative learning are mentioned]. Good as these programs are they potentially mask the power that can be derived from seeing pedagogy as emanating from mathematics itself. (p. 8)

In mathematics education we are concerned to address how issues relate explicitly to the teaching and learning of *mathematics*. Sometimes we need to ask critically, where does mathematics fit into this? How is the fact that we are concerned, ultimately, with students' learning of mathematics related to educational issues in the development of mathematics teaching? One seemingly obvious response to this question is that since the teachers we are working with are teachers of mathematics, their mathematical knowledge is of central importance to their development as teachers. The NCTM professional standards for teaching state; 'The teacher of mathematics should pose tasks that are based on sound and significant mathematics' (1991, p. 25). Cooney (1994b) writes:

> It is difficult to imagine a reasonable argument that says a teacher's knowledge of mathematics is unimportant for that teacher's effectiveness. Yet a precise relationship between a teacher's knowledge of mathematics and his or her ability to be an effective teacher remains elusive. (p. 8)

Nevertheless, (as Cooney points out) a focus on mathematics is and has been a major emphasis in mathematics teacher education programmes, and that is no less true in those described in this book. For teachers at primary (elementary) or intermediate (middle) levels this often reflects a lack of opportunity to study mathematics to a sufficient level in initial teacher education programmes. Papers here reflect the negative effects on teachers of feeling inadequately prepared mathematically (see, particularly, Irwin and Britt, this volume). However, even for teachers with university degrees in mathematics, this does not translate necessarily into good pedagogic practice (see, for example, Farah-Sarkis, this volume). Cooney (1994b) writes:

The evidence does suggest, however, that the study of university level mathematics alone — at least as presently constituted — is not sufficient to ensure that teachers will understand school mathematics deeply enough to realize reform in the teaching of mathematics. (p. 8)

Shulman's concept of 'pedagogical content knowledge' (see, for example, Shulman, 1987) recognizes that different forms of knowledge are required to translate subject knowledge into activities for effective learning in classrooms. That this is true where mathematics is concerned is recognized in several of the chapters (see, particularly, Markovits and Even), which offer a response to Cooney's plea for research:

One could argue that the means by which teachers learn such knowledge is one, if not the, defining point for teacher education and consequently should be the focal point of research on teacher education. (1994b, p. 8)

In many of the programmes described, mathematics itself is central to the philosophy of the programme. This reflects a theoretical position that teachers' own mathematical perceptions and perspectives influence their teaching; that teachers need to recognize and critically reflect on their own mathematical learning in order to understand better the learning of their students (Ball, 1993; Simon and Schifter, 1991). The programmes presented sought to foster alternative conceptions of mathematics, and of ways of thinking and being mathematical, along with a growth of metacognitive awareness of mathematical processes and heuristics (Mason, Burton and Stacey, 1984; Schoenfeld, 1987). Thus, the chapters, in Section Two, from Amit and Hillman, Farah-Sarkis, Weinzweig, Murray et al., Carter and Richards and Irwin and Britt all discuss an element of inviting teachers to engage in mathematical thinking and problem-solving and to reflect on its outcomes for themselves as learners.

Amit and Hillman, discussing parallel programmes in Israel and the United States, focused on 'performance assessment activities', in which students could develop and demonstrate their mathematical knowledge and skills through construction of a solution to a given task. Tasks could involve mathematical or real-world contexts, but an objective of a task was that it allow for multiple levels and types of solutions. Workshops were organized in which teachers were asked to work on tasks of the sort they might then offer their students. The intent of the programme was to encourage teachers to move from their use, with students, of exercises practising basic skills in an isolated way, to a use of more open-ended, real-world problems for learning in context.

Farah-Sarkis, discussing the needs for inservice provision in the Lebanon, asked teachers to work on non-standard problems or answer in-depth questions on mathematical concepts in the curriculum. Most of the teachers had many years of teaching experience, were comfortable with their practice, and mainly believed that knowledge of the subject matter of the syllabus was all they needed to be able to teach it. A major aim of her two-day inservice programmes was to bring teachers up against pedagogical questions which might help them to recognize the value of pedagogical knowledge in teaching mathematics.

Murray, Olivier and Human's work in South Africa focuses on children's intuitive thinking as a way in which to encourage elementary level teachers to rethink their practice of teaching mathematics. In their two-day workshops they asked teachers to work together on solving mathematical problems which they might subsequently offer to their students. These problems were essential to students' development of number sense and construction of meaningful algorithms, including standard algorithms. They also had the goal of increasing teachers' sensitivity to their students' personal ways of thinking. The problems were developed in such a way that teachers solved them using strategies they might observe their own students employing. Through this experience, teachers themselves gained confidence in the mathematical concepts they were expected to teach and the related classroom approaches.

All programmes aimed to help teachers see mathematics as more than standard algorithms and right answers, but there were other objectives leading to the specific problems or types of problems tackled. Weinzweig's purpose was to focus inservice teachers' attention on problem-solving, but with the goal of experiencing and becoming aware of processes of abstraction. To do so, he chose problems which would highlight mathematical processes and enable teachers to move to abstraction. Amit and Hillman asked teachers to work on problems from 'real world' situations in which mathematical modelling strategies would be required. This, they believed would 'have the potential to contribute to the development of higher order thinking and provide information about students' usable mathematical knowledge.' It was expected that after the workshops, teachers would use such problems with their own students.

Farah-Sarkis, taking a different tack, wanted to challenge teachers' assumptions that having mathematical knowledge was all that was required in order to teach mathematics well. She put teachers into student-like situations to help them realize the importance of pedagogical knowledge in teaching. She did this by carefully constructing non-standard problems — those which could not be solved by rote methods — in curricular areas the teachers were required to teach. The teachers then found themselves experiencing the same feelings of frustration and lack of confidence as their own students, and thus considering the importance of their pedagogy — an aim of the course.

Thus practices in the programmes included:

- inviting teachers to solve non-standard problems and model real-world situations in mathematics;
- asking teachers to work on mathematical problems which they might subsequently offer their students;
- engaging teachers in mathematical processes and strategies they might wish their students to employ;
- engaging teachers in student-like situations to increase their sensitivity to students' thinking and appreciate students' learning needs;
- enabling teachers to recognize higher order mathematical thinking and how it can be fostered;
- enabling teachers to recognize and develop processes of mathematical abstraction.

Teachers were encouraged to draw comparisons between their own experiences and those of their students. In doing so, teachers became aware of the consequences of their actions; that is, to 'see' the situation from the students' perspective and to gain critical insight to effective ways of engaging, supporting and challenging students.

All of these programmes reflect a philosophy of mathematics which eschews narrow views of mathematical concepts, and opens up the possibility of students seeing mathematics as more context-related, thinking mathematically themselves, doing their own mathematics, taking responsibility for their growth of mathematical knowledge. For teachers taking part in the programmes it was often the first opportunity they had to see mathematics in this light, and to experience for themselves confidence and ownership in doing mathematics. For some teachers it was a heady experience, as indicated in the following quotation.

> I thought and thought right through the evening and almost couldn't sleep last night. I have learnt the one thing I think is the most important thing I have learnt as a teacher; that is, that if you show somebody how to do a problem you stop him thinking. This is what happened to my mathematics. (Marilyn, quoted in Murray et al., this volume, p. 40)

It raised exciting possibilities for mathematical learning of which the teachers had previously been unaware. However, the promise of such euphoria is lost if teachers are not supported in translating their new visions into effective classroom practice. This became evident in certain of the other programmes described in Section Two.

Working with Teachers in Out-of-school Versus In-school Contexts

Many of the programmes described in Section Two invited teachers to take part in some form of out-of-school course or workshop for all or part of the programme. Murray, Olivier and Human acknowledge that the expectation on which their two-day workshop was founded (namely that 'the workshop should bring about not only a paradigm shift in teachers' perceptions about learning and teaching, but also equip the teacher to establish and maintain on a daily basis a completely different classroom culture') seemed 'unusual and unreasonable'. They describe two-day programmes in which teachers are briefly and sharply brought up against issues deemed essential to their work as elementary school teachers of mathematics. The large numbers of teachers in need of such programmes, and the desire of educationists to raise teaching standards widely and quickly in a large country at a time of enthusiastic expectation and social euphoria, made some form of input, however brief, essential.

Thus the issues for Murray et al. were driven by need and practicality — essentially, what can be achieved in the short time available. It is clear from their report, that teachers' views do change. How this is reflected in the teachers' classroom work, and what follow-up is necessary to facilitate changes in practice are clearly important questions without easy answers, especially with respect to the large-scale development needs in South Africa. It seems undeniable, however, that programmes which take teachers out of school for a short workshop or course are likely to result in less lasting change than longer programmes, especially those with an in-school focus. It is worth noting the words of a teacher in Irwin and Britt's programme:

> I now see that there is little value in one-day teacher development programmes. Even in our ten-week teacher development contract teachers may not progress for the first eight weeks. (p. 93)

The programme described by Weinzweig consisted of workshops which were held over the period of a year with time between them for teachers to try out their new perspectives in classrooms and to develop a collegiality in discussing outcomes with their fellow participants. As the author points out, it is hard to measure the success of the programme without the possibility to assess the change in classroom behaviour of the participating teachers, or any improvement in the achievements of students in their classes. There was, however, evidence of the teachers' enthusiasm, of their development in terms of equipping their classes with more student-centred resources, and of the teachers becoming engaged in other inservice education. All of this pointed to the possibilities of real change in mathematics teaching resulting from the programme.

What might be seen as teacher euphoria with new visions of mathematics and a teacher's own ability to engage with and own that mathematics, is also an outcome of Murray's programme. Similar results are reported by other programmes, that of Amit and Hillman in the US and in Israel and of Farah-Sarkis in the Lebanon. For example, Amit and Hillman say,

> While we do not claim that the experiences described in this paper entirely reshaped the teachers' conceptions, there is evidence that some of their conceptions were challenged. (p. 24)

Farah-Sarkis writes,

> After this experience, the teachers were much more receptive to the training which had been planned for them. Indeed, most teachers asked for more training sessions. (p. 47)

All of these programmes approached teacher education from the perspective of 'doing in your classroom like you were doing in the INSET sessions'. However, evidence from other papers suggests that putting new knowledge and awareness into practice in such a manner is fraught with dilemmas. Carter and Richards' paper addresses such dilemmas. In common with those described above, their programme began with an intensive course for teachers involving exploration of mathematical topics. This course was followed up in schools by programme leaders who visited classrooms and talked with the teacher participants about their teaching. Teachers were encouraged to keep journals, in which they recorded their experiences and issues arising, and to meet to discuss their efforts to put new ideas into practice. The authors write that, 'articulating their understandings and having to defend their ideas forces them [teachers] to grapple with what it means to really understand something.'

From the cases reported, it seems clear that turning into practice the ideas discussed in the workshops was far from simple. Carter and Richards write,

> Although teachers are almost universally excited about the chance to explore mathematical ideas with their peers, and to experience a clearly different way of learning, they find that translating these experiences back into their classrooms is not an easy task. (p. 70)

This is reflected by the quote from Shirley, one of their teachers,

> Am I the only one with nightmares about these issues? I'm floundering. I can't decide what's important. I can't decide how long to stick with something (the old rule of thumb was 80–85 per cent mastery of a skill area by the class). What's mastery any more? What is a skill? (p. 72)

For teachers, the awareness-raising of the workshops was an important step towards making changes in their classrooms, but the experience of putting the new visions into practice provided an even greater learning experience. Here the teachers had no ready-made solutions and had to grapple with choices and decisions which were neither clear-cut nor comfortable. What Carter and Richards make very clear in their chapter is the uncomfortable and unpredictable nature of *real* classroom change. The euphoria of the workshop situation may be a necessary prerequisite for such change to begin, but coping alone in their classroom after the workshop phase is likely to result in frustration for teachers and a return to former practice. The problems encountered are often too great for resolution by teachers working privately to make changes in their practice. The issues here seem to be:

1. There is powerful potential in introducing teachers to alternative approaches to mathematics and its learning, resulting in new visions for teachers of their work with pupils.
2. Although powerful in raising teachers' awareness of the need for change, it is often not clear how such approaches can be manifested with pupils in the classroom. The potential can remain unrealized unless teachers are able to conceptualize and generalize the implications of their new visions to the classroom.
3. Classroom implementation of such new visions is far from straightforward, creating dilemmas for teachers in which ongoing support is paramount.

Programmes Which Focus on Alternative Approaches to Classroom Teaching

The programmes discussed so far have shown teachers inspired to make changes in their teaching practice as a result of new experiences of learning mathematics themselves, and of seeing mathematics from new perspectives. Translating these new visions into ways of working with students is seen to be problematic, even when the teachers themselves are highly motivated.

Other patterns of inservice programmes described in Section Two focus directly on classroom practices, and ways in which these might be developed or changed. Two programmes designed to address ways of changing practices are described in the papers of Markovits and Even in Israel and of Serrazina and Loureiro in Portugal. The former described a three-phase programme in which teachers were invited to consider and to critique a range of classroom processes. The latter focused on a particular aspect of classroom practice in mathematics, namely the use of manipulative materials and calculators in problem-solving activities.

In Markovits and Even's programme, teachers were sent written descriptions of mathematical classroom situations and asked to think about how they would respond in those situations themselves. In a workshop format, the situations and teachers' responses were discussed. Teachers were then offered responses from 'other' teachers, some deliberately contrived by the course leaders to represent particular views and to encourage debate. Through this medium, teachers' awareness was raised as they recognized choices and questions relating to their own teaching. Issues which started to emerge included the importance of student-centred approaches to learning mathematics, focusing on students' own construction of mathematical knowledge. Further awareness-raising was achieved through discussion of articles and research studies, and through teachers' interviews with students to find out about students' perspectives on the situations mentioned above. Markovits and Even acknowledge that, despite considerable evidence of teachers' developing awareness resulting from this programme, the teachers needed more *time* to 'make those ideas a functional part of their pedagogical content knowledge'.

The programme of Serrazina and Loureiro focused on a particular aspect of classroom practice in mathematics, valued for its contribution to children's learning, namely the use of manipulative materials and calculators in problem-solving activities. The programme aimed to encourage teachers to use such materials as part of students' mathematical learning experiences, and also to research the outcomes of their use. This was begun by training sessions in which activities prepared by a research team were tried out over a period of two days with teachers who discussed and evaluated their outcomes. Three months later, the researchers explored the influence of these sessions on teachers' classroom work using questionnaires and follow-up interviews with teachers. As a result of analysis of the data collected, further activities were prepared and further training sessions held. While some teachers had made use of the activities in their classrooms, many others had not done so. This was seen as an important issue in the programme: Why were some teachers unable or unwilling to implement activities in which they themselves had participated and found valuable? An in-depth study of two teachers who made use of materials was conducted to elicit ways of making such activities more accessible to teachers.

Both of these studies illustrate innovative approaches designed to help teachers see ways of manifesting new ideas and visions of mathematical learning in their classrooms. They also illustrate the problematic nature of devising classroom activities which will result in changed classroom practices. In all the above programmes there was evidence of teachers' developing *awareness* of possibilities for their classrooms. Evidence of actual changes in practice, however, was more elusive. Many of the chapters indicate that time is an important factor: more time is needed for the emergence of practical manifestations of theoretical ideas. However, it seemed likely too that additional support was needed for the teachers to turn their visions of practice into realities and to cope with issues and tensions which arose. It may, in retrospect, seem that this is not an unexpected conclusion; however, it is often necessary to see such effects made manifest for them to become powerfully obvious. The implications are that, however good short programmes are at developing an awarenesses for teachers, ongoing forms of inservice education are necessary for any lasting or effective change to be realized in classrooms.

This issue is made clear in the chapter from Goldstein et al., which discusses a longer term programme highlighting a progression of activities over a number of years. Her team's inservice work for teachers started with computer-based tutorial models, moved through out-of-school workshops, and ultimately developed a model for a school-based approach. At the workshop phase, 'small collaborative groups of teachers were encouraged to grapple with mathematical problems . . . and devise and practice methods of dealing with them in the classroom'. Despite indications that the workshops were effective in enhancing teachers' awareness and confidence in alternative conceptualizations of teaching, the teachers 'regressed to established patterns at the chalk front'. Thus the team decided that more direct intervention was necessary to carry changes of teaching through to the children. They adopted the term 'modelling strategies' to describe aspects of this work.

Modelling, here, seems to mean the creation of examples of practice through which teachers can gain more general insights to possibilities for the classroom. Thus teachers' attention would be drawn to particular activities, ways of introducing mathematical topics, approaches to classroom organization, strategies for stimulating students' thinking, etc. Such modelling took a number of forms. In one form, it was implicit in the ways teacher educators interacted with the teachers. For example, a workshop using brainstorming and negotiation of ideas in developing its themes would demonstrate this as a potential mode of working in the classroom. This mode could then be discussed explicitly because it was now part of the teachers' experience and more readily conceptualized in the classroom environment. Another form of modelling involved teacher educators in demonstration lessons, in which they overtly illustrated suggested classroom approaches. As Goldstein et al.'s programme made clear, modelling of such techniques and approaches is only valuable if undertaken alongside other reinforcing and supportive inservice provision.

From these programmes we see a variety of approaches to helping teachers develop activities for the enhancement of mathematics teaching. These include:

- design of classroom materials for use with manipulatives, together with teacher workshops to introduce classroom methods for using the materials;
- descriptions of classroom situations as a basis for teacher discussion and analysis to encourage similar analyses of situations in teachers' own classes;

- modelling activities in which teacher educators make a direct input into teachers' learning by demonstrating the use of techniques and strategies which teachers themselves might use in the classroom.

Teacher-as-researcher Programmes

It seems clear, from patterns reported above, that teacher educators cannot *give* teachers conceptualizations of approaches to teaching. Teachers need opportunities to become aware of issues and work on these issues themselves and with colleagues in order to develop their own conceptions. The programmes discussed above used many strategies in bringing issues to teachers' attention and helping teachers to develop awareness of issues. A major problem for teachers was in sustaining work on the issues and developing their own conceptualizations of classroom approaches. This problem has been addressed, in some programmes, by encouraging teachers to undertake research or inquiry into their own teaching and learning: the 'teacher-as-researcher' inservice paradigm.

Programmes described by Irwin and Britt in New Zealand and Krainer in Austria, discuss teachers' involvement in some form of action research into aspects of their own teaching practice. In both cases, this happened as part of a university, academic or research programme. These were extensive programmes (two years and four semesters, respectively) which were a combination of university meetings and seminars, research work by teachers in their own classrooms, and sharing and discussion by teachers of experiences and issues arising from their classroom work and thinking. In both cases the courses were award-bearing, and teachers were expected to write about their teaching development. As well as teachers engaging in their own research, there were meetings between teachers, workshops for doing mathematics or for sharing research experiences, and visits to the teachers in school by course leaders. In Irwin and Britt's programme, teachers videotaped their lessons for discussion with course leaders. One of the aims of Krainer's programme was to motivate and qualify the participants to organize further education for themselves and for other teachers after conclusion of the course. In these two approaches, not only was the teacher involved in some form of action research into aspects of their own teaching practice, but they were also involved in making public to others their private activity of teaching.

Both reports offer case studies which illustrate the depth of the learning of participants as a result of working on issues of importance to themselves in their classrooms. As Krainer points out, it was not that teachers necessarily produced, as a result of their research, insights which were new to the mathematics education community more widely, but rather that the insights were new for them and so highly significant to their own learning. The development of such insights from the teachers' own practice and thinking was powerful because of the personal practical dimension of their growth of awareness: reading about issues or being told by other people often lacks this important dimension. The keeping of reflective journals and writing about their experiences also led to teacher-developed insights into teaching and learning processes. Teachers were also encouraged to articulate their under-standings and to learn and broaden their experiences from sharing ideas, questions and issues with each other. Thus the knowledge gained individually in the class-room was accessible to others for public examination.

The effective dimensions of these programmes included:

- extended time periods in which teachers worked specifically on developing teaching;
- explicitly encouraged reflective activity generated through the expectations of engaging in classroom inquiry;
- collaborative activity with other teachers and course leaders;
- requirements to keep journals of activity and reflections, and to write accounts of learning experiences.

The multi-dimensionality of these programmes, over a realistic time period, seemed significant to the success of the teaching development for some teachers.

Teacher Educator Learning and Development

Irwin and Britt's report makes comparisons between the learning of intermediate teachers and of the secondary teachers in the programme. The authors reported that differences in teachers' mathematical knowledge, experience and classroom confid-ence resulted in different gains from the course. For example, some intermediate teachers, who had less mathematical experience than the secondary teachers, found the mathematical differential a barrier to their progress. The authors point to the salutary case of the teacher, Emily, who felt she had regressed during the course rather than gained from it. This led to critical reflection on the part of the course leaders to question the philosophy and practice of the course and their own roles within it. As a result, they problematized aspects of their practice, leading to their own development as teacher educators.

Such learning experiences were evident for teacher educators in many of the programmes. For example, Goldstein et al. tried a range of approaches, evaluating results and feeding back to future planning. Serrazina and Loureiro undertook their case studies to find out what difficulties teachers encountered in using manipulative materials in their practice. Markovitz and Even recognized the key nature of 'time' to teachers' classroom development. In many cases, issues which arose were chal-lenging and brought their own tensions and dilemmas for the inservice leaders: for example, Murray et al. recognized the limitations of their two-day programmes, whilst also realizing the enormous pressures for conducting such short programmes which resulted from a societal need to reach many teachers.

It is clear that designing inservice development programmes to enhance math-ematics teaching is problematic in many respects. The programmes described have illustrated many approaches, revealed positive outcomes and further needs, and emphasized a number of key factors on which success of a programme may depend.

137

There is abundant evidence to suggest that out-of-school workshops, however successful, need to be followed up by support for teachers in their ongoing development in schools. It is clear that a major factor is time which often implies a need for further resources and expense. To achieve effective outcomes, programmes need to have adequate resources allocated to teachers' continued professional development. Obvious as this may seem, the reality, even in the developed world, is that inadequate resources reduces potential for success (Walshe, 1998).

As teacher educators reflect on experiences and try to address tensions and dilemmas in planning future programmes, what are the wider issues and concerns — perhaps of philosophical and theoretical or social and political dimensions — which they have to face? The next section of this chapter addresses briefly these dimensions.

Wider Issues and Dimensions

Constructivism as a Perspective for Teaching Development

All the programmes discussed take as given the need to improve the experience of classroom mathematical learning through the development of teachers' knowledge of mathematics and of pedagogy. As we indicated at the beginning of this chapter, most chapters described programmes as being embedded in a reform movement for educational change in mathematical teaching at some level in some culture. Most chapters also indicated that they see learning, both of mathematics by students in classrooms and of pedagogical approaches by teachers, from a perspective influenced by constructivism. It seems important to ask why so many programmes, in different countries, rest on an apparently common perspective, and what are the implications of such an underpinning?

One answer to this question is, simply, to say that constructivism has had such a powerful influence on thinking in mathematics education internationally during the 1980s and early 1990s, that it is impossible for educators not to be aware of it, or not to view development through a constructivist lens. However, it is likely that the influence is the result of far more complex factors. It is certainly true that in the past 15 years, there has been a global shift in perspectives on mathematics learning in a direction away from a transmission view of learning to one involving constructivism. It therefore seems likely that teacher education programmes would incorporate a constructivist view of learning which necessarily influences conceptions of teaching. Still, it is by no means obvious how a constructivist position relates to the practicalities of teaching, let alone to working with teachers.

Constructivism is a perspective on knowledge and learning: it is not a pedagogy for classroom teaching or for teacher education. It seems necessary, therefore, to explicate the relation between a constructivist philosophical position and the various (practical) methodologies employed. We believe that within this explication there is a basis for theory of pedagogy and, concomitantly of teacher education, and this theory needs critique. From the chapters in Section Two we glean some clues.

Amit and Hillman talk of 'challenging teachers' conceptions' and providing opportunities for teachers to reflect on and possibly change those conceptions. Weinzweig states, 'It is our view that children do not receive a concept from without, but construct it from within.' These perspectives fit with a Piagetian view of viability and fit, in which cognitive structuring is reconfigured according to reflection on experience (see, for example, von Glasersfeld, 1987). Serrazina and Loureiro refer to children's learning in terms of the construction of knowledge. For example, speaking of the teacher Miguel, they say, 'He considers that materials allow . . . the construction of pupils' own reasoning . . .'; and of the teacher Rita, they say, 'she feels . . . very upset when the pupils' construction of concepts emerge very slowly'. Carter and Richards state that their inquiry approach is 'framed in a constructivist epistemology', indicating a focus on 'sense-making, building up of one's own ideas'. They emphasize the importance of teachers sharing and reflecting on differences in their experience: 'having to defend their ideas forces them to grapple with what it means to really understand something'. Irwin and Britt indicate that they set out in their programme to test a suggestion that 'if teachers were to develop a new teaching methodology compatible with a constructivist view of learning, the professional development itself should be constructivist in nature'.

Most chapters indicate, explicitly or implicitly, the value of communication and collaboration between students or teachers in aiding mathematics learning or development — classroom processes such as *sharing*, *discussion* or *negotiation* are valued throughout. This includes both negotiation of meanings, as well as personal learning through these classroom approaches. Murray et al. state that their perspectives are based on a 'socio-constructive view of knowledge', which they expand as follows:

> We try to implement these ideas in the classroom through a problem-centred approach to mathematics learning and teaching, where students are presented with problems that are meaningful to them but which they cannot solve with ease using routinized procedures, and where students are expected to discuss, critique, explain and justify their interpretations and strategies. (pp. 33–4)

Further, they recognize the social nature of classroom learning experiences in contributing to learners' constructions of knowledge. Krainer's paper demonstrates the creation of a mutual 'culture of practice' in which regional groups become small 'professional communities' and mutual understanding and constructive criticism are conducive processes. Here we see processes in professional development which go beyond personal construction to public construction of knowledge: that is, the processes involved in creating publically accepted knowledge about teaching. Krainer acknowledges, 'an epistemological understanding of learning which sees the learner as an active producer of knowledge rather than as a consumer.'

The theory to which these perspectives lead is the need to create opportunities for learners (students or teachers) to make sense of situations through collaborative activities which allow articulation and negotiation, and challenge incomplete conceptions. Mutuality and sharing allow supportive structures to emerge through which learner autonomy can be fostered and confident knowledge building can take place. There is evidence of success of this theory in many of the circumstances described where teachers work in small groups under the guidance of educators who are confident in this approach and the goals they are trying to achieve. However, where it breaks down is in situations where conditions are not conducive to the provision of these opportunities, and where those guiding the processes are themselves less confident with the theory or perhaps unaware of the epistemological foundations of the activities in which they are trying to engage.

Goldstein et al. take this further in their criticism of the potential of the constructivist paradigm to radically transform classroom practice. They quote Gordon and Spiegel (1993) to support a view that, 'In the main, political aims remain hidden as programmes are silent on the success of their strategies to reduce class, race and gender inequities in access and achievement.' It is clear that, in order to have any chance of legitimacy, programmes need to address such issues overtly (though few are currently doing so). We might ask, further, whether addressing such issues looks different depending on the cultural contexts in which programmes are implemented.

The Socio-economic, Cultural and Political Context of Mathematics Teacher Education

The papers in Section Two reflect a variety of cultural contexts. While one chapter reports on teacher development in an emergent nation, such as the new South Africa, others describe practices from well-established countries, such as Austria and New Zealand. All of the chapter authors address issues of context for their respective countries. In addition they responded to a set of questions we raised and circulated concerning cultural issues: all saw improving the teaching of mathematics as a high priority in their countries. The following discussion takes account of responses we received.

A striking common characteristic is that, in a fundamental way, all countries are involved in change in which the directions can appear quite similar, while the differences, culturally, are often stark. All are struggling with a similar set of limitations and constraints, but these vary in scale and can be identified broadly in terms of economic and/or social-political issues. The challenge for all countries is to find a means of increasing economic potential in an age of declining material resources. In order to do this, policy-makers argue, the quality of the workforce must be improved to provide highly skilled technical workers. The challenge of this goal is seen in the differences of teacher education between Austria and Portugal. In Austria, on the one hand, there are well-established practices for teachers' professional development, and resources are allocated for this. Teacher education is long term: teachers are aware of their need for continued education; teacher educators are aware of their role in the process of developing teaching. Portugal, on the other hand, has very different concerns for teacher education. Here, until very recently, teachers have lacked basic instruction in mathematics education. Only recently, have resources been provided for teachers educators to work with teachers in mathematics.

In South Africa, the needs of vast numbers of students and teachers in black schools are overwhelmingly predominant in influencing directions of change, regardless of educational philosophy.

Posch (1995) suggests that changes being demanded for the workforce concern the categories of qualifications workers must have (e.g. the ability to cooperate and work in teams) and the necessity for workers to adapt and retrain in order to find and maintain employment in a more dynamic market economy. The United States and South Africa, as countries with diverse cultures, are both attempting to accomplish major transformations in the teaching of mathematics in school. The United States, for example, is attempting to address much needed social change through major efforts to reform schools in general and mathematics education in particular. This issue is related to the enormous social costs of 'producing people who don't make it' (Posch, 1995).

Across the EU countries, the Middle East, South Africa, Australia and North America, top-level reports have been issued which indicate that, globally, education is in a state of flux. Several significant reports have been written detailing the shift from traditional approaches to those which emphasize the changing nature of student roles, knowledge, and concomitantly teachers' roles (c.f., *The Curriculum Redefined: Schooling for the 21st Century*, OECD). These documents chart a call for a shift from traditional teacher-as-authoritarian approaches to those which reflect the responsibility for learning back to the students — a goal which seems compatible with constructivist principles. The underlying assumption is that in order for these nations to accommodate the dimensions of economic and sociol-political shifts taking place, students must be adaptable and flexible in their thinking. This places teachers in a critical role in the process and, for many nations, professional development of teachers is high on the national agenda. A salutary example, as recent international comparisons have shown, is that, despite substantial resources being allocated to the reform movement in mathematics education in the United States, teaching still largely follows a traditional mode of direct instruction and student practice of mathematical exercises. Whereas, in Japan, for example, there is evidence that teachers have established in practice much of what reform in the USA seeks to achieve (Stigler and Hiebert, 1997). While it could be argued that the Japanese results are culturally related, it seems likely that progression in understanding mathematics teaching and INSET could be achieved by learning from the practices and policies of other nations.

Politicization of Mathematics Education

It is evident that proposed changes in mathematics education are tied to international goals for a renewed commitment to democratic processes. Such goals are most strongly evident in the papers of Carter and Richards, Murray et al., and Goldstein et al. However, any critique of the processes and issues in addressing these goals must consider seriously how the term 'democratic' is interpreted in a variety of social and political circumstances. The role of assisting a move from an authorization society to a more democratic one indicates the very social/political nature of education. In some cases goals are overt. For example, issues of democracy are expressed in all reform documents released in the United States.

As a spokesperson for reform, Romberg (1992), claims that a goal for mathematics education, in addition to changing the view of school mathematics and learning, is 'democratic citizenship'. This goal carries with it the issue of generating a citizenry that understands the rights and responsibilities of participation in a democractic society and yet is prepared to be economically productive.

Carter and Richards' chapter shows the dilemmas faced by teachers trying to move from an authoritarian ideology to a more humanistic approach. The constructivist philosophy expressed in the chapter encompasses tenets of democracy, and this may be one reason why there is a current resurgence of interest in constructivism. Adler (1995) views constructivism 'as driven by democratizing intent, with the twin goals of moving away from authoritarian approaches to teaching, learning, and knowledge, and improving socially distributed access and success rates.' However, she argues that adopting such a pedagogy can also inhibit and reduce the development of mathematical knowledge. Something she refers to as the 'democracy–development tension'.

This tension might be seen in efforts to reconcile the democratic ideal with social turmoil and urgent need: more extreme political aspects are revealed in the papers from South Africa. The South African government's dismantling of apartheid in 1990 and agreement to negotiate a democratic society was further strengthened by the coincidental demise of communism. This, according to Gordimer as quoted in Gordon and Spiegel (1993), was 'one of the most extraordinary events in world history — the complete reversal of everything that, for centuries, has ordered the lives of all our people.' One feels a sense of urgency in the writings of Murray et al. and Goldstein et al. Murray speaks of the pressures of brief two-day workshops for teachers who have only the most bare essentials of teacher education. Goldstein situates the work of the Primary Mathematics Centre in the expediency of working with the marginalized majority in South Africa. However, the chapters from South African authors also reveal the strong political dimensions that underlie social transformations: all bring explicitly to the fore the political dimensions of mathematics teacher education not found in the other chapters. And, as Goldstein comments, 'in a country whose economy has been ravaged by greed and self-interest, the implications of such restructuring are overwhelming.'

Constructivism, Culture and Complexity

As an example of the complex relationship between issues in teacher education and the associated socio-political and cultural context, let us look further at Goldstein et al.'s chapter. The programme they describe has evolved over a number of years, and its operation needs to be seen in the context of large numbers of teachers and students in predominantly black schools in a new movement towards educational democracy which is beset with problems at a multiplicity of levels. Not least is the numerical problem of reaching the many teachers in need of support, as also emphasized by Murray et al. More subtle are the perceived needs of schools and teachers. One perception is that 'equality' means having access to the same levels of resource and provision as the more privileged white schools. This leads to uncritical attempts to emulate the educational environment provided by such schools. According to the authors, emulating these environments is not only inappropriate to the wider educational provision, in that it fails to address particular needs, but its educational basis is also suspect in that it perpetuates an undemocratic view of education. Yet, to many black children and teachers, emulating the source of oppression is to gain freedom and equality. This is Adler's tension (1995).

Here seems to be one manifestation of an interface between constructivism and culture. The team of educators, of which Goldstein et al. are members, chooses to work from constructivist principles in the development of educational programmes. They go beyond a transmission approach to mathematics teaching to develop more child-centred classroom approaches, encouraging teachers to question traditional practices, to develop their perspectives of mathematics, and to enquire into children's learning and its consequences for their own teaching. Such practices are uncommon, even in the white privileged schools. Thus, the big question for this team concerns the interpretation of their own constructivist ideology into ways of working with teachers that are consistent with the practices they wish to foster in schools, and often counter to mass perceptions of need.

A Critical Perspective on Mathematics Teacher Education

One chapter from Section Two which has yet to be discussed is that of Breen, who also works in a South African context. Breen speaks persuasively of his personal ideology of how mathematics might be taught, based on the work of Caleb Gattegno, and his attempts to put this into practice over six years of working with teachers. He characterizes his personal belief in a comparison between the authoritarian teacher Mr Smith, the serious Mr Jones who 'teaches for results', and the visionary teacher, Chris, who believes in students' self-discovery and who 'valued students and was prepared to listen to their issues and there was a great deal of group work . . . and fun'.

Breen's own developing world-view emerges from his writing as he describes the tensions faced by the teachers who struggle to implement the approaches which have been fostered in their work with Breen. For some teachers the struggle proves impossibly difficult despite their beliefs and commitment: some regress to established practices; others suffer disillusion and personal distress due to rejection by the system. Such experiences force, for Breen, a critical review of goals and ideology in a context of intense social euphoria, demand for reform, investment of international agencies, and expectation of results. Breen recognizes a growing cynicism in his recognition that the demand for rapid reform forces the pace of events and seduces educators to try to cut corners to deliver results. In so doing, they fail to satisfy in their own practices the demands they are making of teachers.

The consequent inconsistencies of practice result in perpetuation of educational inadequacies and disillusionment for teachers.

Breen concludes that a more honest recognition of the problematic nature of development at all levels is required, particularly on the part of educators. He suggests that the way ahead must be in a spirit of questioning and reflection, involving practitioner research into teaching and learning at all levels. This seems to extend the processes and approaches described in the papers of Krainer and Irwin and Britt, to research into the critical nature of teacher education itself.

Implications for Mathematics Teacher Educators

For mathematics teacher educators the issues discussed above point to a far more demanding role in developing mathematics teaching than has occurred in the past; for example, in addressing the challenge: How can we maintain educational differentiation which respects individual differences in abilities and interest but yet at the same time creates inequities? The chapters in this book are examples of how mathematics teacher educators are attempting to respond to such challenges and to alter their current approaches in developing mathematics teaching.

The shift to presenting mathematics as a dynamic discipline — and one which is accessible for all students not just a few — underlies all contributions. Engaging teachers in 'doing mathematics' was not only to improve content knowledge, but to foster a different view of what it means 'to do' mathematics. Correspondingly, the expectation that teachers will create settings in which students learn to be responsible for their learning as well as developing conditions such that students can access mathematics is of central importance. Clearly, developing teaching in mathematics differs from most disciplines, in that a redefinition of the nature of mathematics — and with this, teachers' beliefs and in some cases anxiety toward the subject itself — underlies all approaches.

It is easy to see how this translates into a constructivist perspective of learning and growth of knowledge. A constructivist view of individual learning is compatible with a more dynamic perception of mathematics, of student autonomy and of expectations for teaching. However, what needs to be recognized from the chapters are the *social* structures which are being developed in classroom settings to further the theoretical goals of the various programmes. It is not always made explicit how these social structures relate to the constructivist position on knowledge and learning, a *socio*-constructivist view, as expressed by Murray et al., may be more indicative of where many of these programmes are philosophically or theoretically based.

This social nature is reflected in the collaborative and communicative aspects of the programmes — in that knowledge construction by individuals is seen as developing relative to that of others in the programme, and, perhaps more importantly, relative to a growing understanding within the learning community of the nature of mathematics and its access and potential for all. The role of the teacher educator is a complex and sensitive one. It involves creating the environment or community in which such values can grow. This is not a case of facilitating socialization into existing cultures and practices, but of dynamically fostering new visions and ways for growth. While essentially constructivist, this is also deeply social, and will depend on the social norms of its participants being respected, even where changes are required. Returning briefly to the South African example, this may be seen as working for democratic or constructivist ideals within a clamour for two-day courses, so that all teachers can start to benefit, but so that the roots of a new community of practice might be established. Of course, the work to be done is enormous.

For teacher educators, the question is how to initiate and maintain an approach to developing mathematics teaching with these goals in mind. Further, how do teacher educators, themselves, incorporate tenets of a *social*-constructivist theory of learning into their own practice? In this regard, the approaches described in the chapters in Section Two reflect a range of attempts to grapple with such issues. It is clear in all approaches, that those involved in teacher and teaching development were attempting to create situations in which teachers experienced and constituted meaning for themselves, rather than being shown what and how to do. However, the chapter authors display a wide diversity in the meaning of constructivism, and subsequently interpretations of the ways in which theory is transformed to practice. A majority of the approaches focused on creating situations in which teachers were expected to reflect on their activity and/or personal experiences. From this comes a growing awareness of a need for mathematics teacher educators themselves to reflect on and reconsider their own practice, to engage in an exchange of ideas, and from this to create a common ground from which to communicate about their work.

Inevitably, as educators and mathematicians, the problems we choose, and the ways we encourage teachers to work on them, is based on our personal philosophies of mathematics and of teaching (Thompson, 1984; Lerman, 1990; Ernest, 1991; Sanders, 1993). This may remain implicit in our work with teachers, given the shortness of time which is available for workshops or courses. In starting to appreciate some of the excitement and potential of new methodologies, teachers might perceive new mathematical ideas, concepts, and approaches as if they are the 'right' or 'preferred' ones in some new ideology, without really appreciating what is needed to implement them effectively in practice. In our attempts to persuade teachers to be critical of former practices, there is the danger that we, teacher educators, become the new guardians of the truth.

In the programmes discussed, the theory–practice dialectic is patently evident: practice is not merely a copy of theory, and it is well accepted that all theories are limited when it comes to practice. For example, we see Goldstein's team operating in a cycle of development of theory and practice: initial computer-based models and out-of-school workshops gave way to more complex models involving working alongside teachers in schools, modelling of preferred practices, and networks of collaborative practice. At each stage the effects of such practices need reconciliation with the theoretical perspectives on which they are based, and the theories are enhanced by what is learned from practice. It is clear that simple statements about an underlying constructivist theory are insufficient to characterize this complexity. As theoreticians in the discipline of mathematics teacher education we have the responsibility to critique the basis of our professional decisions and to explicate our evolving theories. Such critique involves questioning closely what is effective in our practices, and what evidence we have to support perceptions of effectiveness.

It is this that we see as the exciting challenge for the future. The papers we have discussed here all promote practices which contribute to the spectrum of teacher education methodology. We have highlighted their successes and raised issues and questions, making problematic the practices involved. It seems to be this making problematic, with consequent levels of inquiry and critique which will take us forward. The next three chapters in Section Three expand this view.

References

ADLER, J. (1995) 'Participatory, inquiry pedagogy, communicative competence and mathematical knowledge in a multilingual classroom: A vignette', *Proceedings of the Seventeenth International Conference of the International Group for the Psychology of Mathematics Education Vol. 3* (pp. 208–15), Japan: Tsukuta.

BALL, D. (1993) 'With an eye on the mathematical horizon: Dilemmas of teaching elementary school mathematics', *Elementary School Journal*, **93**, pp. 373–97.

BISHOP, A. (1987) 'Mathematics education in its cultural context', *Educational Studies in Mathematics*, **19**, pp. 179–91.

COBB, P., WOOD, T. and YACKEL, E. (1991) 'Small group interactions as a source of learning opportunities in second-grade mathematics', *Journal for Research in Mathematics Education*, **2**, 5, pp. 390–408.

COONEY, T. (1994a) 'Research and teacher education: In search of common ground', *Journal of Research in Mathematics Education*, **25**, pp. 608–36.

COONEY, T.J. (1994b) 'In-service programs in mathematics education', in FITZSIMMONS, S.J. and KERPELMAN, L.C. (eds) *Teacher Enhancement for Elementary and Secondary Science and Mathematics: Status, Issues, and Problems* (Chapter 8), Washington, DC: National Science Foundation.

DAVIS, R.B., MAHER, C.A. and NODDINGS, N. (1990) (eds) 'Constructivist views on the learning and teaching of mathematics', *Journal for Research in Mathematics Education, Monograph Number 4*. Reston, Virginia: National Council of Teachers of Mathematics.

ERNEST, P. (1991) *The Philosophy of Mathematics Education*, London: Falmer Press.

GORDON, R.J. and SPIEGEL, A.D. (1993) 'Southern Africa revisited', in DUEHAM, W.H., DANIEL, E.V. and SCHIEFFELIN, B. (eds) *Annual Reviews in Anthropology*, **22**, pp. 83–105.

HUGHES, P. (1994) 'The curriculum redefined: Schooling for the 21st Century', Washington D.C.: Organization for Economic Cooperation and Development.

JAWORSKI, B. (1994) *Investigating Mathematics Teaching: A Constructivist Inquiry*, London: Falmer Press.

LAMPERT, M. (1990) 'When the problem is not the question and the solution is not the answer', *American Educational Research Journal*, **27**, pp. 29–63.

LERMAN, S. (1990) 'Alternative perspectives on the nature of mathematics and their influence on the teaching of mathematics', *British Educational Research Journal*, **16**, 1, pp. 53–61.

MASON, J., BURTON, L. and STACEY, K. (1984) *Thinking Mathematically*, London: Addison-Wesley.

NATIONAL COUNCIL OF TEACHERS OF MATHEMATICS (1991) *Professional Standards for Teaching Mathematics*, Reston, VA: National Council of Teachers of Mathematics.

PIMM, D. (1988) *Speaking Mathematically*, London: Routledge.

POSCH, P. (1995) 'Teachers and their professional development', Unpublished paper, Klagenfurt, Austria: University of Klagenfurt.

ROMBERG, T. (1992) 'Further thoughts on the Standards: A response to Apple', *Journal of Research in Mathematics Education*, **23**, 432–7.

SANDERS, S.E. (1993) 'Mathematics and mentoring', in JAWORSKI, B. and WATSON, A. (eds) *Mentoring in Mathematics Teaching*, London: Falmer Press.

SCHOENFELD, A. (1987) 'What's all the fuss about metacognition?' in SCHOENFELD, A. (ed.) *Cognitive Science and Mathematics Education*, Hillsdale, NJ: Erlbaum Associates.

SHULMAN, L.S. (1987) 'Knowledge and teaching: Foundations of the new reform', *Harvard Educational Review*, **57**, 1, pp. 1–22.

SIMON, M. and SCHIFTER, D. (1991) 'Towards a constructivist perspective: An intervention study of mathematics teacher development', *Educational Studies in Mathematics*, **22**, 309–31.

STIGLER, J.W. and HIEBERT, J. (1997) 'Understanding and improving classroom mathematics instruction: An overview of the TIMSS video study', *Phi Delta Kappan*, September.

THOMPSON, A. (1984) 'The relationship of teachers' conceptions of mathematics teaching to instructional practice', *Educational Studies in Mathematics*, **15**, pp. 105–27.

VON GLASERSFELD, E. (1987) 'Learning as a constructive activity', in JANVIER, C. (ed.) *Problems of Representation in the Teaching and Learning of Mathematics*, Hillsdale, NJ: Erlbaum Associates.

WALSHE, J. (1998) 'The professional development of teachers', *OECD Observer*, **211**, pp. 31 4.

14 The Enactive Perspective on Teacher Development: 'A path laid while walking'[1]

Sandy Dawson, Canada

Introduction

There seems to be a culture of mathematics inservice education hinted at in the programmes described earlier in the book. Reading between the lines of those descriptions one could argue that this manifestation of inservice culture seems to have the following basic principle: there is something wrong with mathematics teaching world-wide, and that we, as mathematics educators, must fix it. Many mathematics teachers have bought into this culture. Such teachers seem to be seeking new ways to fix their practice. But this places mathematics teachers in a relationship of co-dependence with mathematics teacher educators. Mathematics teachers need someone to fix them, and mathematics teacher educators need someone to fix. The two groups seem made for each other. This culture is based on judging what is right and wrong, paying little attention to what mathematics teachers are actually doing (since it is wrong anyway) in their classrooms, and looking outside themselves for the 'right' way, the newest 'fix'.

But consider for a moment a different approach, a manifestation of a different inservice culture, one based on becoming aware of what you are doing without judging it. Looking with this light, perhaps mathematics teacher educators and mathematics teachers could move from a culture based on judgment to one based on possibility. For example, a mathematics educator with an enactivist bent, who is about to embark on a period of work with teachers on a four month long inservice programme, might well sit in a circle with the assembled group of mathematics teachers and offer these words as a basis for the shared experience which is to follow. Speaking quietly and slowly, distinctly and clearly, the maths educator says:

> As we begin our work together I make a number of assumptions about me and about you, perhaps the most important being the following. I assume:
> - that there is nothing wrong with you as individuals, as teachers, and as learners that needs 'fixing' by me;
> - that you know, however vaguely or ill defined that knowing might be, what you want or need from our work together;
> - that if some of my interactions with you prove useful it is because we will have worked on the group's needs, the group's agenda, and not mine.

The enactive perspective which forms a basis for what this mathematics teacher educator said is being developed by a number of researchers, and has been the focus of discussion groups at PME Conferences in Lisbon (1994), in Valencia (1996), and Stellenbosch (1998), as well as at several PME-NA conferences beginning with the meeting in Baton Rouge (1994). I was a co-leader of some of those discussion groups. I am also one of four members[2] of a research team investigating in the area of curriculum and ecological thought who use the term enactivism as a name for their developing awareness of an alternate way of describing the teaching and learning process in mathematics. In a recent paper another member of that team, Kieren (1995), described the enactivist view of the learning and teaching of mathematics as 'teaching-in-the-middle'. Moreover, Campbell and Dawson (1995) had previously given a brief synopsis of the history and development of this 'middle way' of teaching. More on those matters a bit later.

Part of the motivation behind the development of the enactivist view is a questioning of current views of the nature of knowledge development and acquisition in the mathematics classroom. Those exploring the enactivist view argue that one shortcoming of current conceptualizations of the teaching and learning of mathematics is that it is cast in representationist terms. That is, it is cast in a form where knowledge exists independently of individuals within their environment, that this knowledge can be tested, and that learners' representations of that knowledge can be matched against this external standard. This conceptualization of curriculum raises a number of problems: it casts knowledge as synchronous — a fix on a piece at a time is sufficient for all of it; and as ahistorical especially in personal terms — and this misses the contribution of current thought regarding complexity and chaos (Kellert, 1994; Maturana and Varela, 1992; Varela, Thomson and Rosch, 1991).

From an ecological perspective current disembodied views of knowledge lead to an irresponsible position. Bahktin (1993) makes the point that we are completely responsible for our actions and it is in knowledge garnered through embodied action that ethical responsibility lies. Thus the current idea of representationist knowledge, as a basis for curriculum, is abstracted from human responsibility — the individual is not implicated in it. The thrust of the enactivist work is not to link learners' experiences to an external representation of the curriculum, but to view the curriculum as being occasioned by the learners' experiences in their school environment. In this regard, their work challenges the modern mindset that draws sharp distinctions between self and other, mind and body, and humanity and nature. Ecological thinkers caution that society can no longer afford the luxuries of perceiving of individual identities as fully autonomous or societal actions as without consequences. Rather, individuals must locate themselves within a complex web of relationships, and see their decisions and actions as being both constrained by and influencing all nodes of the web. This is an enactivist orientation to inservice activities. This is inservice-in-the-middle.[3]

Background to the Enactivist Viewpoint

The enactivist view of inservice is adapted from the work of Varela et al., which in turn was guided by the writings of Merleau-Ponty. Merleau-Ponty argues that:

> The world is inseparable from the subject . . . which is nothing but a project of the world, and the subject is inseparable from the world . . . which the subject itself projects. (Merleau-Ponty, cited in Varela et al., 1991, p. 4)

Varela et al. developed their perspective from Merleau-Ponty's *fundamental intuition of double embodiment* (in Varela et al., 1991, p. xvii). In this view our bodies are considered both as outer physical-biological structures and as inner lived, experiential-phenomenological structures between which we *continuously circulate back and forth* (p. xv). In reflection we find ourselves engaged in a fundamental circularity between the two. Here, however, the distinction between self and world is maintained and yet both are embraced within this *double sense* of embodied action.

In this view, objects of thought are not *out there*, independent of our perceptual and cognitive capacities. Nor, for that matter, are they simply *in here*, in some mental space independent of our surrounding biological and cultural world. Rather, conscious experience, loosely constrained by a history of viable connections (which Varela and his colleagues have called *structural couplings*) referred to as natural drift, emerges from a process of mutual specification of organism and environment. Thus, Varela et al. contend:

> It is precisely this emphasis on mutual specification that enables us to negotiate a middle path between the Scylla of cognition as the recovery of a pregiven outer world (realism) and the Charybdis of cognition as the projection of a pregiven inner world (idealism). These two extremes both take representation as their central notion: in the first case representation is used to recover what is outer; in the second case it is used to project what is inner. Our intention is to bypass entirely this logical geography of inner versus outer by studying cognition not as recovery or projection but as embodied action. (1991, p. 172)

When applied to living systems Merleau-Ponty's notion of embodied action is generalized into an intentional theory of immediate experience: '. . . the meaning of this or that interaction for a living system is not prescribed from outside but is the result of the organization and history of the system itself' (Varela et al., 1991, p. 157). The subject is no longer considered separate from the world in any disembodied or objective sense, but rather the two are seen as '. . . bound together in reciprocal specification and selection' (p. 174). The meaning of the phrase *embodied action* is expressed as follows:

> By using the term embodied we mean to highlight two points: first, that cognition depends upon the kinds of experience that come from having a body with various sensorimotor capacities, and second, that these individual sensorimotor capacities are themselves embedded in a more encompassing biological, psychological, and cultural context. By using the term action we mean to emphasize once again that sensory and motor processes, perception and action, are fundamentally inseparable in lived cognition. Indeed, the two are not merely contingently linked in individuals; they have also evolved together. [As a] . . . preliminary formulation . . . the enactive approach (towards a revitalized theory of cognition) consists of two points:

(1) perception consists in perceptually guided action and (2) cognitive structures emerge from the recurrent sensorimotor patterns that enable action to be perceptually guided. (Varela et al., 1991, pp. 172–3)[4]

Teaching and Learning Mathematics from an Enactivist Perspective

Environments for Learning Mathematics

As trees grow they add layers of new material to the outside of that which existed before. In doing so, the new layers alter the older ones even as the newer layers are determined by the older ones; all this occurring as the tree grows. Metaphorically, and perhaps literally, this captures the enactive view of cognition. With respect to humans and their environments (and here we also consider environments for learning mathematics), Varela et al. conclude that:

> . . . living beings and their environments stand in relation to each other through *mutual specification* or *codetermination*. Thus what we describe as environmental regularities are not external features that have been internalized, as representationism and adaptationism both assume. Environmental regularities are the result of a conjoint history, a congruence that enfolds from a long history of codetermination. (1991, p. 198)

They maintain that as a consequence of the relationship of mutual specification between living beings and their environments, intelligence becomes the '. . . capacity to enter into a shared world of significance' (p. 207).[5] This view seems in close agreement with, and may help situate, both Greeno's *environment view* of mathematical learning, and Cobb, Yackel and Wood's *enriched constructive view* of classroom life:

> In the environmental view, knowing a set of concepts is not equivalent to having representations of the concepts but rather involves abilities to find and use the concepts in constructive processes of reasoning . . . The person's knowledge . . . is in his or her ability to find and use the resources, not in having mental versions of maps and instructions as the basis for all reasoning and action. (Greeno, 1991, p. 175)

> . . . [we] emphasize that mathematics is both a collective human activity . . . and an individual constructive activity. (Cobb Yackel and Wood, 1992, p. 17)

Two brief examples of recent work give a somewhat fuller picture of this enactivist, ecological view of the teaching and learning environment. Kieren (1994) presents an analysis of a mathematics class of 8-year-olds which uses the Varelan (1987) metaphor 'laying down a path while walking' to describe the interactions amongst these young learners. Kieren observes that 'children's knowing acts bring forth aspects of a mathematical world'. The world brought forward is not one which exists outside the learner, though it is constrained by the environment within which the 'bringing forth' occurs. Nor is the world brought forward a private one, but is one that the learner brings forth with others. Viewing learning as the product of a mutual specification among learner, classroom culture, classmates and the teacher, Kieren brings to light the co-determinate nature of cognition in this classroom.

As a second example, Sumara (1993) lived with a secondary school, academic stream English class as it studied the novel *Chrysalides*. The teacher, Ingrid, chose this novel in response to the increasing racial tension in the inner-city school where she taught. In summarizing this experience, Sumara found, among other things, that readings of literary texts will not 'give' students understandings which fall outside their previous lived experience: 'Some paths are simply not possible, even with the assistance of literary imagination' (Sumara, 1993, p. 17). The lived experience is crucial to the development of individual and shared awareness.

Meaning Making

The meaning of any particular situation cannot be prescribed or determined from outside the learner, because the meaning attributed to a situation is a result of the organization and history of that learner. What any learner does in a particular situation can only be understood in terms of what took place previously as the learner interacted with the environment — the history of structural coupling between learner and environment. Meaning is co-determined by the learner and the environment. Meaning doesn't exist independent of the learner. There aren't external regularities and meanings that learners are attempting to find or discover.

Not even words have meanings independent of people and situations — people in situations give meanings to their environments and invent words through which they attempt to express the meanings they have ascribed. In his book, *The Universe of Babies: In the beginning there were no words*, Gattegno concludes from his study of babies learning their mother tongues that all meaning is subject to reinterpretation as the baby gains more and more experience of the world (Gattegno, 1973). Arnold put the idea nicely in his doctoral dissertation:

> Because the signification of words can derive from words yet to be uttered, as well as words which have been uttered, the meaning to be attributed to words is in a *state of becoming*, it is never complete, never saturated, never stable, until perhaps the last word has been uttered. (Arnold, 1992, pp. 73–4, my emphasis)

Teaching and Learning Mathematics

The classroom of today, when viewed from an enactive viewpoint, would be construed as a dynamic system '. . . not structured in a serial or linear way, where chains of input/output, instruction/outcome, cause/effect can be isolated and explicated . . .' (Arnold, 1992, p. 70). An enactive environment is seen as an open system in which students, through interaction with peers and parents, teachers and technology, create order — make sense — out of disorder. As dynamic systems (learners) operating within a dynamic system (the classroom), the learners and classrooms mutually specify each other. Some pathways are open to learners in classrooms and others are not. Viable pathways which do exist within classrooms may or may not be selected by learners.

Although Kieren agrees that 'teaching can be thought about in terms of underlying and facilitating the lesson or in terms of overseeing and directing it,' he argues that an alternate and perhaps more fruitful way of viewing teaching is available. He describes this alternate way as 'teaching-in-the-middle'. In this latter view:

> . . . the learning and the teaching are not clearly distinct but are better thought of as being reciprocal in nature. The children's mathematical actions were occasioned by the teacher acts but that teacher actions were in turn occasioned by the children's mathematical activity. This reciprocity was not a simple 'back and forth' activity. This reciprocal teaching/learning occurred in a complex web with each person's actions resulting in new possibilities for all of the others. (Kieren, 1995, p. 10)

'Teaching-in-the-middle' puts both teachers and learners in-the-middle. It is not the case, as in direct instruction modes of teaching, that the teacher-in-the-middle tells, interrogates, and evaluates the responses which learners present, and in so doing oversees the lesson. The direct instruction teacher listens for particular answers to see if they match with the pre-existing (and pre-scriptive) knowledge the teacher wishes the students to learn.

Nor does the teacher-in-the-middle, like her constructive counterpart, only facilitate the learner activities based on her careful planning of the underlying themes of the lesson, listening to the students attentively over their shoulders as they carry out their investigations so as to formulate a vision of their learning which when matched against the teacher's view of how students learn can then be used to formulate a response to give assistance as needed. The constructive-oriented teacher listens to children so as to decide what is the most appropriate teaching act to do next.

These ways of being in classrooms with learners keep separate the teaching and learning acts. For the enactivist teacher, however, teaching-in-the-middle does not separate teaching and learning. And the listening which an enactivist teacher does is different in kind and motivation from her two colleagues. As Kieren notes:

> The teacher was listening not to check or model the students . . . she was listening to participate *with* her students. (Kieren, 1995, p. 13)

The teacher listens with her students

> . . . so as to build a world of mathematical significance. Her thinking about her teaching with respect to a mathematical idea is co-determined by what the students are thinking about that idea . . . By the same token the students' actions are shaped by the way in which they can take advantage of the possibilities in the classroom. (Kieren, 1995, p. 17)

Hence, teacher and students are aware of and open to possibilities which arise, and it is this creation of and action upon possibilities which, along with listening in a different way (e.g. see Davis, 1994, 1996), provides a contrast to both direct instruction and constructivist ways of teaching. The direct instruction teacher presents and controls a limited range of possibilities. Student responses, by and large, are not meant to extend these possibilities. Teaching from a constructivist view actively encourages all students to extend their own possibilities, but without all students necessarily becoming aware of the range of possibilities being offered by others around the classroom. By engaging and listening *with* learners, the enactivist teacher engages with the entire class. Kieren writes that

> . . . rather than possibilities being pre-given or determined on an individual basis, listening with students implies that the teacher deliberately holds open many possibilities, and that in the interaction . . . the possibilities will grow. (Kieren, 1995, p. 18)

There is not in the enactive view of cognition a straight path between a learner and the activities into which that learner may have been invited to engage. Rather, the learner chooses to stress certain aspects of the activities and to ignore others. It is not just a one-way street with the learner being the predominant force. The environment exerts itself by putting limits on what pathways the learner is able to pursue. Learning occurs at the interstices where the learner meets the environment, stresses particularities within that environment, and generates a response whose viability in the environment is then determined. The realm of the possible must intersect with the predilection of the learner to take notice of it. The particular pathway mutually determined by the learner and the environment is rarely unique. Other pathways are possible. The one selected is but one of many possible ways of *satisficing* the demands of the interaction as seen by the learner and permitted by the environment[6].

The learning, which teachers hope will occur, does not happen simply as the result of engaging learners in particular activities, whether those activities are, for example, a teacher talking to/with learners, learners watching a film, or learners using a computer running *Sketchpad* or *Cabri*. However, if learners *don't get it* (whatever *it* might be), it doesn't follow that there is something wrong with the learners, or that the learners weren't listening, or weren't paying attention. It is just that the learners were at that point in time *stressing* things other than those which the teacher might have anticipated, or that environment and those learners — given their particular history of structural couplings — did not opt for the pathway expected by the teacher. It is evident, then, that teaching is not telling.

Teaching Is Not Telling

The enactive view of cognition contends that feedback is provided by the environment to learners. Knowledge and/or information is not transmitted to learners from the environment. The transmission model of knowledge acquisition, the metaphor of the *tube of communication*, in the enactive view of cognition, is not tenable. Maturana and Varela contend:

> ... each person says what he says or hears what he hears according to his own structural determination; saying does not ensure listening. From the perspective of an observer, there is always ambiguity in a communicative interaction. The phenomenon of communication depends on not what is transmitted, but on what happens to the person who receives it. And this is a very different matter from *transmitting information*. (1992, p. 196)

The message sent may not be the message received. A colleague was once delivering a lecture to a room of 300-plus mathematics educators. A voice from the back of the room was heard to shout, 'That's utter rubbish!' Our colleague's swift reply was, 'It may have been rubbish when it reached you, sir, but I can assure you it was not rubbish when it left me!' In the enactive view, both people were right. In that situation a discussion needed to take place in which the meaning intended by the speaker and the meaning detected by the listener are explicated and adjudicated. They needed to negotiate their meaning.

Cognition Is Not Problem Solving

If a very significant part of what takes place in classrooms is negotiation of meaning, and the finding of pathways which are satisficing, what then can be taken to be a problematic situation for learners in the mathematics classroom? When is a problem a problem for the learner? The answer, from an enactive point of view, is that a problem is only a problem when the learner and the environment mutually determine that there is something missing in the situation, a something which seems in need of rectification. There is always a *next step* for the system, i.e. the learner within an environment, even if that step is to do nothing! Hence, it is the learner and the environment within which the learner is functioning that together '... poses the problems and specifies those paths that must be tread or laid down for their solution' (Varela et al., 1991, p. 205).

In the case where the learner takes a positive next step (and in a very real sense *all* next steps are positive ones), the notion of finding the optimal step does not operate. Learners try things out and see if they work. If they don't work, then another step may be tried or the activity may be abandoned. If the next step fills the missing link in the situation in a satisficing fashion, then again the learner may pass onto another activity, or the learner may, having found one acceptable solution, seek another. In this manner, pathways out of situations are generated. The decision as to whether or not a proposed step is viable is based on the individual's assessment of responses from the environment, including the learner's teacher and peers. The new pathways which are generated play a dynamic role in the structural history of the learner. The direction that classroom interactions will take, the pathways that learners will choose, the situations that learners will view as problematic cannot be determined in advance. There are no guarantees that the lesson planned will unfold in the way expected!

In the next section of this chapter some inservice activities are described which are based on enactivist principles and ideas of teaching and learning. These are provided so that the reader can perhaps gain some insight as to how enactivist approaches to inservice would be played out with classroom teachers and teacher educators where the cycle of co-dependence between these two groups postulated earlier is broken.

Some Current Enactivist Inservice Activities

Two inservice activities based broadly on enactivist principles and ideas are described below. The first one is currently in process, and is taking place in Canada. The second, of five weeks duration, was completed in March 1998 in Colombo, Sri Lanka.

The Canadian Programme

In a suburban area of Vancouver, Canada, 85 teachers, predominantly with a focus on the primary and middle grades but including a few secondary teachers as well, are in the second phase[7] of a seven-phase inservice programme. The programme is offered for credit by Simon Fraser University, and though it has a theme it does not have a pre-set curriculum. The overall theme of the programme is described as the exploration of issues in the teaching and learning of mathematics and science, but the focus of the programme for each teacher is that person's own perceived needs in one of those subject areas. Teachers are encouraged to look at their current practice non-judgmentally, and to note the strengths and areas of concern they have about what occurs in their own classrooms. They are assisted in this task by their peers and the inservice leaders. Teachers were asked to identify some aspect of their practice which they would like to alter, or which they would like to reinforce and strengthen in their classrooms. Hence, the path chosen by the teachers was based on their own perceived needs and aspirations, and the manner in which they decided to journey along that path will be 'laid down while walking'.

The programme consists of seven segments, alternating between study and implementation experiences. The first experience, which involved thirteen, four-hour meetings, one evening per week between January and early April 1998, entailed a beginning exploration of issues around mathematics and science instruction, the issues initially being suggested by the inservice leaders. However, the teachers quickly expanded and broadened the discussion to encompass issues and concerns they brought with them. It was out of the discussion about such matters that participating teachers were to identify particular needs that they proposed to investigate in greater detail. These were not just talk sessions: the teachers were expected to think about ways that their concerns could be addressed and their classroom practice modified as a consequence. The outcome of this first experience was that the teachers were to develop action plans[8] (Norman et al., 1989), plans which they were to implement during the second phase of the programme.

The inservice leaders' role (there were three such leaders) in this first experience was to work with the teachers to identify and sharpen the focus on aspects of their classroom practice, and to assist the teachers with the development of a viable plan as to how to alter or reinforce that practice. The inservice leaders were not there to judge these plans, or to tell the teachers what they should do, or to tell the teachers what was wrong with their practice and how to fix it. Examples of action plans, which some of these teachers are currently implementing, include: the introduction of journal writing in a grade three classroom; the use of literature — children's stories — for the enhancement of their teaching of mathematics with kindergarten-aged children; and the use of manipulatives with a secondary algebra class. All the plans were selected, devised and implemented by the teachers.

The action plans are being implemented in the teachers' classrooms during April, May, and the first part of June 1998. The large group of 85 was subdivided, primarily on the basis of the geographical location of the schools where they taught, into seven smaller groups with 10–15 teachers in each group. These smaller groups were convened once every three weeks, for three hours after school in the early evening, by a mathematics or science teacher educator whose role it was to mentor these teachers as they implemented their action plans. Of the seven teacher educators involved with this phase, two had also been involved in phase one.

If one generalization can be made at this point in time about the first implementation phase, it is that the action plan never proceeds as planned, it is always a 'path laid down while walking'. The product which the teachers are expected to produce at the conclusion of the implementation phase takes this fact into account, however, because the teachers are required to create and maintain a portfolio *describing their journey* — the zigs and zags, the ups and downs, the advances and the withdrawals — that occurred as they attempted to translate their plan into action. The action plans get altered 'on the fly', as it were. The goal for the teachers becomes one of finding a viable implementation path, not the perfect path, or the best path, but the one which is satisficing for the teachers and their students. The teachers are attesting to the fact that the plan as implemented is jointly and interactively determined by the students, the classroom and school environment, and the teachers themselves. During a meeting at the end of phase two, the inservice leaders noted positively that '. . . the amount of reflection on the part of the teachers was amazing . . .' '. . . it was humbling to see how much the teachers have gone through in attempting to implement their plans', and '. . . some of the teachers went a whole lot deeper into issues than was anticipated . . .' They also noted that '. . . for some teachers the resistance to doing anything was palpable . . .' 'some were clearly there for the credit and the increase in salary, so if they gained one new awareness that would be a bonus . . .', and that '. . . there was a great range in the detail provided in the portfolios which described the teacher's journey'.

The third phase of the programme, which will commence in July 1998, is a two week, five hour per day, five day per week, intensive study of issues and concerns which arose from the implementation phase just completed. As with phase one, the outcome being sought from the teachers in phase three is a *new* (or renewed) action plan. This plan would then be implemented in phase four of the programme starting in September 1998.

And so the process goes: study issues and concerns, devise an action plan, implement the action plan, study issues and concerns arising from the implementation and revise the plan or devise a new one, implement this new plan, then study and revise, and so on through the seven phases of the programme. The programme will be completed over a two calendar year period, at the conclusion of which the teachers will be eligible for the awarding of a Post Baccalaureate Diploma by Simon Fraser University. This diploma enables the teachers to receive an increase in salary, so the rewards for completion of the programme are financial as well as academic and pedagogical.

The Sri Lankan Programme

A more intense, and of shorter duration, enactivist inservice programme was completed in March 1998 with a group of 30 Sri Lankan teacher educators. The Sri Lankan Government has undertaken the task of rethinking the education offered in its schools. To make the changes they hope for, they decided that teacher educators in their 15 Colleges of Education should undertake professional development. Hence, one significant aspect of this programme was that it was, in part, designed to select approximately 15 teacher educators to come to Canada for advanced study at the Masters and Doctoral levels. One might well query how an inservice programme with such a defined goal could operate on enactivist principles and ideas. How can a 'path be laid down while walking' when the end point of the journey is predetermined? The answer lies in the nature of the criteria which were used to determine who would be selected.

One criterion focused on the participants' ability to design a potentially viable action plan which outlined an issue or concern they had about their current practice as teacher educators in their local Colleges of Education located in all regions of Sri Lanka, and how their plan might be implemented upon their return to Sri Lanka after a one-year period of study in Canada. A second criterion was how well the participants could communicate, orally and in written form, about their action plan to the selection committee. The participants were expected to reflect on the activities and challenges offered during the programme, and this ability to reflect was the third main criterion used in the selection process.

The conversation which began the programme in the last week of February 1998 invited the participants to talk about themselves, their professional work and their academic education, and to situate this within their own complex web of professional and family relationships. For a substantial number of the participants, this initial presentation was the first time they had spoken formally in public in English. This was a very stressful and challenging situation for most of the participants.

From these personal histories of the participants' structural couplings, the inservice leaders took their cues for the development of programme activities. The curriculum was mutually specified and determined among the inservice leaders and the participants as part of the daily dialogue. Though the inservice leaders had to make a judgment about who would come to Canada, the particulars of the programme arose out of discussions with the participants. The programme path was indeed 'laid down while walking'. There was not a curriculum that the inservice leaders set out to 'cover', though it was clear from the outset that work on written and spoken English would be needed by all the participants since none of them had English as a first language. Indeed, for many participants, English was a third language, after Sinhalese and Tamil, and most participants had never experienced any sort of formal instruction in or about English. As it turned out, the path laid down included such activities as having the participants reflect about their thoughts and feelings as they tackled a mathematical problem, drew their own self-portrait, and engaged in a variety of writing activities. All discussions and all writing was done in English.

The participants were strongly encouraged to write. They wrote paragraphs, summaries of readings, and essays. They wrote personal pieces, and more academic, professional pieces of work. They kept reader-response journals, and journals of their thoughts and feelings as they struggled with the mathematics problem, and the drawing task. They were also engaged in discussion groups, sometimes as small as 3 or 4, sometimes 10 or so, and sometimes with the entire large group. Their confidence and knowledge grew, layer upon layer being added daily.

Even though Sri Lanka is embroiled in a civil war, even though programme participants came from various viewpoints regarding that war, over the five-week period the group developed a cohesiveness, cooperativeness, and spirit of mutual support that surprised, indeed astonished some, both the participants and their senior colleagues in the Ministry of Education and the Colleges of Education from whence they were recruited. Despite the fact that half of the participants would not be selected, there was mutual support, assistance and respect among the entire group.

The inservice leaders were also changed. Their knowledge and understandings were broadened and deepened. The path they thought they might be travelling when planning for the inservice programme was not the one they in fact traversed. They were open to possibilities as these arose in the interactions with the programme participants and the cultural and social environment of Sri Lanka. Along with the participants they devised the programme, they mutually specified what would be emphasized and what would not, and in so doing brought forth a world of inservice substantially different than that which anyone, inservice leader or participants, government or university and college officials, had anticipated. Even for those participants not selected to come to Canada, this inservice programme was, by their own testimony, a highly positive professional development experience.

Conclusion

The enactivist mathematics teacher educator we met at the outset is setting the stage to listen *with* the assembled mathematics educators. There is not a predetermined, pre-set curriculum, but rather a curriculum which will be co-determined by the interactions amongst the members of the group. The goal in the listening is to expand the range of possibilities so that the ultimate curriculum which emerges is co-determined by all the participants, a co-emergent curriculum.

The above accounts of these inservice programmes have been offered, not as systematic evaluations of practice, but as illustrations of the enactive approach in practice. Such an approach to inservice activities is in marked contrast to programmes which are designed, for example, to: 1) improve teachers' mathematical knowledge; or 2) improve teachers' pedagogical understandings; or 3) assist teachers in making their teaching practices problematic; or 4) to show teachers how to make their classrooms into places where doing 'investigations' or having a problem-solving orientation is paramount. The enactivist mathematics teacher educator does not set out to accomplish such goals though some of those things may occur as a by-product of what happens during the inservice programme. The enactivist mathematics teacher educator does not set out to 'fix' what others might perceive to be wrong with teachers. Rather, the enactivist teacher educator embarks on a journey with the assembled inservice mathematics teachers. This group 'lays down its own path while walking'. This path is co-determined, devised from a rich and growing set of possibilities. Interactions among inservice group members is characterized by all listening with their colleagues, looking for opportunities and possibilities for their own thinking, their own learning, their own practice, their own classroom, and the learners within those classrooms, including the teachers themselves, and indeed the teacher educator.

Notes

1　The first part of this section is based in part on an SSHRC grant-supported project entitled *Curriculum and Ecological Thought* under the direction of A.J. Dawson, Simon Fraser University, and D. Sumara, York University.

2　The other members of the team are Brent Davis, York University, Tom Kieren (Prof Emeritus) University of Alberta, and Dennis Sumara, York University.

3　Campbell and Dawson's work (1995) is used extensively in what follows as a source for describing the background to Varela and his colleagues' development of the enactivist viewpoint.

4　Varela et al. eventually propose a more technically refined definition of the enactive view of cognition situated within an evolutionary context, however this preliminary formulation is sufficient for our purposes here (Varela et al., 1991, p. 206).

5　This encapsulates an important implication of the enactive view of cognitive science regarding recent developments in the philosophy of mathematics education. From a pedagogical perspective a number of mathematics educators (e.g. Schoenfeld, 1987; Janvier, 1987; and Clements, 1991) have provided informative accounts as to how developments in cognitive science are particularly germane to mathematics education. The implications of the enactive view of cognition for mathematics education warrants a comprehensive analysis particularly with respect to the current developments in constructivism (e.g. Cobb et al., 1992; Ernest, 1991; and Kilpatrick, 1987) and situated learning (e.g. Greeno, 1991).

6　*Satisficing* means good enough, workable, satisfactory and acceptable.
7　June 1998, as this book was being prepared to go to press.
8　Designed by Peter Norman (1989), from materials developed by Maurice Gibbons, David Hopkins, Peter Norman, and Gary Phillips. Illustrated by Dennis Smith. *The Self-Directed Learning Contract: A guide for learners and teachers*, Vancouver, Canada: Simon Fraser University.

References

ARNOLD, M. (1992) 'Educational cybernetics: Communication and control of and with Logo', Unpublished doctoral dissertation, Deakin University.

BAHKTIN, M.M. (1993) *Toward a Philosophy of the Act*, Austin: University of Texas Press.

CLEMENTS, K. (1982) 'Visual imagery and school mathematics', *For the Learning of Mathematics*, **2**, 2, pp. 2–39; **2**, 3, pp. 33–9.

COBB, P., YACKEL, E. and WOOD, T. (1992) 'A constructivist alternative to the representational view of mind in mathematics education', *Journal for Research in Mathematics Education*, **23**,1, pp. 2–33.

CAMPBELL, S. and DAWSON, A.J. (1995) 'Learning as embodied action', in Mason J. and Sutherland R. (eds) *Exploiting Mental Imagery with Computers in Mathematics Education* (pp. 231–46), New York: Springer-Verlag.

DAVIS, A.B. (1994) 'Mathematics teaching: Moving from telling to listening', *Journal of Curriculum and Supervision*, **9**, 3, pp. 263–82.

DAVIS, A.B. (1996) *Teaching Mathematics: Toward a Sound Alternative*, New York: Garland Publishing, Inc.

ERNEST, P. (1991) *The Philosophy of Mathematics Education*, London: Falmer Press.

GATTEGNO, C. (1973) *The Universe of Babies: In the Beginning There Were No Words*, New York: Educational Solutions Inc.

GIBBONS, M., HOPKINS, D., NORMAN, P. and PHILLIPS, G. (1989) *The Self-Directed Learning Contract: A Guide for Learners and Teachers*, Vancouver, CA: Simon Fraser University.

GREENO, J.G. (1991) 'Number sense as situated knowing in a conceptual domain', *Journal for Research in Mathematics Education*, **22**, 3, pp. 170–218.

JANVIER, C. (ed.) (1987) *Problems of Representation in Mathematics Learning and Problem Solving*, Hillsdale, NJ: Lawrence Erlbaum Associates.

KELLERT, S. (1994) *In the Wake of Chaos*, Chicago, Ill: University of Chicago Press.

KIEREN, T. (1995) 'Teaching in the middle: Enactivist view on teaching and learning mathematics', Invited plenary lecture at the Queens/Gage Canadian National Mathematics Leadership Conference: Queens University.

KILPATRICK, J. (1987) 'What constructivism might be in mathematics education', in BERGERON, J.C., HERSCOVICS, N. and KIERAN, C. (eds) *Proceedings of the Eleventh International Conference for the Psychology of Mathematics Education Vol. 1* (pp. 3–27), Montréal, PQ: Université de Montréal.

MATURANA, H.R. and VARELA, F.J. (1992) *The Tree of Knowledge: The Biological Roots of Human Understanding*, revised edition, Boston, MA: Shambhala Publications.

SCHOENFELD, A.H. (ed.) (1987) *Cognitive Science and Mathematics Education*, Hillsdale, NJ: Lawrence Erlbaum Associates.

SUMARA, D.J. (1993) 'Occasioning reading relationships in the classroom', Paper presented at the annual meeting of the Canadian Society for the Study of Education, Calgary, CA.

VARELA, F.J. (1987) 'Laying down a path in walking', in THOMPSON W.I. (ed.) *GAIA: A Way of Knowing: Political Implications of the New Biology* (pp. 48–64), Hudson, NY: Lindisfarne Press.

VARELA, F.J., THOMPSON, E. and ROSCH, E. (1991) *The Embodied Mind: Cognitive Science and Human Experience*, Cambridge, MA: The MIT Press.

15 Approaching Teacher Development: Practice into Theory

Terry Wood, USA

Introduction

It should be clear by now that each chapter in Section Two and the chapters in this section assume images of 'good' teaching. Each of the approaches to teacher education is derived from a view of the processes that underlie learning and the development of knowledge in mathematics. These views about learning and knowledge reflect trends in cognition and the nature of knowledge influenced by modern or postmodern philosophies. Further, these trends suggest different views for what it means to learn and teach that are articulated by both Dawson and Jaworski in this section. Implicit in their discussions is the recognition that the epistemic beliefs held by teacher educators about (i) how one learns and the processes involved in learning; and (ii) about mathematical knowledge and the source of this knowledge, strongly influence their view of teaching.

However, I contend that the changes in the conceptions of 'good' teaching that are held among teacher educators are not yet well conceptualized or developed. This is due to the fact that the changes in teaching that are advocated are still undetermined and indefinite. Currently, the reformed view of teaching is largely drawn from theoretical and epistemological tenets of learning and the sources of mathematical knowledge generalized to a hypothetical view of teaching, rather than a perspective grounded in the practice of teachers (to which Dawson speaks). Moreover, I claim that without empirical inquiry into teaching it is difficult to create an approach to teacher education that is meaningful to teachers and therefore effective in approach.

In this chapter, I argue for the necessity to develop, in our understanding of teaching, beyond the level of description and personal insight to create theoretical constructs of pedagogy. I argue that this can best be accomplished through a process that is grounded in findings from empirical data gathered in classrooms, to the formation of descriptive categories for the empirical work, to the generation of theoretical constructs in the formulations of teaching. As evidence, I describe three theoretical formulations of teaching that were developed following this process. Following the description of each theory, I present an approach to inservice teacher education which evolved from each perspective on teaching. In the end, I claim that this process of theory generation is essential by virtue of the fact that it draws from descriptive inquiry into teaching to generate theoretical frameworks. But beyond this, the generation of teaching theory creates the capability for prediction. It is the advent of prediction that is essential to the development of effective approaches in teacher development. I begin by locating the discussion in the context of the current situation in mathematics education in the United States.

Dilemmas for Mathematics Teacher Educators

The fundamental goal of the ongoing effort in the United States of the National Council of Teachers of Mathematics (NCTM) and others (e.g. National Science Foundation) is to reform and improve mathematics instruction for all students, not just the academically elite. To add to the complexity of the situation, the alterations proposed in the nature of school mathematics differ substantially from the conventional beliefs about mathematics and doing mathematics in school held by the wider society. Although this endeavor is grounded in evidence of the poor performance of US students in mathematics (e.g. TIMSS; see, for example, Beaton, Mullis, Martin, Gonzales, Kelly and Smith, 1996), the criticism in reality is directed at teachers — what they do in their teaching of students. As Little (1993) asserts, implicit in the goals for the current reform is the underlying assumption that teachers will make significant and substantial changes in their ways of teaching in the classroom — a view which is also supported by the standards documents issued by NCTM (1989, 1991). Therefore, to bring about the changes in teaching as envisioned entails providing inservice education for all teachers — even those who are disinclined.

Yet, the goal to change instructional practices in addition to making changes in the goals of mathematics is exactly what Dawson (this volume, Chapter 14) argues against; making judgments about teachers and their ways of teaching. It might be the desire of many teacher educators' to work in ways that allow teachers to develop means to address their own concerns and issues. However, it is evident that this does not seem possible in the current situation in which the assumption is that something is wrong with the way in which mathematics is taught in school.

This situation creates amongst mathematics teacher educators several dilemmas in their attempts to develop approaches to teachers' professional development. One dilemma arises from the fact that the recommendations for teaching are drawn from research on students' learning rather than inquiry into teaching and its connections to students' learning. Teaching mathematics, as seen by reformers, is a process of taking perspectives of learners and their ways of learning as the basis for teachers' instruction. The shift in perspective on learning emphasizes students' active involvement, and the goal to involve students in higher-order thinking and reasoning processes as a means for their learning. This view of learning, combined with changes in the focus of school mathematics on problem-solving, represents a major shift from the long-standing emphasis on single computational procedures that create additional demands on teachers (e.g. MSEB, 1989). As envisioned, these pedagogical changes demand a more complex and sophisticated form of mathematics teaching than that used in conventional practice (NCTM, 1991). Thus, the form of teaching envisioned requires far more of teachers than simply making adjustments in their present ways of teaching.

In addition, the proposed changes in teaching call for a shift in the role of the teacher from a position of authority to more indirect and collaborative relationships with their students. Unmistakably these recommended changes in teaching go beyond simply suggesting adjustments in current pedagogical strategies and instead require that teachers make foundational shifts in their beliefs and fundamental transformations in their ways of teaching. Thus, another dilemma for mathematics teacher educators resides in trying to help teachers accomplish a form of pedagogy that is not only lacking in clear formulation but also requires substantial changes in teachers' beliefs.

Further, without knowledge of an alternative pedagogy, let alone the ways in which such teaching develops, mathematics teacher educators are confronted with the dilemma of trying to create approaches to inservice teacher education that successfully promote and assure that teachers accomplish the substantial changes advocated in the reform, while allowing teachers to make the self-initiated changes of which Dawson speaks. Cooney (1994), in his review of mathematics teacher education, addresses the heart of the matter by asking what teachers need to know in order to become effective teachers of mathematics? Moreover, what sort of experiences are needed for teachers to acquire this knowledge, and what are the processes by which teachers develop in their knowledge of this teaching?

Theoretical Perspectives on Teaching

In this section of the chapter I discuss the way in which inquiry into practice forms the basis for the formulation of teaching theory. In order to do this, I describe three theories of teaching that are empirically based to illustrate how research into teaching is used to generate theoretical perspectives on teaching. In addition to discussing each teaching theory, I present samples of approaches to inservice teacher education that developed from each of the theoretical perspectives.

Teachers' Knowledge

The first example of a theory of teaching is Lee Shulman's (1986, 1987) work on teacher knowledge that was a move away from the process–product research that was predominant at the time. Shulman's work began as a counterpoint to the focus of research on how teachers manage their classrooms to consider what Shulman referred to as the 'missing paradigm': 'the *content* of the lessons taught, the questions asked, and the explanations offered' (1986, p. 8). Considerations of teaching then became questions of what do teachers know and when do they come to know it. The central question of concern for Shulman was the transition from expert student to novice teacher to veteran teacher. Consequently, in addition to general *pedagogical* knowledge, the focus shifted to teachers' *content* knowledge and, more importantly to a new category, *pedagogical content* knowledge. Pedagogical content knowledge he describes as the 'dimension of subject matter knowledge *for teaching*' (1986,

p. 9). This new category of teacher knowledge became the central emphasis of Shulman's inquiry and those that followed for the next decade. Barbara Jaworski's chapter, which follows, offers a list of each of the knowledge categories as it relates to mathematics teaching.

However, one aspect of Shulman's work not generally recognized is the fact that his analysis is grounded in empirical evidence and a conceptualization of teaching based on a traditional view of teaching as transmission in much the same way as was Mehan's (1979) classic analysis of classroom interaction and discourse. Consequently, while his central interest in conceptualizing teacher knowledge was an important contribution to thinking about teaching, the nature of the knowledge categories may need to be recast when considering alternative forms of teaching. As an example, pedagogical content knowledge, as conceived by Shulman is described as

> the most useful forms of representation of those ideas, the most powerful analogies, illustrations, examples, explanations, and demonstration . . . the ways of representing and formulating the subject that make it comprehensible to others . . . the teacher must have at hand a veritable armamentarium of alternative forms of representation. (1986, p. 9)

Moreover, the shift in instruction to an emphasis on students' conceptualizations and representations of their knowledge as a central source of knowledge for classroom instruction, calls for forms of teacher knowledge that are quite different to those described by Shulman. Two approaches to teacher education that have attempted to redefine teacher pedagogical content knowledge are Cognitively Guided Instruction (CGI) (Carpenter, Fennema, Peterson, Chiang and Loef, 1989; Carpenter, Fennema and Franke, 1996; Fennema, Carpenter, Franke, Levi, Jacobs and Empson, 1996) and Schifter's (along with Simon) Learning Mathematics for Teaching (Schifter, 1993, 1997; Simon and Schifter, 1991).

Approaches to inservice based on teacher knowledge

Cognitively Guided Instruction (CGI). The primary focus of CGI is on children's mathematical thinking which is revealed by the strategies children use to solve a variety of word problems which are categorized by their underlying structure. This approach began as a research project with the goal of attempting to connect research with practice. Carpenter and Fennema wanted to find out what would happen if they shared their 'research-based knowledge' about children's learning of mathematics with teachers. They were interested in how teachers might use these research results in their classrooms as a possible way to address the issue of bridging theory and practice.

Teachers learn about the findings of the research on children's strategies during workshop sessions held in the summer. CGI workshop leaders spend time sharing with teachers the findings from research on children's learning. These results are demonstrated with videotape recordings of children solving word problems in one-on-one clinical interview settings. During this time, teachers also conduct their own student interviews in order to gain experience in learning about students' strategies and the ways they respond to changes teachers make in the type of word problems and number size.

Following the workshop, teachers then take the information given by the researchers about children's strategies and the word problem types to their classrooms to learn about the strategies of their own students. A central goal of the CGI approach is for teachers to change their practice from telling children how to solve problems to making 'decisions that enable children to use their knowledge to solve problems' which is compatible with revisionists' calls for change in the goals of pedagogy. Although the setting of the classroom is understood to be important for teachers' learning, follow-up visits to teachers' classrooms by the researchers do not occur during the school year.

The approach is highly compatible with Shulman's notions of pedagogical content knowledge. CGI teachers come to 'believe that they need to find out what children know and then use that knowledge to enable each child's knowledge of mathematics to mature' (Fennema, 1996, p. 5). The research findings from this approach to teacher development are extensive and consist of the use of both quantitative and qualitative methods. Carpenter and Fennema have investigated both teachers' and children's learning in CGI and conventional classes. The main question of interest to the researchers is how teachers' knowledge of children's thinking, which was presented in the CGI workshops, influences their decisions for instruction and their students' learning. In addition, attention is given to investigating the relationship of the changes that occur in teachers' beliefs and knowledge and the instructional decisions they make. Fennema and Carpenter conclude that changes in teaching occur as teachers gain knowledge about children's thinking revealed to them in the strategies their pupils use to solve the word problems.

The results of the research indicate that teachers' knowledge of their own students' strategies is strongly linked to teachers' knowledge of the research-based information about word problems and students' strategies provided by the researchers in the CGI workshops. In addition, other research conducted on the relationship between teachers' knowledge and change in teaching revealed that increases in teachers' knowledge of children's strategies is linked to changes in teaching (Carpenter et al., 1996). In a recent longitudinal study of changes in teachers' beliefs and knowledge, Fennema et al. (1996) found that the role of the teacher changed from one of demonstrating procedures to engaging students in solving word problems and encouraging talk about their strategies. Case studies of selected CGI teachers also reveal some further insights into the nature of teachers' use of knowledge of children's thinking and their daily practice (Warfield, 1997).

Learning mathematics for teaching. Learning Mathematics for Teaching is an approach to teacher development, generally ascribed to Schifter (1993, 1997), that has as a primary focus teachers' understanding of mathematics and, thus, addresses the shift in the goals for learning mathematics as advocated by revisionists. In her original work, Schifter with Simon (1991) created a model of teacher development that derived from Piaget's theory of cognitive development. Fundamental to the approach, according to Schifter (1997), is the central notion that:

> ... developing a successful practice grounded in the principles of the current mathematics education reform effort requires qualitatively different and significantly richer understanding of mathematics than most teachers currently possess. (p. 2)

Moreover, teachers can deepen their understanding through explorations of 'disciplinary content led by project staff' on topics from the elementary mathematics curriculum and through the analysis of the mathematical issues that arise from students' thinking in the classroom. Underlying this approach is the assumption that teachers, who have a deeper understanding of the content students are learning, are better able to comprehend their pupils' ways of thinking about mathematics and thus enhance their own ability to teach.

Therefore, the approach Schifter takes is content specific and represents her long-standing efforts to create an approach which focuses on teachers developing an understanding of mathematics and the relationship of this cognizance to their teaching. This approach can be seen to address Shulman's category of teachers' content knowledge. However, Schifter's notion of content knowledge differs from the earlier ideas and approaches which attempted to increase teachers' knowledge of advanced mathematical content. From Schifter's perspective, it is not teachers' acquisition of increased mathematical knowledge that is crucial, but rather their conceptual understanding of the content their students learn that is central to improving their ability to teach.

In her most recent project, 'Teaching to the Big Ideas' (TBI), the primary focus is on teachers coming to understand through their own thinking the major conceptual ideas which underlie the mathematics that students encounter in elementary school (Schifter, 1997). In this approach, teachers meet in two-week summer institutes that are accompanied by extensive and intensive follow-up in the classroom by teacher educators throughout the school year. Summer institutes are used to provide teachers with an opportunity to engage in mathematical investigations of the content that they encountered in the school curriculum. These investigations are designed to enable teachers to enhance their conceptual understanding of the mathematics that they teach. The follow-up classroom visits made by the teacher educators provided opportunities to identify mathematical issues that arose in practice; these topics were then used as the basis for further learning in the bi-weekly seminars. Schifter (1997) reports that through this process teachers develop an understanding of mathematics as they 'move back and forth reflectively between the teacher education seminar and the mathematical experience of their classroom' (p. 19).

The research on the influence of this approach on teachers' learning and change in practice is qualitative and descriptive in nature. Many of Schifter's research findings are drawn from teachers' written narratives of their experiences, coupled with fieldnotes of the classroom observations. From this data, using qualitative methodology, conclusions are drawn about the influence of an approach that encourages teachers' 'back and forth' reflective movement between their mathematical experience in the class and the teacher education seminar on changes made in teachers' practice. Evidence of the effectiveness of the approach is presented in case studies of individual teachers. These are given as illustrative examples of the approach and how teachers then use the mathematical understandings they learned in the development sessions in their classroom lessons as a means to enhance their students conceptual understanding of mathematics. These findings provide insights into teachers' perceptions of changes in their teaching. In addition, the case studies shed light on how teachers' personal experiences in learning to understand the fundamental concepts of elementary school mathematics influence their teaching both in the selection of student materials and in their interaction with pupils. Teachers' writings also address the concern among some teacher educators (e.g. Cochran-Smith and Lytle, 1993) for the need of teachers' voices in the research on teacher change.

The Teaching Triad

The second example of a theory of teaching is Barbara Jaworski's (1994) investigation of teaching in secondary mathematics classrooms. In her research, Jaworski engaged in extensive fieldwork in the classrooms of a few secondary mathematics teachers using inquiry forms of teaching. Here she observed the teacher and students in action, taking fieldnotes and writing reflective summaries of her observations. In addition, she spent a considerable amount of time talking with the teachers about her observations and gathering their impressions of their lessons. From her empirical data, she generated a conceptual model of teaching that she called the teaching triad. Briefly, this model is composed of three components of the teacher's activity: management of learning; sensitivity to students; and mathematical challenge. It is an example of theory arising from classroom data, subsequently reconciled with the theoretical basis of the research (constructivism) from which it emerged.

This approach differs from Shulman's knowledge conceptualization in that it does not focus specifically on cognition and the 'knowledge' teachers are thought to hold. Instead, Jaworski's model is derived from teachers' actions in their classes, in conjunction with their thoughts about these actions, to consider all the aspects of teachers' work. However, in this conceptualization, teaching activity includes management that is related to student learning. The connection between the development of the normative structure of the class and student learning lies in the teacher's *management of the learning* environment relative to *sensitivity to students* within the environment.

Jaworski's empirical research and theoretical conceptualization of mathematical challenge as a significant component of the teaching triad contributes more directly to the understanding of mathematics teaching and thus improves Shulman's general teaching approach to subject matter. Important, in addition, is the move away from a focus on investigating teachers' knowledge to a consideration of growth in knowledge in teaching.

An approach to inservice based on the teaching triad

The ways in which the teaching triad has informed Jaworski's approach to teacher education is chronicled in her chapter, which follows. The inservice teacher education projects in England and Pakistan that she describes in her chapter serve as examples of this effort.

Theoretical Framework for Teaching and Learning

The third example of a theory of teaching is from my own research that is also a field-based examination of practices in the context of the classroom. In my case, I have examined mathematics teaching at the elementary level in which the mathematical knowledge of teachers, in general, is less well-structured. In earlier work with Paul Cobb and Erna Yackel, we worked collaboratively for one year with a group of classroom teachers to develop classes which were highly interactive and focused on children's thinking (Cobb, Wood and Yackel, 1990). Over the next four years, these teachers continued to teach mathematics in this manner and to develop their practice. For my research, I returned to these same teachers and gathered extensive data in their classes for one year. In our empirical examination of reform-oriented elementary mathematics classrooms, differences in teaching are defined by the social and cognitive parameters established for learning.

In order to examine the extensive data collected from the classrooms, my students and I developed a set of categories for coding. The coding categories that were developed to analyze the interactive and discursive patterns were drawn from the literature on teacher questioning and student responses. In particular, the work of Dillon (1990) in examining the ways in which teachers, who varied from the traditional recitation format, used their statements and questions to enable students to participate in discussions. Additionally, in mathematics education, the work of Ainley (1988) and Labinowicz (1985) was used to examine the ways in which teacher questions acted to promote students' thinking. The categories were refined in the process and applied to pilot protocols until the coders could reliably identify the classifications. The combination of the two perspectives, participation and student thinking, allowed for the analysis of teaching actions in relation to opportunities for children's conceptual understanding.

Applying the categories developed through this process, enabled us to bridge the gap between the results from the empirical analyses and the theoretical aspects of our research. From the analyses of the empirical data, we condensed the results into generalizable patterns of interaction and discourse and from this created a theoretical framework. Conceptualizing this framework in this manner allows for the abstraction of the empirical results into generalizable categories, and for connections to be drawn to theoretical perspectives on participation from micro-sociology and children's thinking from developmental psychology. Therefore, the empirical dimensions of social interaction and discourse could be related to one another in a meaningful way in order to gain insight into the relationship of the activity of teaching and children's mathematical thinking.

In brief, the findings from this investigation reveal a stable form of pedagogy that is characteristically distinct from traditional mathematics teaching. This general finding is similar to that of my earlier qualitative studies of the teacher from the experimental year (e.g. Wood, 1995) and to the work of others (e.g. Carpenter et al., 1989). However, the findings also indicate that the pedagogy in these reform-oriented classes consists of three definitive forms of teaching that we believe influence the contexts created for students' thinking and consequently their developing conceptions of mathematics. Teaching differs on two dimensions: the ways in which teachers develop interactive and discursive contexts for participation; and, the ways in which they promote children's thinking through the questions and statements they make.

From these analyses, we are able to create a theoretical framework to link our empirical findings with constructs drawn from psychological and sociological theories (Wood, 1997, in press; Wood and Turner-Vorbeck, in review). These findings have since been further corroborated by findings from data collected in classes of additional teachers using the problem-centered program. In addition to describing the practice of teaching, the formulation of a theoretical framework brings together two aspects of teaching traditionally viewed as separate entities. One is 'knowing how to manage the classroom', which we view as establishing and maintaining social norms. The other is 'knowing the subject matter', which we conceive of as knowing not only mathematics but how to sustain students in their ways of thinking about mathematics. This enables us to indicate how these two aspects of teaching activity are linked to students' processes of learning.

The combination of Jaworski's investigation of secondary teachers and mine of elementary teachers presents a conceptualization of mathematics teaching unlike that found in the research on teachers' knowledge. The teaching triad brings to the fore three essential aspects of the activity of teaching cast in terms which represent the current shift in cognition and in the development of knowledge.

Mapping my research findings from fine-grained analysis of teachers' activity of establishing and maintaining the routine interactive and discursive patterns found in the classroom onto the teaching triad provides insight into the link between social norms, teacher activity, and student mathematical thinking and reasoning.

An approach to inservice teacher development

Background. The approach developed to teacher education was generated from my earlier work with Paul Cobb and Erna Yackel (e.g. 1990) as the result of a research and development project in a second grade class (ages 7–9). The major research goal of the project was to investigate children's learning from a constructivist perspective in the natural setting of the classroom. The development goal for the project was to create a set of problem-centered student materials in tandem with observations of students' use of them in the classroom. The observations we made of children's thinking as a result of using the activities in the classroom were used to revise and develop new materials. In addition, the neo-Piagetian theory of the role of social interaction in learning influenced the selection of classroom arrangements involving pairs of students working collaboratively followed by whole class discussion.

The approach to teacher development grew out of our experiences in working with the classroom teacher during this project. Although the project goal was children's learning, we soon realized that the setting created opportunities for the teacher to learn as well. The highly interactive and discursive settings in the classroom created opportunities for the teacher to learn about her students' mathematical thinking. Throughout the year, the problematic situations arose between the teacher's previous ways of teaching and the constructivist orientation to children's learning. Accordingly, she began to resolve her dilemmas and change her ways of teaching to accommodate the sense she was making of children's thinking (Cobb et al., 1990). These changes in teaching, observed by us and the teacher's own insights, formed the basis of the approach to working with additional teachers in the next year. According to Cobb et al. (1990):

> . . . attempts to influence teachers' knowledge and beliefs will not be at their most effective unless they draw on teachers' first-hand experiences of interacting with their students during mathematics instruction. (pp. 141–2)

Description of the initial approach.　The teachers involved in the approach to inservice education, following the experimental year, met in a one-week summer workshop for the purpose of becoming aware of the distinctions between the traditional goals of mathematics and learning and those of a constructivist approach which were similar to the reform agenda:

> [The] initial goal . . . was to develop situations that would make it possible for the teachers to begin to question their current practices and thus have a reason to consider an alternative approach. (Cobb et al., 1990, p. 140)

These differences were illustrated with classroom and interview videotapes of children's mathematical understanding when using a textbook approach versus a problem-centered approach to learning mathematics. As they watched these videotapes, teachers became aware of the differences in children's understanding of mathematics when learning from traditional instruction versus pupils using problem-centered activities. In addition, teachers solved open-ended mathematics problems in pairs followed by whole group discussions of their solutions and thinking; read articles assigned; visited an experimental classroom and conducted an individual interview with a child from the experimental class.

During the first year, we made follow-up visits to the classroom once every two weeks for the purpose of continued dialogue with the teachers about their questions or concerns as they used the student materials and social organization in their classrooms. Additionally, the teachers participated in four after-school working sessions during the year. However, further investigation of the influence of the approach on their teaching did not extend beyond this initial year of working with these teachers.

Findings from analysis of the project focused on children's learning in these classrooms in comparison to pupils in traditional textbook classes (Cobb, Wood, Yackel, Nicholls, Wheatley, Trigatti and Perlwitz, 1991). Quantitative data analyses using standard norm-referenced measures as well as project-developed items revealed that students in problem-centered classes after one year of reform-oriented instruction had better conceptual understanding of arithmetical concepts and held different beliefs than did their counterparts in conventional textbook classes. More recent analyses of students' learning in problem-centered classes, conducted by Pat Sellers and myself, continue to support differences in children's learning between problem-centered classes and textbook-based instruction (Wood and Sellers, 1996, 1997).

Current approach to teacher education

Since that time, in my own work, I have examined more extensively the nature of teaching in these classes. Tammy Turner-Vorbeck and I examined the nature of teaching of those teachers involved in the initial teacher development approach four years later in their classrooms. The goal of this research was to gain a better understanding of the nature of the practice teachers had developed during the time period. In part, this research was conducted for the purpose of addressing the dilemma of formulating a new pedagogy that was confronting mathematics teacher educators. It was also an attempt to describe the teachers' practices that were shown to be effective through the results of our observations of significant differences in children's mathematical understanding and beliefs in these classes compared with pupils in textbook-based classes. The findings from this investigation revealed forms of teaching that were distinct from other approaches to mathematics teaching, as I shall discuss shortly.

We used the results of our findings about teaching in these classes to develop an approach to inservice teacher education that we have been conducting with a group of elementary teachers for the past two years.[1] Three central themes underlie this approach. One theme, drawn from tenets of constructivism in psychology, is to make use of the cognitive processes commonly thought to be involved in personal learning, which include: (i) careful observation and reflection on one's actions and mental thought; and (ii) social interaction as a means for creating opportunities for reflection and observation. Implicit in this theme, is the notion that the creation of confusion and conflict in personal thinking promotes change in thought. A second thesis, derived from a social-constructivist perspective in psychology, makes use of the processes involved in the social construction of knowledge and the development of common meanings to foster communication and understanding among members. The third theme, drawn from sociology, is the importance of norms and social structure in the creation of patterns of interaction and discourse as a means of establishing a professional community of practice among teachers. The second and third themes also provide opportunities for private knowledge to become shared public knowledge through processes of examination and critique. Thus, the stance taken in working with teachers is that they have individual ways of developing their teaching and that sharing their individual ways of teaching not only develops their personal capacity for teaching, but that working in this manner contributes to the generation of a community of professional practice in which inquiry and critique are the hallmarks in the formation of public knowledge about teaching.

We think the uniqueness of this approach resides in the fact that it combines empirically based research knowledge about children's mathematical thinking

(Carpenter and Moser, 1984; Steffe, von Glasersfeld, Richards and Cobb, 1983) with knowledge about the complexities involved in teaching drawn from our empirically grounded research in reform-based classes. It is becoming well accepted that an important approach to teacher development is to enable teachers to learn about children's ways of thinking (e.g. Carpenter et al., 1996) and to incorporate this with situations for improving teachers' mathematical understanding (e.g. Schifter, 1997). What is less well understood is the way that pedagogical research can be incorporated to enable teachers to learn about their teaching.

We have created an approach in which teachers learn to examine their own classroom situations in ways that allow for private examination of their teaching as well as for public inquiry within a community of practice. To do so, we have relied on certain aspects of technology to provide tools for teachers' learning. In the short run our goal is to examine the ways in which this approach enables teachers to develop their teaching. The long-term goal is to develop effective approaches to education that allow teachers to continue in their professional development.

Description of the approach.   Of central importance in our approach are teachers' personal reflections on their own teaching. Therefore, we have created a component in which teachers reflect on their teaching activity in conjunction with their children's mathematical thinking during mathematics lessons. Specifically, teachers reflected on a lesson in which class discussions followed their students' work in pairs. This particular lesson was selected for discussion with teachers based on previous research that indicated class discussions are not only the most revealing of teaching but are also the most challenging for teachers to conduct.

We incorporated the use of videotape as a tool or a means of support for the teachers' learning. Instead of them using videotape to view 'preferred practice' as illustrated by others, the teachers made video-recordings of their own lessons in order to examine the events that occurred. Later, they used these videotapes to examine the events that occurred during their classroom lesson. However, in order to engage in investigation of their instruction, teachers needed to develop their skills in making observations and reflecting on videotaped classroom events. Therefore, the examination of their lessons followed a structured sequence of reporting, inquiring and critically examining their practice. To support teachers in the development of these skills, we created a three-step procedure for responding to the tapes in 'reflective journals'. These steps were to: write their expectations for the lesson prior to teaching; make detailed records of the discourse during class discussion; and, compare and contrast the records of the actual events with their expectations. In this process, it was anticipated that teachers would come to realize the potential of using video-recordings and would continue to use them to examine their practice.

Our approach to working with teachers also attempts to resolve the second dilemma encountered by teacher educators, of finding ways that allow teachers autonomy in their development but yet meet the external demands for reform in mathematics education. A variety of approaches was used to create a community of practice in which the teachers' practices became public. In the first year, teachers shared selected segments of video-recordings of their classrooms that were illustrating a particular teaching issue that they encountered. The videos were discussed using a format similar to that used by the teachers in critiquing their own videotapes. The teachers described the dilemma that concerned them and showed the videotape segment to the others. The other teachers made detailed written records of the discourse in the segment. Then, together, they discussed and critiqued the segment, focusing on the dilemma presented by the teacher.

In the second year, in order to focus teachers' attention on the mathematical thinking of their children, research-based information on children's mathematical thinking was given. Following this, teachers interviewed their students to learn about their thinking, taped those interviews and, at subsequent meetings, shared the tapes. The discussions of the videos focused on understanding the ways in which the child in the tape was making sense of mathematics and on the ways the teachers' questioning helped clarify the children's thinking. Through these discussions, we learned about the teachers' understanding of their children's thinking as well as their understanding of the mathematics involved in the problems.

Third, a critical component of the professional community was the teachers' involvement in decisions about their next activities as a group. At the conclusion of each working session, discussion was held about the activities in which the teachers had been involved, and they made plans about what to do next.

Finally, videotape proved to be a useful tool for focusing teachers on classroom observations and stimulating them to reflect on their own teaching practices. Working sessions provided opportunities for public examination of videotapes and inquiry into both children's thinking and instructional practices. However, both teachers' examination of videotapes and working sessions were intermittent in nature.

After the first year, in order to overcome this limitation and extend teachers' reflections beyond the working sessions, we turned to the Internet as a tool for linking the participants and building a community of professional practice. An electronic mail listserver and a Website were established to support the project and to provide opportunities for the creation of an ongoing dialog about professional practice. Significantly, the use of the Internet has the potential to engage a broad cross-section of teachers from widely disparate locations in reflection on, and development of, their teaching. Our approach focused initially on the use of e-mail and the Web to help the teachers acclimatize to this medium of communications and develop a participatory routine. Subsequently, the Internet served as a tool for public inquiry into teaching. Teachers presented common mathematics problems, adjusted in difficulty for differing grade levels, to their classes. These common problems, the students' approaches, and the teachers' own pedagogy were then discussed and analyzed via the e-mail forum. Participants commented on and asked questions about one another's experiences, and we, as teacher educators, probed their understandings and practices through questioning and feedback about observations. Through this process, the teachers developed a public community of practice that provided opportunities for growth extending beyond those provided by the videotape observations and the working sessions.

Preliminary Findings

Although analysis of the data is ongoing, preliminary analyses reveal that the teachers' capacity to observe and reflect on their practice improved significantly. Teachers provided more detailed observations of students' strategies and thinking about mathematics both in viewing videotapes of their own class and others. As a community of professionals they were comfortable: exchanging videotaped episodes of situations in teaching they found problematic; discussing openly students' actions or thinking they did not understand; and, deciding how they wished to proceed as a group.

Most participating teachers also embraced the use of e-mail and the Internet as tools for dialog and communication. Teachers already comfortable with the technology quickly adapted to its use. With the exception of one participant, who was never able to become at ease with the use of the Internet, the teachers became more sophisticated in their use of the technology and were able to use it to focus their reflections on common mathematics problems in the classroom. They were comfortable in discussing classroom issues, sharing details of their classroom activities, and responding in one-on-one fashion to critiques of and questions about their observations of classroom activities and their roles in the classrooms.

Although the reflections on their students' mathematical thinking became more explicit and thoughtful, the critiques of their role as teacher in the interaction were more difficult and infrequent. When teachers made these critiques, these created opportunities for us, as teacher educators, to pose questions and make challenges of their thinking. In some cases, this resulted in teachers rethinking their actions and making changes that were evident in later lessons; however, in other cases, the teachers provided rationalization and justification of their actions. In addition, the teachers were uncomfortable and hesitant to analyze the practice of others in the working sessions. Further, the on-line discussion on the Internet rarely developed into the spontaneous and self-perpetuating discussion of teaching practice that we had hoped would emerge.

Analysis of the videotaped lessons indicated that although teacher growth occurred in these processes, teachers struggled to make revisions in their actual classroom practice. Preliminary analysis indicates that teachers in the second year anticipated children's thinking in some situations and used this knowledge in their teaching. In other cases, however, the teachers' limited knowledge of children's mathematical thinking and mathematics hindered them in anticipating pupils' thinking and/or making sense of that thinking. Although a few teachers developed more complex forms of pedagogy, others vacillated between using their previous traditional teaching methods and the initial approaches to reform-based teaching.

Conclusion

Still, there is one aspect that pertains to teacher development that we seemingly know little about, and that is the processes that are involved as teachers make changes in their teaching. We have gained insights into their thinking from their self-reports in interviews and from their writings in reflective journals and papers. We also have information about teachers' beliefs and knowledge before and after using a particular approach from which to find the particulars of change (Warfield, 1997). But, we do not know much about the interplay between the teacher education sessions and their classroom experiences. Granted we know that the classroom setting is a very powerful site for teachers' learning and that much of teachers' thinking about their practice is grounded in the specific events of their class. But, what I am referring to is an understanding of the processes involved as teachers' transform their experiences in teacher education situations to their classrooms to create a meaningful form of practice to meet the demands for students learning mathematics.

As a consequence, we, as yet, do not have well-developed conceptual frameworks that allow us to understand more fully how teachers progress themselves in their development of teaching and what influence our role, as teacher educators, plays in this process. Much of the criticism directed at the current more 'constructivist' approaches to teacher education are a result of this lack of knowledge (Richardson, 1997). From a theoretical perspective, empirical findings from inquiry into the ways in which teaching develops, as well as interrelation between teaching and learning, need to be abstracted and generalized into theoretical frameworks for aiding knowledge of the processes involved in developing teaching. From a point of practicality, knowledge of the dimensions involved in teaching is crucial to knowing how and why different forms of teaching are effective in supporting student learning. This information becomes all important when policy decisions are made, such as those currently occurring in Britain which reflect a shift from the alternative practices of teaching advocated in the 1967 Plowden Report and the 1982 Cockcroft Report back to the traditional forms of teaching (Ball, 1994; *The Economist*, 1998).

Note

1   In addition to Tammy Turner-Vorbeck, Janet Warfield, James Lehman and Kathy Cennamo have been involved in the development of the various components in the approach to teacher education.

The writing of this paper was supported by the National Science Foundation under award number RED 925–4939. All opinions are those of the author. I would like to thank Janet Warfield and James Lehman for their comments and contributions to the section describing our current approach to teacher education.

References

AINLEY, J. (1988) 'Perceptions of teachers' questioning styles', *Proceedings of the Twelfth International Conference on the Psychology of Mathematics Education* (pp. 92–9), Vesprém, Hungary: Psychology of Mathematics Education.

BALL, S.J. (1994) 'Culture, crisis and morality: The struggle over the National Curriculum', in ATKINSON, P., DELAMONT, S. and DAVIES, W.B. (eds) *Discourse and Reproduction: A Fetschrift for Basil Bernstein*, Cresskill NJ: Hampton Press.

BEATON, A.E., MULLIS, I.V.S., MARTIN, M.O., GONZALES, E.J., KELLY, D.L. and SMITH, T.A. (1996) *Mathematics Achievement in the Middle School Years: IEA's Third International Mathematics and Science Study*, Chestnut Hill, MA: Center for the Study of Testing, Evaluation and Educational Policy, Boston College.

CARPENTER, T., FENNEMA, E. and FRANKE, M. (1996) 'Cognitively Guided Instruction: A knowledge base for reform in mathematics instruction', *Elementary School Journal*, **97**, pp. 3–20.

CARPENTER, T., FENNEMA, E., PETERSON, P., CHIANG, C. and LOEF, M. (1989) 'Using knowledge of children's mathematics thinking in classroom teaching: An experimental study', *American Educational Research Journal*, **26**, pp. 499–531.

CARPENTER, T. and MOSER, J. (1984) 'The acquisition of addition and subtraction concepts', in LESH, R. and LANDAU, M. (eds) *Acquisition of Mathematics Concepts and Processes* (pp. 7–44), New York: Academic Press.

COBB, P., WOOD, T. and YACKEL, E. (1990) 'Classrooms as learning environments for teachers and researchers', in DAVIS, R.B., MAHER, C. and NODDINGS, N. (eds) *Constructivist Views on Teaching and Learning of Mathematics* (pp. 125–46), *Journal for Research in Mathematics Education Monograph Series No. 4*, Reston, VA: National Council of Teachers of Mathematics.

COBB, P., WOOD, T., YACKEL, E., NICHOLLS, J., WHEATLEY, G., TRIGATTI, B. and PERLWITZ, M. (1991) 'Assessment of a problem-centered second grade mathematics project', *Journal of Research in Mathematics Education*, **22**, pp. 3–29.

COCHRAN-SMITH, M. and LYTLE, S. (1993) *Inside/Outside: Teacher Research and Knowledge*, New York: Teachers College Press.

COONEY, T. (1994) 'Research and teacher education: In search of common ground', *Journal of Research in Mathematics Education*, **25**, pp. 608–36.

DILLON, J. (1990) *The Practice of Questioning*, New York: Routledge.

FENNEMA, E. (1996) *Cognitively Guided Instruction*, Madison: University of Wisconsin-Madison.

FENNEMA, E., CARPENTER, T., FRANKE, M., LEVI, L., JACOBS, V. and EMPSON, S. (1996) 'A longitudinal study of learning to use children's thinking in mathematics instruction', *Journal of Research in Mathematics Education*, **27**, pp. 403–34.

JAWORSKI, B. (1994) *Investigating Mathematics Teaching: A Constructivist Enquiry*, London: Falmer Press.

LABINOWICZ, E. (1985) *Learning from Children: New Beginnings for Teaching Numerical Thinking*, Menlo Park, CA: Addison-Wesley.

LITTLE, J.W. (1993) 'Teachers' professional development in a climate of reform', *Educational Evaluation and Policy Analysis*, **15**, pp. 129–51.

MATHEMATICAL SCIENCES EDUCATION BOARD (1989) *Everybody Counts: A Report to the Nation on the Future of Mathematics Education*, Washington, DC: National Academy Press.

MEHAN, H. (1979) *Learning Lessons*, Cambridge, MA: Harvard University Press.

NATIONAL COUNCIL OF TEACHERS OF MATHEMATICS (1989) *Curriculum and Evaluation Standards for School Mathematics*, Reston, VA: NCTM.

NATIONAL COUNCIL OF TEACHERS OF MATHEMATICS (1991) *Professional Standards for Teaching Mathematics*, Reston, VA: NCTM.

'Plowden's Progress' (1998) *The Economist*, **347**, pp. 63–5, 26 June.

RICHARDSON, V. (ed.) (1997) *Constructivist Teacher Education*, London: Falmer Press.

SCHIFTER, D. (1993) 'Mathematics process as mathematics content: A course for teachers', *Journal of Mathematical Behavior*, **12**, 3, pp. 271–383.

SCHIFTER, D. (1997) *Learning Mathematics for Teaching*, Newton, MA: Center for the Development of Teaching.

SHULMAN, L. (1986) 'Those who understand: Knowledge growth in teaching', *Educational Researcher*, **15**, pp. 4–14.

SHULMAN, L. (1987) 'Knowledge and teaching: Foundations of the new reform', *Harvard Educational Review*, **57**, pp. 1–22.

SIMON, M. and SCHIFTER, D. (1991) 'Towards a constructivist perspective: An intervention study of mathematics teacher development', *Educational Studies in Mathematics*, **22**, pp. 309–31.

STEFFE, L.P., VON GLASERSFELD, E., RICHARDS, J. and COBB, P. (1983) *Children's Counting Types: Philosophy, Theory, and Application*, New York: Praeger Scientific.

WARFIELD, J. (1997) 'Kindergarten teachers' knowledge of their children's mathematical thinking: Two case studies', Paper presented at the annual meeting of the American Educational Research Association, Chicago, IL.

WOOD, T. (1995) 'An emerging practice of teaching', in COBB, P. and BAUERSFELD, H. (eds) *The Emergence of Mathematical Meanings: Interaction in Classroom Cultures* (pp. 203–27), Hillsdale, NJ: Lawrence Erlbaum Associates.

WOOD, T. (1997) *Creating Classroom Interactions for Mathematical Reasoning: Beyond 'Natural' Teaching*, Setubal, Portugal: International Commission for the Study and Improvement of Mathematics Education (CIEAEM).

WOOD, T. (in press) 'Creating a context for argument in mathematics class' *Journal for Research in Mathematics Education*.

WOOD, T. and SELLERS, P. (1996) 'Assessment of a problem-centered mathematics program: Third grade', *Journal for Research in Mathematics Education*, **27**, pp. 337–53.

WOOD, T. and SELLERS, P. (1997) 'Deepening the analysis: Longitudinal assessment of a problem-centered mathematics program', *Journal for Research in Mathematics Education*, **28**, pp. 163–86.

WOOD, T. and TURNER-VORBECK, T. (in review) 'Developing teaching of mathematics: Making connection in practice', in BURTON, L. (ed.) *Learning Mathematics: From Hierarchies to Networks*, London: Falmer Press.

16   The Plurality of Knowledge Growth in Mathematics Teaching

Barbara Jaworski, UK

This chapter draws on a number of theoretical positions regarding learning and the growth of knowledge, and models and perspectives of teaching development to address the complexities of development for mathematics teachers and teaching. It takes as examples two research projects into teaching development, one in the UK and one in Pakistan, to highlight relationships between theory and practice, and to suggest that a perspective of 'plurality' is neither simplistic nor far-fetched. Plurality will be defined later in the chapter. In the initial sections, the reader is invited to consider its meaning through a number of theoretical and practical perspectives in the development of mathematics teaching. The chapter is thus in three major sections: Perspectives of *Theory*; Perspectives of *Practice* and Perspectives of *Plurality*. Within these sections, issues of the nature of knowledge and its growth in mathematics teaching, and the relationship of knowledge to the theory–practice dialectic feature prominently.

Explicit in considerations of mathematics teaching development is the role of inservice provision by teacher educators. Chapter 13 of this book synthesized a number of themes relative to inservice provision and identified issues associated with these themes. This chapter will extend some of the themes and contribute to a discussion of the issues within an overall linking of theory and practice.

Perspectives of Theory

The Problem for Mathematics Educators

Central to the concern of mathematics teachers, who are seeking to enhance students' mathematical knowledge, is the question of how students come to know mathematics, and, moreover, *what is mathematical knowledge*? For teacher educators, thinking about inservice provision, the parallel questions are about teachers coming to know mathematics teaching; and *what is knowledge in mathematics teaching*? Just as teachers seeking to teach mathematics need to address fundamentally the nature of mathematics and the growth of mathematical knowledge, so teacher educators, seeking to teach teaching, need to address the nature and growth of knowledge in mathematics teaching.

Jill Adler (1996) has written, 'Knowledge about teaching is not acquired in courses about teaching.' This quotation captures one of the issues raised in earlier discussions in this book. Just *how* is knowledge about mathematics teaching 'acquired', and what can educators do to help its acquisition?

Mathematics teacher education has a range of theories, beliefs, ideas and visions about what constitutes good teaching. Many of these are reflected in official documents such as the Cockcroft Report, a major government report into mathematics teaching in the UK (DES, 1982), and the Curriculum and Evaluation Standards and Professional Standards for Teaching in the USA (NCTM, 1989, 1991). Since these reports were published, and even before this, mathematics educators have addressed the thorny problems of how to translate these theories, beliefs, ideas and visions into forms of practice which will ensure students develop a confident and meaningful understanding of mathematics as a result of their classroom experiences. The recent TIMSS video study of classrooms in three countries (Japan, Germany and the USA) has been immensely revealing about current practices in the teaching of mathematics in these countries (Stigler and Hiebert, 1997). There is clear diversity in teaching practices, with that in the USA seemingly at odds with the widely known and well-regarded professional standards. Why is it that in some cases practices reflect the standards, and in others they do not? What are the ingredients of 'success' or lack of it?

It is important to recognize three levels of consideration here, as they tend to become intertwined. In inservice provision for the development of mathematics teaching, it is impossible to avoid questions of what makes good teaching. Such questions have to take into account mathematical learners in classrooms. Hence the learning of mathematics has to be a key consideration for inservice provision. Thus the three levels for teacher educators are:

1. Mathematics and provision of classroom mathematical activities for students' effective learning of mathematics.
2. Mathematics teaching and ways in which teachers think about developing their approaches to teaching.
3. The roles and activities of teacher educators in contributing to developments in 1 and 2.

In developing theories of teacher inservice education, leading to practices at level 3, teacher educators need to consider theories of development in 1 and 2; for example, common errors as cognitive obstacles in mathematical learning (1); the Teaching Triad (Jaworski, 1994) as means of conceptualizing teaching (2).

As an example of a theoretical construct related to the development of effective teaching, consider the notion of 'pedagogical power' introduced by Tom Cooney (1994). Tom Cooney and Barry Shealy (1997, p. 105, citing Cooney, 1994) point to pedagogical power as 'the essence of intelligent problem solving within the context of teaching mathematics'. If we think of *mathematical power*, for the learner of mathematics, as 'the ability to draw on whatever [mathematical] knowledge is needed to solve problems' (Cooney, 1994, p. 15), then *pedagogical power*, can be defined similarly — the ability to draw on whatever pedagogical knowledge is needed to solve problems. Cooney wrote 'pedagogical problem solving has to do with recognizing the conditions and constraints of the pedagogical problems being faced' (1994, p. 15). I would add to this the aims, possibilities and opportunities provided by such problem-solving. Pedagogical power is seen to be vested in such pedagogical problem-solving through processes of reflection and analysis. In this context, Cooney and Shealy ask, 'But how can we *engender* such an orientation among teachers with whom we work?' (1997, p. 105, my emphasis). This is a level 3 question. The constructs of mathematical power and pedagogical power can be seen to apply respectively at levels 1 and 2 above. At level 3 are questions about the roles teacher educators can play in the development of pedagogical power by teachers.

Here we have an example of a theory espoused by educators: that is, the importance of the link between pedagogical power and intelligent problem-solving in mathematics teaching. The word 'engender' carries a wealth of meaning with it, and encapsulates the problem for educators. *What is it that educators can do that will result in teaching which manifests in practice such theoretical concepts?* Moreover, and this is not always asked, what exactly might such theoretical concepts — in this case, 'intelligent problem-solving' — look like in the community of practice of teachers and teaching? How would we recognize it, and would we like what we see? These questions lead to a scrutiny of links between theory and practice, and ways in which practice fits with or mirrors theory. Through such questions we shall search for insights into the development of practice in terms of its desired theoretical outcomes.

Influences on Teaching Development

A fuller version of the Adler quotation above is as follows:

> Knowing about teaching and becoming a teacher evolve, and are deeply interwoven in ongoing activity in the practice of teaching. Knowledge about teaching is not acquired in courses about teaching, but in ongoing participation in the teaching community in which such courses may be a part. (Adler, 1996, p. 2)

Adler does not deny the value of *courses*, but rather emphasizes the importance of the community through which teaching evolves. She follows sociocultural theorists Jean Lave and Etienne Wenger (1991) in conceptualizing teaching as a process of apprenticeship into a community of practice with its novices and old-stagers, with newcomers growing into the community through their participation in its practices. Lave and Wenger speak of the development of communities of practice within which novices develop as full members of the community through apprentice-type relationships. Learning is seen to be a process of enculturation where learners as 'peripheral participants' in the community grow into 'old-stagers', those who represent the community of practice. They write, '. . . newcomers legitimate peripherality . . . involves participation as a way of learning — of both absorbing and being absorbed in

— the "culture of practice" . . . mastery resides not in the master, but in the organization of the community of practice' (p. 95). Thus, knowing, or cognition, is *situated* in the practice. According to Adler, Lave's theory suggests that, 'Learning is located in the process of co-participation, and not in the heads of individuals'. Adler comments, 'This is thus a social theory of the mind where meaning production is taken out of the heads of individual speakers and located in social arenas that are at once situationally specific and in the broader society' (Adler, 1996, p. 3).

Adler reminds us: 'We know only too well from teacher education courses that a prospective teacher's ability to write a good essay on what is good teaching . . . often bears little relation to good teaching in practice.' We also know 'only too well' that the most significant influence on a new teacher's teaching is the way she or he was taught (c.g. Lortie, 1975). We know too that when new teachers move from teacher education courses into the reality of schools, the school ethos, including the way in which teachers in the school operate, is often far more influential on the new teacher's teaching than principles from their education course (e.g. Thompson, 1984). So, a conceptualization of the development of teaching deriving from Lave's theories is not far-fetched. It fits with much of our experience, but sits there none too comfortably, since, as long as there exist *in*effective practices, a theory of socialization emphasizes the inevitability of such practices being perpetuated.

Brown and McIntyre (1993) present an alternative perspective in linking theory and practice in teacher education. They write,

> Inspectors, evaluators, advisors of teachers and inservice teacher trainers often remark on the 'good practice' displayed by individual teachers and exhort others to learn from them. This implies a model for inservice teacher education in which there is a deliberate and determined sharing among teachers of their diverse and successful approaches to teaching: a 'building on strengths model'. (p. 13)

The focus here appears to be on the importance of using a socialization process deliberately to build on strengths, and perpetuate good practices. However, the authors continue,

> In practice, that is rarely the case. Almost always inservice has been based on a 'deficit model' of teaching. By that we mean the emphasis has been on the identification of what it is thought teachers ought to be doing and are not doing, and on appropriate action to remedy matters. (p. 13)

The deficit models appear to be ones in which educators try to remedy perceived deficiencies (as discussed by Sandy Dawson, this volume, Chapter 14) in contrast to potentially more positive models which promote socialization into good practices. A tension between theoretical positions here lies: firstly, in contrasting *natural* socialization or apprenticeship, as in the theory of Lave and Wenger, with *deliberate* socialization (presumably involving teacher educators) as proposed by Brown and McIntyre; secondly, in recognition of the difference between 'good' and 'ineffective' practices. Natural socialization seems not to discriminate between these whereas Brown and McIntyre wish to perpetuate the good but presumably not the ineffective.

We might go further to suggest that, if indeed the 'good practice' of which Brown and McIntyre speak is available for sharing, and if teaching development is a process of socialization according to the theories of Lave and Wenger, then 'good practice' will be seen to permeate teaching. There would then be no need for teacher educators to operate any kind of model, deficit or otherwise. However, the proliferation of theories and models for improving teaching supports our wider experience to suggest this is not the case (see, for example, Anderson and Burns, 1989).

According to Brown and McIntyre, the lack of success of the so-called deficit models is due to problematic relationships between theory and practice in which the theories of educators are seen not to take account of the conditions and constraints of learners and classrooms which affect teachers and teaching. There is thus a need to explore, further, ways in which existing good teaching might become more widely practised. This is the motivation for their research which focuses on the practical knowledge which expert teachers bring to their teaching. This research aims to throw light on the nature of such knowledge which might provide insights into its development by other teachers.

The above discussion has aimed to emphasize that we have, on the one hand, educators' theories about teaching, with questions about ways in which such theories might be manifested in practice. We have, on the other, good or 'expert' teachers, who practise effectively (according to the judgments of students and others with whom they work), with questions about the knowledge which underpins such teaching. We recognize that much teaching might not be described as good or effective, and ask what might improve this teaching. We have questions about judgments such as 'good' or 'effective', and on what assumptions such judgments are based. We might also ask in what ways the forms of practice recognized as good or effective reflect the theoretical positions proposed by educators. In all of this we need to bear in mind the special nature of mathematics and in what ways perceptions of mathematics influence teaching practices.

The issues here are complex and fascinating. Fundamentally, they concern relationships between theory and practice in the growth of knowledge. Indeed they are concerned with what counts as knowledge in teaching and how such knowledge is communicated or constructed. The basic question motivating this chapter is:

> In all of this complexity, what is it that mathematics educators do, or can do, to promote, enable, facilitate, support, or engender (or even *recognize*) effective mathematics teaching in classrooms?

What Do We Mean by Knowledge in Teaching?

A familiar caricature of teaching is that of 20 years' teaching experience which is no more than 20 repetitions of one year's experience; a syndrome of 'I've been giving this lecture for 20 years. I don't need my notes any more'. An alternative caricature is encapsulated in, 'I reinvent this lecture every time I give it'. In oversimplifying complexity in order to make a telling point, caricatures can be useful in pointing to key elements of the complexity we are trying to fathom. The mathematical knowledge on which the lecture is based might be seen as fixed or changing, which would influence the lecturer's perception of the lecture to be given. The lecturer's concept of teaching as represented by the lecture goes beyond mathematics per se into a philosophy of mathematical pedagogy which seems particularly limited in the caricatures. Maybe critical appraisal of last year's lecture leads to a better lecture this year. Maybe an overt synthesizing of the knowledge which derives from such critical appraisal is of more value than the improved lecture, because it determines future practice, of which the improved lecture is just one example. Critical appraisal, and overt synthesizing of knowledge can be seen as key elements in knowledge growth, not evident in the caricatures. Characteristics and deficiencies in the caricatures prompt recognition of the elements of knowledge which are brought to an act of teaching. The point here is what we mean by *knowledge* in teaching.

Shulman (1987) identified a minimum set of 'categories of knowledge that underlie the teacher understanding needed to promote comprehension among students' (p. 8). These include content knowledge; general pedagogical knowledge; curriculum knowledge; pedagogical content knowledge; knowledge of learners; knowledge of educational contexts; and knowledge of educational ends, purposes and values.

Content knowledge, for mathematics teachers is *mathematical* knowledge. Its importance for teachers of mathematics is undisputed. Such knowledge goes beyond mathematical topics or processes per se, to mathematical philosophy and the perspectives and perceptions which guide our mathematical practices (e.g. Davis and Hersh, 1981; Ernest, 1991). For example, in their analysis of belief structures of mathematics teachers, Cooney and Shealy (1997) draw attention to the importance of new paradigms in the development of mathematical knowledge; the work of Kuhn and Lakatos, for example. These influence not only the mathematics which is taught, but fundamentally our perceptions of the ways in which people come to know mathematics. The consequences for teaching are enormous, which was reflected in many of the programmes discussed in Section Two of this book.

Shulman's concept of *pedagogical content knowledge* recognizes a need for teachers to translate their perceptions of mathematics into classroom activities which provide opportunity for learners to 'come to know'. For effective teaching of mathematics, mathematical knowledge by itself, however powerfully or insightfully perceived, is limited. Effective teaching requires some understanding of how mathematics might become accessible to learners; for example, how mathematical generalization and abstraction can be *learned* (e.g. Sierpinska, 1994). Pedagogical knowledge itself goes beyond mathematics to the wider social and cultural issues in school and society through which students 'come to know' mathematics (e.g. Bishop, 1988).

There is some literature on the development of knowledge in subject disciplines in classroom settings (e.g. Stodolsky, 1988), but surprisingly little which results from a study of the practical environments in which teachers and students interact with these various forms of knowledge. This is starting to be remedied in mathematics education as might be seen in a number of studies in the United States, highlighted by Terry Wood (this section).

Belenky, Clinchy, Goldberger and Tarule (1986), in their study of women in practice, synthesized a range of 'ways of knowing' (as opposed to *particular* knowledge such as mathematical or pedagogic knowledge) based on Perry's positions (Perry, 1970). From *silence*, 'a position in which women experience themselves as mindless and voiceless and subject to the whims of external authority'; through *received knowledge*[1], capable of receiving, even reproducing, knowledge but not of creating knowledge; *subjective knowledge*, where truth and knowledge are conceived of as personal, private, and subjectively known or intuited; *procedural knowledge*, learning and applying objective procedures for obtaining and communicating knowledge; to *constructed knowledge*, 'a position in which women view all knowledge as contextual, experience themselves as creators of knowledge, and value both subjective and objective strategies for knowing' (p. 15). Many of these positions can be aligned with observations of teachers' knowledge as may be seen through the research of, for example, Brown and McIntyre (1993), Yusof Othman (1996), and Deborah Schifter (e.g. 1993, 1997). Ways of knowing, as opposed to forms of knowledge, have parallels with dichotomies between theory and practice — *forms of knowledge* being usually a synthesis arising from theorizing, with *ways of knowing* emerging from practice. In order for teacher educators to find ways of bridging the theory–practice divide in working for teaching development, greater recognition of teachers' ways of knowing seems essential.

Communication of Knowledge in Teaching

The very words we use to discuss processes of learning highlight issues in conceptualizing such ways of knowing. I deliberately placed quotes around the words 'come to know' (above) because I was using them very particularly to carry a dynamic sense about the construction of knowledge. 'Coming to know' mathematics might reflect a constructive process conceptualized perhaps in Piagetian terms or according to von Glasersfeld's radical constructivism (Piaget, 1970; von Glasersfeld, 1987), or it might, however, reflect some socialization process — a 'social theory of the mind', as discussed above (Adler, 1996). It seems necessary to be aware of how such language use affects our conceptualization of the knowledge to which it refers, and it is as well to point out that this might be mathematical knowledge, knowledge of teaching mathematics, or indeed knowledge of 'the growth of knowledge' in mathematics or in teaching. A sociocultural view of knowledge growth, based in Vygotskian theory, emphasizes this influence of language: seeing language as fundamental to the *forming* of ideas, rather than just as a vehicle for their communication. A danger in charting knowledge growth is that as syntheses of knowledge are made by theoreticians, conceptualizations become shrouded in obscure language forms which have meaning only for the initiated. For example, postmodernist approaches to seeing knowledge in terms of text and discourse have resulted often in powerful ways of knowing being undermined by the language forms in which they are communicated. To highlight the pre-eminence of social interchange over any attempts to map or picture the world, Gergen (1995) writes, 'In principle, this is no more a table before me than it is a Gouda cheese or a griffin'. It is what is understood in the community and context which provides meaning. However, his example illustrates graphically a dilemma of language. How many of us could be sure that a griffin was not a name for a particular type of table unfamiliar to us?

In the study of Brown and McIntyre (1993), attempting to capture and chart the knowledge of expert teachers, a dilemma for the teachers was finding language forms to communicate the knowledge in or behind their classroom practice. Once such language forms are coined, their usage grows and develops within a community. Outside the community they have little meaning or relevance. In studying the development of teaching, it seems important to distinguish between language development which is integral to knowledge growth, and imposed language which is often an impediment to knowledge growth: the former representing the growth of knowledge in practice, and the latter the imposition of external theoretical knowledge. Knowledge in practice is part of the community of teachers which is different from the community of teacher educators. These differing cultures have different discourses so that cultural transformation or enculturation produces different effects and creates different problems.

As an example here, I recall a teacher (Mike) in my research in the later 1980s, who conceptualized some aspect of his teaching as encouraging 'cognitive density', or the lack of it (Jaworski, 1994, p. 130). The words 'cognitive density', for Mike expressed succinctly a concept in his students' learning which, for him, was highly meaningful. The concept and its language form were, for him, a central part of the culture in which his teaching developed. However, suppose, as a result of reflection on this concept, Mike or others wished to teach other teachers of the value of 'cognitive density'. How might this be achieved, if both language and concept are outside the direct experience of other teachers? The concept could certainly be described or explained, but how would it be possible to *engender* the practical understanding that made the concept important for Mike? How can such a concept become a cultural phenomenon? It is this critical link between the concept itself, and its expression theoretically through language, which forms one of the essential issues in teacher inservice education, and the communication of knowledge central to developing teaching. For teacher educators such synthesizing of practice in theoretical terms is part of the community of practice. For teachers, the opportunities to talk and reflect in such theoretical terms are less common, so other means of appreciation through links with practice need to be found. Some such opportunities will be discussed in the second section of this chapter.

Perhaps even more fundamental than the problem of language for teachers in communicating their knowledge is the often *tacit* nature of that knowledge (e.g. Polanyi, 1958). Until such knowledge has been recognized overtly, there exists no means of articulating it. Donald Schön (1983, 1987) has addressed the tacit nature of knowledge in professions, and the problems in gaining access to it at a theoretical level. *Knowledge-in-action*, as he has called it, is fundamental to how professionals behave effectively in a professional context, i.e. in their professional *action*. Gaining access to this tacit knowledge can occur through *reflection*, first of all *on* the action, and ultimately *in* the action. Reflecting-*on*-action is the process of reviewing and analysing what has occurred *after* it has occurred. This starts the process of developing awareness of the what, how and why of teaching acts which can lead to a making explicit of the underlying personal theories and beliefs which motivate those acts. Schön's theory is that this growth of awareness leads to reflection-*in*-action where the explicated knowledge becomes available to influence the practice as it is practised.

We might see teachers' knowledge, albeit tacit, as part of the community of practice of teachers and teaching, with cultural transmission and communication within the practice. Schön's theory, on the other hand, presupposes a perspective of knowledge growth for the individual teacher. We might ask in what ways such knowledge growth enters into the community of practice. How might it become a cultural phenomenon? Although Schön's work, at least in the beginning, was not explicitly addressed at the profession of teaching, it is much quoted in educational writing. His theoretical perspective has resonated strongly with *educators'* perceptions of knowledge growth in teaching. However, as Eraut (1995) points out, Schön's theory is not empirically researched where the practice of teaching is concerned, and we have little evidence of teachers reflecting-in-action from which to judge its effectiveness for teaching development. Indeed, Eraut questions the compatibility of the notion of reflection-in-action with the immediacy of decision-making demands for a teacher in the classroom.

A theory–practice dialectic

We need to ask, rather fundamentally, whether the theory *describes* a way of acting and thinking through which knowledge grows and teaching develops — in which case we can ask how valid a description it offers — or whether, as educators, we want to go further and propose Schön's theory as a process which can be offered to teachers to aid their development of teaching. The latter has profound implications, both practically and philosophically, for teacher educators in their relationships with teachers. In my earlier research (Jaworski, 1994) I charted a process of teacher reflection leading to enhanced awareness and noticing in-the-moment (Mason, 1994) which could be seen to be a form of reflection-in-action, in Schön's terms. In subsequent research with teachers acting as inquirers into their own practice (see the MTE project, below), such reflection-in-action was further evident. It seemed that the activity of overt inquiry into the teaching process could be seen to lead to this kind of reflection. Here, there was no attempt at any stage to engender, or inculcate, reflection-in-action. However, if reflection-in-action is seen to be a theoretical goal for developing effective teaching, educators would need to address questions of how such practice might be initiated.

A study of theories, such as reflection-in-action, by educators experienced in grappling with abstract concepts, and a relating of them (still theoretically) to practical knowledge is very different to a study of those theories in practice. (I remind the reader of the discussion of 'pedagogical power' above.) The complexities of knowledge and practice which the theories encapsulate are beyond quick description or reference in a few sentences. Meanings are invested in technical terms, which carry all the language problems mentioned earlier. Also, meanings, in practical terms, go beyond the understandings of those who contemplate them only from a theoretical viewpoint. Only the practitioner can ultimately have access to such meanings which are part of teachers' personal theories, even if tacit. However, teachers do not normally have access to external theories, and, moreover, teachers who engage every day of their professional lives in the ways of knowing and being to which the theories refer might perceive such external theory as extraneously irrelevant to what matters in classroom teaching and learning. Yet, as educators, we invest immense value in the terms and concepts involved as they enlarge and represent our own understandings and knowledge growth. It is a case of the culture of teaching versus articulations or theorizations of this culture. Ideally, as teacher educators, we should like our theorizations to be evident in the development of teaching. The responsibility for this is ours; we cannot expect it just to happen for teachers.

There is evidence of teachers' growth of awareness of theories of teaching, often their own personal theories, through interaction with educators or researchers. Yusof Othman (1996) talks of his research into the craft knowledge of mathematics teachers proving highly illuminating for the teachers themselves, who had little perception of the complexities of the knowledge they brought to 'simple' classroom decisions. The researcher's questions about their teaching stimulated teachers to become aware of their own decisions and their reasons for making them. When articulated as knowledge, these decisions become momentous in pointing to a pedagogy of practice. A theoretical account of this practice is essential to representing and learning from it.

The research of Brown and McIntyre has been directed at developing such a theoretical account from the personal actions and theories of teachers, and enhances our understandings in general terms, although not specifically in mathematical terms. This follows work in a general educational tradition by Elbaz (1983) and others. The research of Othman, quoted above, is seeking to take such theories into the realm of *mathematics* teaching. In my own research, I have sought to provide an articulation of teachers' voices regarding their conceptualization of mathematics teaching. I have tried to capture manifestations of theory in practice, and the theorizing of practical issues, but yet the value of such theory to the growth of knowledge of teaching remains elusive for the teachers who practise it.

Perspectives of Practice

*Linking Theory to Practice in Conceptualizing Knowledge Growth
in Teaching*

In this chapter, so far, I have tried to set the scene for seeing teaching as a complex enterprise in which theorizing is essential to conceptualizing the development of mathematics teaching. Yet at the same time, paradoxically theorizing can divert attention from the goals of using theory for the development of mathematics teaching. I intend now to move into an essentially practical domain, in which the dilemmas of teaching development become the central focus, and where I try to develop links in a productive way with the theories expressed above. This will lead to a clarification of what I see as the *plurality* of knowledge growth in teaching, and its implications for mathematics educators. I will refer to two projects which have been extremely significant in my own development as a teacher educator over the last five years. One is a research project undertaken in the UK, the Mathematics Teacher Enquiry (MTE) Project, and the second is an enterprise in teaching development in which I have been privileged to take part in Pakistan. Together these projects highlight methodologies through which teaching develops as well as epistemological, social and ethical questions regarding the situation of teaching knowledge relative to the individuals and cultures concerned. The role of the teacher educator in these examples of developing teaching will be a key concept.

The Mathematics Teacher Enquiry Project

In 1994, at the University of Oxford in the UK, a pilot project was initiated to explore developments in mathematics teaching arising from classroom teachers of mathematics undertaking research into self-chosen aspects of their own teaching. A small number of teachers volunteered themselves, as a result of an invitation to teachers in an initial teacher education partnership programme with local schools. The teachers agreed to undertake research (into questions of their own choosing), to discuss their research with a researcher from the university, and to participate in twice-termly meetings of all researchers in the project. The project was designed and funded, initially, for one year, but, due mainly to the interest of the teachers, it was extended to two years.

Detailed discussion of processes and practices in the project, research methodology, and issues arising for the teachers and for mathematics teaching development are discussed in Jaworski (1997, 1998). Evidence showed that the teachers' thinking and practice developed relative to their research activity, which was described as *evolutionary* rather than systematic. Cycles of action and reflection in the research led to new awarenesses and realizations which stimulated further activity and reflection. Here I shall focus on issues in knowledge growth for some teacher participants in the project, relating these to theoretical positions outlined above. It is my aim to exemplify plurality in the knowledge, practices and development of these teachers through their engagement in research.

The three teachers, Julie, Sam and Jeanette (pseudonyms) are all established practitioners in comprehensive schools in largely middle-class, semi-rural, small-town environments in southern England. They emerge from a period in which progressive educational values have both gained wider perception among teachers (during the 1970s and early 1980s) and subsequently been suppressed through political back-to-basics movements in recent successive governments. A culture of statutory control of curriculum and testing has placed severe limitations on what is possible in classrooms through high bureaucratic demands and accountability pressures on teachers' time. The project sought to capitalize on teachers' desire to offer students better opportunities for mathematical understanding and development (level 1 above) relative to forces which are perceived as reducing opportunity for the sake of narrowly defined goals. It was thus recognized as running counter to political pressures, and concomitantly as attractive in its vision and potential for resisting perceived oppression. Supported by the school principals, it provided a legitimate opportunity to focus on more idealistic aspects of teachers' beliefs in teaching, despite the external constraints.

Julie came from a traditional approach to mathematics teaching with a strong element of direct instruction. She wanted to move towards practices which might be considered 'investigative', and to develop a more activity-based classroom in which mathematics was discussed by students. She had recently read about some research which suggested that children learned better in a formal environment, seated in rows; more akin to traditional teaching methods than the investigative ones she sought to develop. She knew that she lacked a clear sense of what more investigative teaching might mean for her classroom and did not know how to begin research. However, she was aware that her resistance to seating students in rows was that she felt this seating would not encourage the mathematical talk which she believed to be important to mathematical understanding. Thus, mathematical talk became the focus of her study. She moved through a number of cycles of devising activities to explore the talk in her classroom. Early, naively formulated activities led to developing awareness of both substance and methodology of her research. Her research questions matured, as did her means of exploring them. She came to an understanding of her own value system in terms of the mathematics she wanted students to learn and the manifestations of that learning accessible through students' talk. In her writing[2], she acknowledged that she had come to know more clearly her own philosophy of mathematical learning, and the implications of ideas which had formally been instinctive and vague.

Julie might be seen as moving towards a form of teaching in which the quality of students' thinking was becoming increasingly important to her own construction of teaching. In the initial stages of her research, she operated from a vague and instinctive awareness which fits well with notions of teachers' tacit knowledge. In terms of her own beliefs, she 'knew' that traditional approaches were not achieving what she hoped in terms of students' learning, but found it hard to articulate the improvements she sought or how to go about implementing them. The research allowed her actively to explore her own thinking, and through analysis of methods which proved unsatisfactory in revealing the way forward, she came to know more clearly what it was that she sought. There was considerable evidence of her growth of knowledge in the project, both of mathematics pedagogy and of her personal theories of teaching, indicating a significant shift in her position as a teacher.

Sam came from a clear perspective of mathematics and of ways in which he believed mathematics is best learned. He had a charismatic approach to presenting activities in his classroom, aiming to engender in students a love of mathematical thinking and exploration akin to his own. He observed some students to work 'productively' with the activities he offered them, whereas others appeared to 'resist' his approaches. His research was directed at finding out more about this *productivity* or *resistance* — his words. He used visitors to his classroom to observe groups of students and inform him of their activity and thinking when he was not able to be present himself in their group. Some of the feedback he received proved extremely salutary to him. Whereas certain students seemed to relish a high degree of challenge and a rapid pace to lessons, others gave evidence of needing a gentler approach with more time to practise and assimilate ideas, and more opportunity for support and reinforcement. It seemed that there were affective factors in these students' responses to the teaching they experienced which proved to be obstacles to mathematical progress and which produced a seemingly resistant attitude to the teachers' expectations. Given the opportunity to express their views, some of these students were very vocal in their criticism of the teaching methods they perceived.

The teacher came to appreciate a need for a clearer understanding of the work and thinking of all students in his class, and especially a consideration of affective factors which influenced mathematical development. From a cognitively focused view of students' construction of knowledge he seemed to move towards a greater awareness of social factors in students' learning of mathematics. Ignoring such social factors was seen to be leading to the observed resistance. Thus again we see a growth of knowledge and a concomitant shift in thinking and perspective resulting in reconsideration of practices and alternative approaches to classroom teaching.

A third teacher, Jeanette, started from a position of caring about her students' personal self-esteem in their mathematical development. Her style of teaching was to devise activities through which students could engage with mathematics, feel able to express their thinking and difficulties, and gain a personal sense of achievement and satisfaction. Her research was focused on types of mathematical activities which would engage and challenge students with mathematical learning difficulties, while providing scaffolding and reinforcement which was not hugely teacher-intensive. The issue of students' self-esteem was for a long time the main focus of her attention. However, a shift in her focus occurred as she came to question the degree of cognitive challenge which was evident in learning outcomes. For example, while students showed an active involvement in tasks set, and a clear participation in and enjoyment of lessons, Jeanette felt that there was not enough evidence of mathematical generalization arising from activity. Many students remained at the level of an appreciation of the particular, without being able to appreciate or justify general principles. Jeanette's research moved into a questioning of what teaching approaches might lead to enhanced cognitive development while maintaining students' confidence and self-esteem. This might be seen as a shift from a socially embedded teaching approach to one with a more psychological focus, perhaps looking more closely at students' individual knowledge construction relative to the social domain of the classroom — in contrast perhaps to Sam's shift, which could be characterized as a move from psychological to more social considerations.

I have tried to highlight in the above accounts the important shifts in teachers knowledge and awareness which occurred as a result of their engaging in classroom research into their own teaching. There was considerable evidence of the growth of knowledge for each teacher, although this knowledge was different for each of the three. These results relate to Level 2 above. In all cases, the main focus of the teachers was on the particular activities devised for pupils, and pupils' responses to these activities. For each of the teachers there was evidence of changes in thinking with regard to the construction of activities, which led to variations in experience for their pupils. This relates to Level 1 above. What it was not possible to ascertain during the timescale of the project was the degree to which changes in pedagogy and thinking of teachers resulted in enhanced mathematical learning for pupils. A greater time period and more overt scrutiny would have been required for such evidence to emerge.

Where Level 3 is concerned, undoubtedly, the university researchers, themselves teacher educators, had a role to play in this development. Their chief role was studying the practices, processes, theoretical perspectives and issues arising in the teachers' research. There was no overt role for them as teacher educators. There was no intention to act as change agents or to develop the teachers. However, the interactive nature of the project, encouraging communication and collaboration had to be analysed as part of the data relating to shifts and changes observed. Researchers' presence in school and in project meetings provided not only levels of support to foster teachers' research activity, but also implicit role models. Questions asked influenced teachers to think in particular directions. Although the questions were not explicitly designed for this purpose, they undeniably contributed to changing awarenesses. Where teachers asked overtly for help and support this was provided; for example, in the undertaking of research observations in classrooms, or by recommending books or articles relevant to issues arising from the teachers' research. The university researchers encouraged teachers to raise questions, explore problematic areas and to feel at ease with notions of research. In regular project meetings of all researchers, a sharing of practice and individual learning led to the airing of issues which could be seen as generic to the practice of all the teachers. They were, thus, instrumental in the growth of a small community of practice (Adler, 1996; Lave, 1996) where the practice was the development of teaching through classroom research, and analysis of its outcomes. The above examples of growth of knowledge and shifts in thinking for individuals were seen to be strongly related to the ethos of communication and cooperation within this community.

An example of theoretical development deriving from this collaboration between teacher researchers and university researchers involved appropriation of a theoretical construct, the 'teaching triad' arising from earlier classroom research by Jaworski (1994). This triad involves elements of 'management of learning', 'sensitivity to students' and 'mathematical challenge' and it was offered originally to characterize observed teaching, and as an analytical device for scrutinizing teaching. It was offered during one of the project meetings in response to issues which arose, and it proved attractive to the three teachers in deriving, independently, conceptualizations of their practice. All pointed to its relevance in terms of their seeking a balance between challenge and sensitivity to achieve effective learning. Relationships between challenge and sensitivity were seen to characterize shifts between cognitive and social aspects of students' learning seen in the examples above. Teachers' (common) desire to create a classroom environment which fostered mathematical thinking and approaches to learning mathematics seemed to be captured by notions of management of learning. Each teacher was able to fit the three domains of the triad to elements of their teaching and resulting classroom practices, and they became very excited about the triad's potential to help them think about their teaching. These outcomes were so significant that they led to a further research project into the potential of this triad to describe mathematics teaching and act as an analytical tool for understanding teaching (e.g. Jaworski and Potari, 1998).

Three elements of the above discussion seem especially significant for the main focus of this paper:

- the shifts in awareness and conceptualization of practice which were evident for each of the teachers;
- the diversity of practices and theoretical underpinnings associated with these shifts;
- the role of university researchers as teacher educators within the developmental process.

These elements will be discussed further in the section on 'plurality' to follow.

Mathematics Teaching Development in Pakistan

In 1994, the Aga Khan University in Pakistan inaugurated an Institute for Educational Development (IED) with a mission to enhance teaching and hence schooling in Pakistan and beyond. I have been one of a team from Oxford which has participated in the IED's teacher/teaching development programme.

The IED's initial framework had 'twin goals of enhancing teachers' skills by enabling [teachers] to reflect on their practice, their classroom situation, and the way in which children learn; and rewarding teachers' progress by the granting of internationally recognized qualifications', the first of which was a masters degree programme (MEd) in teacher education for selected experienced teachers.

At the end of the MEd programme (18 months, then; now 2 years full time), graduates returned to their own schools as Professional Development Teachers (PDTs) with responsibilities to develop their own teaching relative to their learning in the programme and to work with other teachers in their school to facilitate development and contribute to school improvement. They were also contracted to devote six months of each year, for three years, to delivering two-month education programmes at the IED for *Visiting Teachers* (VTs) from schools. Thus an aim of the programme was that these people would not only develop as teachers, they would take on the mantle of teacher educators. Thus a study of the outcomes of this programme adds an extra dimension to the three levels of consideration for teacher educators. It might be seen as a split at Level 3:

3a. Mathematics teacher education and ways in which educators think about developing their approaches to teacher education.
3b. (The old 3). The roles and activities of teacher educators in contributing to developments at 1, 2 and 3a above.

This new level involves the development of teachers to become teacher educators working in ways similar to those who are instrumental in their education. Models of apprenticeship might be seen to describe this situation, with novice teacher educators apprenticed to the old-stagers — those who are 'teaching' them (Lave and Wenger, 1991).

The initial framework for the IED included the following statement on complementarity between research, reflective practice and teaching programmes:

> ... inquiry is at the heart of both teaching and learning. Teachers who view learning as inquiring into the natural and social world relate to subject matter in characteristic ways. These ways differ markedly from those that characterize teachers who view themselves as conduits for received knowledge and their students as empty vessels. Teachers who view themselves and their students as inquirers rather than receptors are more inclined to encourage students to challenge their own thinking and that of others, to foster the kind of open debate and discussion critical to sharpening and refining ideas and concepts. (The Aga Khan University Institute for Educational Development, 1991, p. 24)

Thus, the IED set out to encourage inquiry, mutual challenge and critical reflection. Consistent with the above aims, MEd participants wrote reflective journals which were shared with tutors and peers for communication and feedback. Theories of cooperative learning were pursued in the practice of the course, leading to the development of a community of learners for support and challenge. During taught modules, participants worked with students and/or teachers in schools on the same campus as the IED. Gaining practical experience alongside theoretical input, with encouragement to reflect and critically review their learning, was central to the philosophy of the programme (see, for example, Halai, 1998).

Within the aims and practices of this academic and professional programme, I will refer to the development, as teacher educators, of three of the MEd graduates who specialized in mathematics teaching. I shall draw on their own words as written in their journals, dissertations and personal communications. Through their own voices, I shall demonstrate practical aspects of their development and issues which this raised, and relate these practice-based elements to theoretical positions outlined above. In doing so I shall be developing notions of plurality of knowledge and its growth in mathematics teacher education, this time within the environment of a formal programme in which teacher educators (the IED's faculty) aimed to develop future teacher educators to work in university and school contexts.

In seeking insights into their development, I asked the three teachers a number of questions, including:

- How would you characterize your thinking/teaching before the MEd course?
- What were the key elements of your learning in the MEd course? How did you relate these to your actual teaching with students in the classroom?
- How would you characterize your teaching now?

One teacher wrote,

> A significant aspect of my learning during the MEd programme was a deeper understanding of how learning takes place. In pre-MEd days, I had an idea that pupils had different needs regarding the kind of support they needed in learning mathematics. However, I looked at these needs being different because I thought one was bright, the other dull, and so on. In the MEd . . . I was exposed to a variety of learning strategies which allowed me to learn by interacting with people and materials. I also had an opportunity to find out by reading and in sessions what others had found out about how learning takes place. I now realize the significance of allowing pupils to make meaning in mathematics. An important aspect is acknowledging that different people will make meaning and hence represent their ideas and understanding through different ways.

The teacher also acknowledged various forms of input which had contributed to her growth of knowledge in the formal programme (such as modelling of learning strategies, interactions with people and materials, opportunities to read what others had written) and their significance for her own learning — for example, in emphasizing meaning-making in mathematics.

In response to my questions, another teacher offered me excerpts from her journal which exemplify aspects of her learning and her ways of expressing her learning. As with the teacher quoted above, she pointed to what she saw as 'limitations' in perception which her studies had revealed.

> What a different vision is being developed. Yes, I allowed my children to share, but that sharing was not to explore or to investigate; that was only to help weak children to complete the problems in the book, and assurance of everyone's understanding . I [would] never ask thinking questions, only check their work or explain. Yes, talk was there, but not for the purpose discussed today.

Her reference to 'thinking questions', and to new ways of seeing 'sharing' and 'talk' provided exemplars of her developed perceptions. Further examples of her developed thinking arose in references to her work with children on mathematical topics during the mathematics module of the MEd programme. Her remarks reflect both her awareness of the mathematics per se and some analysis of qualities of the classroom environment which contributed to the children's mathematical development.

> Mathematics is fun. The children were so happy while doing activities; how they were convincing each other: 'No, this is half, give me two thirds, 1/6 is less than 1/3.' When they were talking they were very relaxed and comfortable. Why? Did they feel they were in a safe environment? Is it because they were allowed to talk and do themselves? I was surprised to see their level of confidence, and making decisions.

She emphasized her enhanced perceptions of the nature of mathematics and of mathematical activity, comparing it with her previous practice in teaching. She drew attention to the value of working with children to try out new perceptions and see the children's responses.

> Today I saw myself that algebra begins from primary [school]. Patterns emerge from the child's early life when they arrange things. This is something new for me. I did this with my niece with two colour beads and she got the pattern quickly. Then I did with her odd + odd = even. She got it — surprisingly!

The very specific nature of the examples in these remarks are evidence of the learning of the teachers, and no doubt resonate strongly with readers who have experienced this process for themselves. The honesty and clarity of this recognition are significant elements of the learning process and growth of knowledge in teaching — as I recognize in my own development as a teacher educator. In working with these teachers over a four-year period, I was aware of growth and change in their thinking and ways of working both personally in their classroom teaching and in their work with other teachers which paralleled my own experiences over many years. I thus felt able to ask them,

> Assuming there has been a shift in your awareness (as a teacher) of the effective teaching of mathematics (Is this a reasonable assumption?), what have been the key elements of this shift? How would you characterize the shift for you — perhaps in terms of your *original* knowledge and beliefs about mathematics, teaching and learning compared to your *current* position

I was here using the language of 'shifts' which had arisen for me from the MTE work. No doubt my use of this term influenced their responses. As I had asked about *knowledge*, it was unsurprising that the teachers addressed the concept of knowledge directly. However, their responses indicated a deeply thoughtful consideration of what knowledge meant for them, and their shifts in knowledge. For example, one teacher wrote,

> Reading books and listening to teachers lecture was the important tool of receiving knowledge. I never thought that knowledge always has context and meaning. But as I am getting experience to work with other teachers my own knowledge or understanding about knowledge is being changed. Knowledge is not only to learn new subject or content, but understand and get meaning. Knowledge should include: what is being taught, to whom it is being taught, e.g. students' background, learning style, level . . . why it is being taught.
>
> Knowledge is power.

The words 'knowledge is power' captured the importance for us all of our knowing, our ways of knowing and our ways of relating this knowing to constructions of the practices of teaching and teacher education. Theoretical conceptualizations of changes in practice were highlighted by one teacher who listed decisions which 'reflect my changed thinking as a result of this wider understanding about learning'. Her list included new uses for textbooks, a variety of teaching strategies ('to allow pupils room for active participation and social interaction in class') and the representation of mathematical ideas in pictures, words, concrete models or symbols.

These are concrete manifestations of the general principles highlighted by the teacher who spoke of knowledge, above. Although my questions might be seen to pre-empt the teachers' responses, presupposing shifts of thinking and changes in practice, the teachers' words provided ample justification for my assumptions. All the teachers sent me either quotations from, or portions of, their journals to read. These were not constructed for my benefit, to answer my questions, but documented, over considerable time periods, deep and searching reflections into knowledge and practice.

I felt that the responses I received provided many examples of the different levels of knowing quoted from Belenky et al. (1986) earlier, particularly of personal, procedural and constructed knowledge. Such growth and development was not always comfortable as reflected in the statement:

> In one task of the module I took the initiative to be the group presenter, and describing the task I wrote 'roll model' instead of 'role model'. The facilitator of the group laughed at my English, and I was so hurt that immediately I lost all my confidence. Read my reflection of the day: 'Today is the worst day of my life. I am very stupid. Why did I have a desire of learning? High qualification is only for the people who have the power of English language.'

As I read such elements of the journals I recognized elements of all the three levels above — my own personal reflections on my role in this process being central to Levels 3a and 3b. Alongside these teachers, and putative teacher educators, my own knowledge as a teacher educator was a significant element of the process, its synthesis, and the ability to communicate this process to others.

After MEd graduation, the three teachers, now PDTs, took part in a research project which had similarities with the Oxford MTE Project, above. They each worked with two teachers in their school, encouraging and supporting the teachers' inquiry into self-chosen aspects of their practice, and documenting outcomes and issues. One PDT sent me 100 pages from her journal, written during research with her two teachers (pseudonyms, Habiba and Farah). My analysis of this writing resulted in a categorization of the substance of remarks in the journal which are significantly indicative of knowledge and growth. Out of 125 items recorded, the largest categories were:

1. *Personal learning/evaluation of the PDT* (21 items). For example, 'I have learned that you can't do something to teachers, you need to do it *with* them — or even better they must feel the need to do it themselves.'
2. *Issues related to reading of the literature by the PDT and her associated teachers* (19 items). For example, 'The meeting with Habiba was very interesting. Her reading of Hargreaves has led her to reflect on the issue of empowerment.'
3. *The learning/growth of her associated teachers* (13 items). For example, 'Through the action research Farah has started examining her role as a teacher, not only in a particular classroom but in a school and in society. . . .

When did this interest in self emerge? Was it the reading? Was it her ability to apply that reading to her experiences? Was it that while working on a project she saw a difference in approach between [another teacher] and herself?'

Here is evidence not only of the development of the PDT, but also of the two teachers with whom she was conducting research. Her report of her research project, written for publication provides ample further evidence as well as insights and issues into teaching development through classroom research. The significance of professional and academic literature to development of all three was potent, and their perception of its importance was a significant outcome of the MEd programme. There were clearly cognitive outcomes for each teacher. The collaborative nature of the work, and the supportive structures it created proved also significant to its success. Thus these teachers operated in an environment which encouraged personal knowledge construction within cooperative and collaborative structures which both facilitated and challenged learning. As they experienced the challenges themselves and recognized social and cognitive demands, they were more able to appreciate the complexity of issues which they and the teachers they worked with had to face. One PDT wrote about her own struggles with teaching, 'Teaching Class VI through the use of multiple strategies was not a smooth affair. The issues and concerns can be seen in my journal entries'. From her journal I extracted the following quotation:

> I must do something about the issues which are coming out of my teaching. First, pupils are not used to working with each other — it is obvious from the way they work, the individualistic approach to group tasks, the squabbles and so on. This means that, for meaningful learning to take place, I have to focus more on using strategies specific to cooperative learning. I also feel that in a whole school day, just 35 minutes of working with each other, and the remaining time working individually, competing against each other, is not going to help. I will have to convince other teachers also to use cooperative learning in their class.

As a result of working with other teachers in her school, and observing the problems they had in conceptualizing changed practices, she wrote,

> Now I understand why teachers just resort to plain telling. It is so easy compared to pupils' reasoning out the whole problem themselves with appropriate support and guidance from the teacher.

When back in their schools after the MEd course, as new PDTs, they were obliged to work with their colleagues to contribute to developing practice within the school. The comments above reflect the PDT's recognition of her need to interact with and gain feedback from other teachers. Her role in this was not easy to define.

In addition to working with colleagues in school, she took part in running 8-week courses for Visiting Teachers at the IED. Teachers from her school were part of this programme. My observations of these programmes provided overwhelming evidence of PDTs' knowledge, understanding and expertise, consolidated during their

MEd programme and in their subsequent work in school. Their work with other teachers indicated a deep understanding of issues in teaching and learning, and they struggled with ways of communicating their knowledge to others and enabling others to develop and grow. Unsurprisingly, their own knowledge and understanding was both questioned and strengthened during this time. One of them wrote, 'I have not found all this easy. Teachers depend on me and sometimes I have no solutions. At times I have felt quite alone.'

These quotations reflect poignantly the dilemmas all teacher educators have faced in their transition from teacher to educator: the personal difficulties which shame or embarrass us; the recognition of imperfections in our own practice; the dependence of others and our knowledge that we don't have all the answers; our own needs for support and encouragement. Too often when we, as teacher educators, report on teacher education projects we point only towards our aims and objectives for the course or programme, along with an evaluation of teachers' progress within the programme, and the programme's successes and failures. How often do we recognize overtly the fallibility, not only of the course or programme, but of our own abilities to make good choices, or live up to our espoused theories and expectations. In our (legitimate) efforts and desires to 'engender' in teachers the theories we espouse, how ready are we to critique our own practices and their outcomes? I recognize in the above discussion not only elements of all the 3 levels of consideration in teacher education, but also strongly and, increasingly, humbly my own learning and development in this process.

Perspectives of Plurality

What Is Plurality?

It is clear that teaching is a very *complex* activity — it encompasses many facets, issues, philosophical positions. Through the various stages of writing this chapter, I personally struggled with the difference between plurality and complexity, feeling intuitively that plurality was more than just complexity, but finding it hard to articulate this intuition.

Another term which crops up in educational theory is *diversity* — alternative ways of doing and seeing, not always compatible with each other. In our theoretical debates it is all too easy to define ourselves into narrow corners rather than to celebrate diversity. Jere Confrey (1991), for example, in her critique of Davydov (1990), accuses activity theorists of lacking diversity because 'the outcomes of one's activities culminates in access to true reality, which is disturbingly uniform across any setting' (p. 31). Often such narrow corners result in ridiculous stances, such as, for example, a so-called 'constructivist' pedagogy in which the teacher never engages in explanation or exposition because this would be seen as 'transmission teaching'.

The act of writing the chapter has enabled me to see more clearly what plurality encompasses. Plurality acknowledges both complexity and diversity, but goes further in my view. As well as 'numerousness', the Chambers dictionary offers 'a philosophy that recognizes more than one *principle of being*' (my emphasis). I find helpful the idea of 'principles of being'. It seems to accord with Belenky's exposition of ways of knowing, recognizing that there are many such ways and that they coexist and support each other, and that there exist transitions between them. I have indicated important shifts observed in the ways of being and ways of thinking of the teachers on whose thinking and practice I have drawn in providing snapshots of teaching development in practice.

The notion of *principles of being* seems to carry with it a non-tacit nature, indicative of a critical awareness of issues and dichotomies and sources of challenge. Such principles of being are reflected through our theoretical perspectives, our ways of acting in classrooms and courses, and in the many questions which challenge and direct our ongoing development.

In this section I attempt to draw together the two earlier sections in an appraisal of theoretical and practical considerations for the development of teaching, and the role of teacher educators in the processes involved.

Pedagogical Power

I should like to start with Cooney's notion of pedagogical power — 'the essence of intelligent problem solving within the context of teaching mathematics' (1997, p. 298). I used 'pedagogical power' both as an example of a theoretical principle of which we might seek manifestations in practice, and as a theoretical principle in its own right. In my examples from the practice of the various teachers in the second section of this chapter, I believe I have provided manifestations of pedagogical power.

For example, the MTE teachers were very explicitly problem-solvers in their classroom situations. This was the nature of their enterprise. They set out to ask questions and to inquire into their practice. What we see, as we scrutinize the processes of these teachers' research, are ways in which pedagogical power is manifested. It is clearly an emancipatory power in so far as the teachers concerned all gained insights into their own practice which made their knowledge, or principles of being, more evident to them. They recognized qualities which they valued, and objectives which they wanted to pursue. This recognition brought with it a confidence in pursuing their questions and objectives, despite the barriers they encountered. None of the teachers would claim they had found answers to the problems. Identifying the problems and gaining insight into ways of tackling them made clear that looking for answers was too simplistic.

When we looked closely at the particularities of their problem-solving, we saw shifts of theoretical significance. For example, shifts from social to psychological positions or vice versa. The 'vice versa' is important. It is popular in the mathematics education literature to offer 'solutions' to pedagogical problems in terms of particular paradigms in particular domains. For example, the constructivist movement of the 1980s operated within a largely psychological domain, in which it was accused of ignoring social factors (e.g. Lerman, 1996). The situated cognitionists (e.g. Lave,

1996) position learning as a product of social situations and working practices in which cognitive structures are at best derivative. *Constructivism* and *Situated Cognition* are examples of paradigms that often take on a monolithic status, exclusive of each other. Neither paradigm, in my view, accounts for the entire complexity of classrooms, students' learning or the issues teachers face. In moving towards a perspective of plurality we open up the possibilities for a diversity of paradigms to act dialectically in providing lenses into the theory–practice interface which is our focus.

A recognition of pedagogical power, its centrality to developing teaching, and its characterization in mathematical epistemology, cognition and pedagogy through diverse paradigmatic representations acting in dialectic and dialogic modes is the basis of plurality in mathematics teacher education. It needs elaboration in terms of one of the key issues of this chapter, i.e. the notion of 'engendering' certain theoretical principles in practice. Such theoretical principles lie in the domains of mathematical epistemology, cognition and pedagogy. One way of approaching the notion of 'engendering' is through paradigmatic lenses.

To Engender or Make Manifest Theoretical Principles in Practice

It seems clear to me that the MTE project resulted in pedagogical power for the teachers who participated in it. Thus, perhaps, we might conclude that one means of 'engendering' pedagogical power is to create opportunity for teachers to engage in research into aspects of their practice. The MTE project was not a course. The teachers were not 'taught' as part of the project. However, it would be naive to suggest that the project provided no influences; that the teaching or teacher development observed was solely a product of teacher activity. Reports from the project have acknowledged, critically, the position of the project leaders in influencing its progress and perhaps acting as role models for the participating teachers (e.g. Jaworski, 1998). Nevertheless, the learning and development which took place was both clear to participants and specific to individuals. What was 'engendered', if such a term can be used, was a form of reflective practice which was judged to fit with Schön's principles of reflection in action (1983, 1987). The learning and development of the individual teachers provided manifestations of 'reflection-in-action' in action.

On the other hand, the Pakistani teachers did engage in a course – an MEd degree programme. In this they were taught, and addressed deeply, the literature related to their study. Such teaching and literature clearly affected their thinking and further development, although it was the challenges posed by practical application of such theory which arguably influenced growth.

As a teacher educator and researcher, my deepest learning experiences arise from tackling serious challenges within practical situations, relative to theoretical principles from a variety of sources. In responding to such challenges I gain pedagogical power and influence my own development. I might be seen as overcoming the learning paradox indicated by Bereiter (1985) through the process of critical reflective practice, actively constructing not only my own learning, but also the mechanisms for this learning. I believe that the teachers discussed in this paper were all engaged in such a process.

Thus 'engendering' can be seen as growth of: a) a diversity of perspectives, alongside; b) a critical awareness of their relations to practice and the issues arising from practice, in an environment which fosters particular views and practices either explicitly through direct teaching or literature, or implicitly through the role models of the associated educators, programme leaders or researchers. A key element of this view is that the developing critical perspective is manifested in challenges to the forces of influence, which then demand critique of the very fabric of the social situations in which the various perspectives have developed. Current considerations of equity and social justice are one element of such challenge and critique (Restivo, Van Bendegem and Fischer, 1993). A danger of the process is that it becomes self-destructive, as critique ultimately demolishes all the 'wise' principles on which the edifice has been founded.

As an example, which fits with a paradigm underpinning a large proportion of this book, I will look briefly at how *constructivism* might be seen to inter-relate with the developing of pedagogical principles in the teaching and learning of mathematics, and some of the problems faced by those seeing constructivism as an all-encompassing paradigm.

The Overt Construction of Teaching Development in Social Settings

The MTE project provided an environment in which the teacher researchers could be seen to construct their own developmental process. The supporting structure encouraged communication and collaboration. All researchers met periodically in project meetings to share experiences and issues. Although each teacher's research was unique to their own interests and experience, the issues which arose had much in common with the research of other teachers. The teachers felt that they not only learned from each other, but they gained mutual support and inspiration from the processes of sharing. As well as each constructing their own research process, which led to developments in their thinking about teaching and ultimately in the teaching itself, there was a construction of a research community in which the leaders of the group also participated. Thus teachers, in a cooperative enterprise, came to know what research meant for them and for their colleagues. This was not enculturation into an existing community of practice with its old-stagers[3], but rather the creation of a community through intersubjective construction, and what Steffe (in press) refers to as 'experiential abstraction'.

Steffe, von Glasersfeld, Richards and Cobb (1983) introduced the idea of first and second order models to explain such intersubjectivity within a constructive process. *First order* models concern the knowledge the subject constructs to order, comprehend and control his or her experience. For the MTE teachers, first order models included models of mathematics, models of children's learning of mathematics, and models of approaches to teaching mathematics, as well as complex interrelationships between these models.

According to Steffe et al., *second order* models are models that observers construct of the subjects' knowledge in order to explain their observations. Steffe writes (in press), 'Second order models are necessarily constructed through social interaction because they are the observer's models of the observed. One can legitimately say that they are co-constructed by the observer and the observed and refer to intersubjective knowledge.' Thus, according to Steffe, intersubjectivity involves 'making second order models of the concepts, schemes, actions, goals and ultimately feelings and emotions of the other' (in press). In these terms, the MTE teachers made sense of each other's experiences and problems, and the issues arising from them. Negotiation within the constructive process allowed second order models to be tested, modified and used as a basis of developing first order models. Steffe (personal communication) makes the point that '. . . any knowledge of another's knowledge can be made one's own — that is, any second order model can be constituted as a first order model when abstracted from the context of the establishment. If this were not the case we could never learn from each other.'

Although this process may seem deeply psychological, it is also a social process. It may not fit notions of 'socialization' within a community of practice in that the community here is not well established. However, it might be envisaged that, over time, such establishment would take place and it would be of interest to trace the development of socialization within the community. This would include development of language forms as means of abstracting from experience. It would involve the making explicit of tacit knowledge by members of the community. There might be elements of knowledge growth relative to the practices of the community in which knowledge seems rooted in the practice and even derivative of it. However, currently a metaphor of construction seems to fit better than one of socialization for growth of knowledge in the teacher/researcher group. Steffe's models provide a means for reconciling the constructive/social processes involved.

Shifting between paradigms brings us to serious questions concerning the commensurability of paradigms (notably, here, paradigms of construction and socialization) which have been aired extensively elsewhere (see, for example, Confrey, 1995). Bruner (1996), in his address to the conference to celebrate 100 years since the births of the two 'giants' of educational theory, Piaget and Vygotsky, acknowledged this incommensurability, but nevertheless pointed to ways in which apparently diverse paradigms might coexist in contributing to our growth of understanding. It is necessary to be critical but open-minded. At a naive level, a constructivist paradigm focuses on the individual cognizer at the expense of the sociocultural domains in which cognition develops; a paradigm of socialization, positing cognition as derivative, fails to explain the creativity of individual invention; in both, a critical dimension is needed to expose paradigm-boundedness.

The emancipatory nature of pedagogical power may be rooted in a constructivist paradigm in which individual creativity is valued above social acculturation. It would need to be asked what emancipation would look like in a culture of practice in which cognition is seen as derivative. Thus to talk of emancipation, might be seen to presuppose paradigmatic dominance. Issues of language aired earlier in this chapter, contribute to the paradigmatic imperialism of the arguments presented. As I use language to express the ideas I attempt to communicate, I betray the paradigmatic origins of my argument. I cannot use the language of constructivism to express with integrity a sociocultural view, or a situated view of knowledge growth. Similarly critiques of constructivism fail to convince constructivists because they are couched in language which seems to side-step the principle elements of constructivist belief. The debate between Lerman and Steffe (Lerman, 1996; Steffe, in press) exemplifies to some extent such language dichotomy. In an attempt to get beyond paradigm-boundedness through proposing plurality, I have to take care that I am not simply seeking another version of paradigm imperialism.

In Conclusion

Plurality is seen in complexity and diversity and in multiple 'principles of being'. This is manifested in teachers and teacher educators exploring practices, identifying and critiquing theoretical perspectives, and being open-minded to ways of seeing, expressing and justifying practice. Plurality extends to the domain of overarching theoretical paradigms in an attempt to breach incommensurability through a making transparent of the language forms which bind us to particular paradigms to allow us to extend our critiques to the roots of the social situations in which practices are formed.

In the practices described in this chapter, the fundamental nature of the success of teacher and teaching development seemed to lie in teachers taking responsibility to explore practices and theories, raise questions, expose problems, use communication and negotiation to confirm or challenge practices, and to open up new ways of seeing and understanding. The collaborative nature of developmental processes were significant to effective outcomes.

However, to talk of collaboration and negotiation, one presupposes interactions between individuals, which root us within particular paradigms in which certain issues and relationships may remain hidden. If, for example, emancipation depends on cognitive processes which are derivative of a middle-class educated community, the socially oppressed, for whom emancipation is most necessary, may have no chance of achieving it if they cannot begin to fulfil the baseline criteria it requires. In the cases discussed here, this refers to engagement in exploration, inquiry and critique.

The teachers in the studies quoted were small in number, self-selected or institution-selected (in either case indicating special qualities), and in close communication with educators with strong views and incentives to promote practices deemed to be emancipatory for teachers and thus advantageous to children's mathematical development. What of the multitudes of teachers who do not fall into these specialized categories? Where are the communities which will introduce them to exploration, inquiry and reflective practice? Where are the supportive structures which will enable them to develop and sustain practices based on inquiry and critique? Where is the financial backing which will support felicitous environments, free, for example, from poverty, overcrowding, intolerance, and political oppression?

It is clear from the many chapters in this book that educators, working with teachers, have worthy principles and ideals for mathematics education which strive to develop teaching within local or national communities and settings. Despite considerable diversity in the settings, common goals and principles emerge and issues are shared. Theoretical paradigms are seen to prevail over local conditions, while local conditions often spike goals and principles. The South African situation discussed in Section Two and chapter 13 is a prime example. In a recognition of the overwhelming nature of local conditions it can be tempting to throw out the baby with the bathwater, abandoning principles to social demand. The centrality of critique to plurality demands we resist such abandonment, yet keep social conditions and constraints to the forefront of our paradigmatic thinking. The processes which have been seen to have success in the programmes described should neither be seen as blueprints to success, if only the conditions can be replicated; nor should they be seen as futile in the face of overwhelming social conditions.

By recognizing connections between plurality and open-mindedness we need to strive to rationalize theories and practices with the social conditions in which learning and teaching take place. While we might expect teachers to be able to undertake classroom research in Oxford, this might not be as readily expected in Pakistan[4]. The practices are different in the two places, depending heavily on social conditions, cultural traditions, and economic circumstances — just as South Africa, or Israel, are again different. However, the principles on which programmes have developed are not so different.

Relating the variety of programmes and practices described in this book, first from paradigmatic principles, then from national, social and cultural perspectives, we see much in common and much that is different. What is common needs subjecting to critique relative to what is different. Teacher educators, in seeking to 'engender' practices and their theoretical groundings, cannot afford to ignore the national, social, economic and political. A challenge for us all is to find language forms which cut through paradigmatic boundaries to address the social and cultural issues which present the real problems which teachers have to face in developing effective mathematical education for children.

Author Note

My sincere thanks go to Razia Fakir-Mohammed, Anjum Halai, and Yasmin Mehta, who participated so willingly in my explorations into their thinking and development, and who, over the years in which we have worked together, have become my friends. I should also like to thank Les Steffe for insights arising from our e-mail discussions, and Anne Watson, Paul Ernest and my co-editors for their critiques on earlier drafts of this chapter.

Notes

1 I perceive that these 'ways of knowing' are synthesized in terms of 'knowledge'. I leave it to the reader to consider whether the distinctions are epistemological or a matter of language, as discussed later in this section of the chapter.
2 Problems arise when quoting published work of *anonymous* teachers. It seems necessary, however, to acknowledge such publications, hence I refer here to (Hall, 1997). I believe my analyses in this chapter accord with what this teacher has written of her own experiences and perspectives.
3 I feel obliged to quote my colleague Anne Watson here, from her critique of an earlier draft of this chapter. She wrote: 'Now hang on! You were in there and you are an old-stager — remember, Lave says that no explicit teaching takes place. Don't you think that your questioning, your ways of working and your concerns were 'old-stager' characteristics? Don't you think teachers would have developed differently if I or [another colleague] had led it?' I leave it to the reader to consider the relative merits of our two interpretations, and where they fit in perspectives of plurality!
4 In fact teachers in Pakistan *did* engage in research, which led to a realization and questioning of social and cultural issues in the Pakistan context, the discussion of which is outside the scope of this chapter.

References

ADLER, J. (1996) 'Lave and Wenger's social practice theory and teaching and learning school mathematics', in PUIG, L. and GUTIERREZ, A. (eds) *Proceedings of the Twentieth Conference of the International Group for the Psychology of Mathematics Education* Vol. 2 (pp. 3–10), University of Valencia, Spain: Psychology of Mathematics Education.

ANDERSON, L.W. and BURNS, R.B. (1989) *Research in Classrooms: The Study of Teachers, Teaching and Instruction*, Oxford: Pergamon Press.

BELENKY, M.F., CLINCHY, B.M., GOLDBERGER, N.R. and TARULE, J.M. (1986) *Women's Ways of Knowing: The Development of Self, Voice and Mind*, New York: Basic Books.

BEREITER, C. (1985) 'Towards a solution of the learning paradox', *Review of Educational Research*, **55**, 2, pp. 201–26.

BISHOP, A.J. (1988) 'Mathematics education in its cultural context', *Educational Studies in Mathematics*, **19**, pp. 179–91.

BROWN, S. and McINTYRE, D. (1993) *Making Sense of Teaching*, Buckingham: Open University Press.

BRUNER, J. (1996) 'Celebrating Divergence: Piaget and Vygotsky', Keynote address delivered in Geneva on 15th September, 1996 at a joint meeting of the 'Growing Mind Conference' in honour of the centennial of Jean Piaget's birth, and the 'Vygotsky–Piaget Conference' of the 2nd Congress of Socio-Cultural Research.

CONFREY, J. (1991) 'Steering a course between Vygotsky and Piaget', *Educational Researcher*, November.

CONFREY, J. (1995) 'How compatible are radical constructivism, sociocultural approaches and social constructivism?' in STEFFE, L.P. and GALE, J. (eds) *Constructivism in Education*, Hillsdale, NJ: Erlbaum.

COONEY, T. (1994) 'Teacher education as an exercise in adaptation', in AICHELE, D.B. and COXFORD, A.F. (eds) *Professional Development for Teachers of Mathematics: 1994 Yearbook*, Reston, VA: NCTM.

Cooney, T.J. and Shealy, B. (1997) 'On understanding the structure of teachers beliefs and their relationship to change', in Fennema, E. and Scott-Nelson B. (eds) *Mathematics Teachers in Transition*, Mahwah, NJ: Erlbaum.

Davydov, V.V. (1990) *Soviet Studies in Mathematics Education: Volume 2. Types of Generalization in Instruction*, (trans. Joan Teller; ed. Jeremy Kilpatrick), Reston VA: NCTM.

Davis, P.J. and Hersh, R. (1981) *The Mathematical Experience*, Boston: Houghton, Mifflin.

Department of Education and Science (1982) *Mathematics Counts: The Cockcroft Report*, London: HMSO.

Elbaz, F. (1983) *Teacher Thinking: A Study of Practical Knowledge*, London: Croom Helm.

Eraut, M. (1995) 'Schön shock: A case for reframing reflection-in-action', *Teachers and Teaching: Theory and Practice*, **1**, 1.

Ernest, P. (1991) *The Philosophy of Mathematics Education*, London: Falmer Press.

Gergen, K.J. (1995) 'Social construction and the educational process', in Steffe, L.P. and Gale, J. (eds) *Constructivism in Education*, Hillsdale, NJ: Erlbaum.

Halai, A. (1997) 'Secondary mathematics teaching: Should it be all chalk and talk?' *Mathematics Teaching*, **161** pp. 18–19.

Halai, A. (1998) 'Mentor, mentee and mathematics', *Journal of Mathematics Teacher Education, **1**, 3.

Jaworski, B. (1994) *Investigating Mathematics Teaching: A Constructivist Enquiry*, London: Falmer Press.

Jaworski, B. (1997) 'Developing understanding of developing teaching', in Zack, V. Mousely, J. and Breen, C. (eds) *Developing Practice: Teachers' Inquiry and Educational Change in Classrooms*, Geelong Australia: Centre for Studies in Mathematics, Science and Environmental Education, Deakin University.

Jaworski, B. (1998) 'Mathematics teacher research: Process, practice and the development of teaching', *Journal of Mathematics Teacher Education*, **1**, 1, pp. 3–31.

Jaworski, B., and Potari, D. (1998) 'Characterising mathematics teaching using the teaching triad', in A. Olivier and K. Newstead (eds) *Proceedings of the 22nd Conference of the International Group for the Psychology of Mathematics Education*, **3**, pp. 88–95.

Lave, J. and Wenger, E. (1991) *Situated Learning: Legitimate Peripheral Participation*, New York: Cambridge University Press.

Lave, J. (1996) 'Teaching as learning, in practice', *Mind, Culture and Activity*, **3**, 3. pp. 149–64.

Lerman, S. (1996) 'Intersubjectivity in mathematics learning: A challenge to the radical constructivist paradigm?' *Journal for Research in Mathematics Education*, **27**, 2.

Lortie, D.C. (1975) *Schoolteacher: A Sociological Study*, Chicago: University of Chicago Press.

Mason, J. (1994) *Researching from the Inside in Mathematics Education: Locating an I–You Relationship*, Milton Keynes: Centre for Mathematics Education, Open University.

National Council of Teachers of Mathematics (1989) *Curriculum and Evaluation Standards for School Mathematics*, Reston, VA: NCTM.

National Council of Teachers of Mathematics (1991) *Professional Standards for Teaching Mathematics*, Reston, VA: NCTM.

Othman, M.Y. (1996) 'A pilot study into the teacher craft of three mathematics teachers and its relation to learning in the classroom: Methodological issues and indications for future research', Unpublished MSc thesis, University of Oxford.

Perry, W.G. (1970) *Forms of Intellectual and Ethical Development in the College Years*, New York: Holt, Rinehart and Winston.

Piaget, J. (1970) *Genetic Epistemology*, New York: Columbia University Press.

POLANYI, M. (1958) *Personal Knowledge*, London: Routledge and Kegan Paul.

RESTIVO, S., VAN BENDEGEM, J.P. and FISCHER, R. (1993) *Math Worlds: Philosophical and Social Studies of Mathematics and Mathematics Education*, NY: SUNY Press.

SCHIFTER, D. (1993) 'Mathematics process as mathematics content: A course for teachers', *Journal of Mathematical Behavior*, **12**, 3, pp. 271–83.

SCHIFTER, D. (1997) *Learning Mathematics for Teaching*, Newton, MA: Center for the Development of Teaching.

SCHÖN, D.A. (1983) *The Reflective Practitioner*, London: Temple Smith.

SCHÖN, D.A. (1987) *Educating the Reflective Practitioner*, Oxford: Jossey-Bass.

SHULMAN, L.S. (1987) 'Knowledge and teaching: Foundations of the new reform', *Harvard Educational Review*, **57**, 1, pp. 1–22.

SIERPINSKA, A. (1994) *Understanding Mathematics*, London: Falmer Press.

STEFFE, L.P. (in press) 'Intersubjectivity in mathematics learning: A challenge to the radical constructivist paradigm? A Reply to Lerman', *Chreods*.

STEFFE, L.P., VON GLASERSFELD, E., RICHARDS, J. and COBB, P. (1983) *Children's Counting Types: Philosophy, Theory and Application*, New York: Praeger.

STIGLER, J.W. and HEIBERT, J. (1997) 'Understanding and improving classroom mathematics instruction: An overview of the TIMSS video study', *Phi Delta Kappan*, September.

STODOLSKY, S. (1988) *The Subject Matters*, Chicago: University of Chicago Press.

THE AGA KHAN UNIVERSITY INSTITUTE FOR EDUCATIONAL DEVELOPMENT (1991) *A Proposal to the AKU Board of Trustees*, Karachi, Pakistan: Author.

THOMPSON, A. (1984) 'The relationship of teachers' conceptions of mathematics teaching to instructional practice', *Educational Studies in Mathematics*, **15**, pp. 105–27.

VON GLASERSFELD, E. (1987) 'Learning as a constructive activity', in JANVIER, C. (ed.) *Problems of Representation in the Teaching and Learning of Mathematics*, Hillsdale, NJ: Erlbaum Associates.

Final Remarks

What insights might be drawn from the last three chapters? Terry Wood contends that there is one aspect that pertains to teacher development that we seemingly know little about, and that is the processes that are involved as teachers make changes in their teaching. Sandy Dawson argues that such a state of affairs is not surprising, because in his view the enactivist teacher educator embarks on a journey with a group of inservice mathematics teachers, a journey wherein the group 'lays down its own path while walking'. This would seem to imply that the process of change might be different for each teacher. Jaworski seems to support this point of view when she concludes that plurality is seen in complexity and diversity and in multiple 'principles of being'. This is manifested in teachers and teacher educators exploring practices, identifying and critiquing theoretical perspectives, and being open-minded to diverse and pluralistic ways of seeing, expressing and justifying practice.

The issues, of course, do not stop here. There is ongoing need for international debate of the practices, theories, issues and dilemmas which the papers of this book have revealed and raised. We should like to see this book as a stepping stone in this wider debate.

Notes on Contributors

Miriam Amit, Ministry of Education and Culture and Ben-Gurion University, Israel. National Chief Superintendent of Mathematics, responsible for the mathematics education programme in Israel, including K-12 programmes and teacher training. At BGU, responsibility for development and application of research-based programmes for inservice teacher training.

Chris Breen, Associate Professor in mathematics education, University of Cape Town, South Africa. Formal teaching duties include preservice courses at both primary and secondary school level. Involvement in inservice teacher education has been mainly through the Mathematics Education Project (MEP), which he directed from 1989–95.

Murray S. Britt, Auckland College of Education, Auckland, New Zealand. Lectures in mathematics education at Auckland College of Education. Background in mathematics curriculum development with considerable experience of working with practising primary and secondary school teachers towards advanced qualifications. Teaches in the college's mathematics education programmes for preservice primary and secondary school teachers.

Richard C. Carter, Senior Scientist, BBN Learning Systems and Technologies, USA. Developing technology-based professional development materials including video case studies of mathematics teachers who are trying to implement mathematics reform in their classrooms and on-line collaboration environments for teachers implementing new curriculum.

Sandy Dawson, Professor, Faculty of Education, Simon Fraser University, Vancouver, Canada. Sandy was Director of teacher education program (PDP) at Simon Fraser University from 1985 to 1994. His current work focuses on both pre-service and inservice education, but his main interest is on Inservice at diverse locations around the province of British Columbia. He mentors graduate level Inservice courses for cohorts of Masters students who are elementary and secondary teachers from the greater Vancouver area.

Ruhama Even, Senior Researcher Department of Science Teaching Weizmann Institute of Science, Israel. Director of the National Mathematics Teacher Center at the Weizmann Institute of Science since its establishment. Designed and operates the MANOR Project — a teacher-leaders preparation programme, and the preparation of resource materials for teacher-leaders. Research and development work focuses on teachers' knowledge and understanding about mathematical topics and concepts, and processes involved in the development of mathematics teachers and teacher-leaders.

Fairouz Farah-Sarkis, Lebanese University, Lebanon. From 1985 until present: advisor for several private school boards mainly in inservice training. From 1990–94: Director of the Educational Services Unit at the American University of Beirut, where the main services were inservice teacher training. From 1996 until present: Director of the Office of External Projects in the Lebanese University of which a major part is inservice training.

Susan L. Hillman, Assistant Professor of Mathematics Education, Penn State Harrisburg, USA. Teacher of mathematics education courses for the elementary and secondary education programmes, and the graduate programme in Teaching and Curriculum. Involved in developing partnerships with several local schools to enhance mathematics education and provide practical experiences for preservice teachers in urban settings.

Piet Human, University of Stellenbosch, South Africa. Part-time professor and director of research unit, independent mathematics educator and curriculum materials writer. Currently involved in several teacher education projects in rural areas in South Africa. These projects focus on providing academically disadvantaged teachers who received minimal training with opportunities to deepen their understanding of the mathematics they teach.

Colleen Goldstein, Parktown, South Africa. Works as a consultant to various NGOs, mainly working on teacher development programmes and teaching support materials. She is part of a Provincial Government Curriculum Studies task team which is mapping mathematics development levels and producing illustrative learning programmes for the new curriculum.

Kathryn C. Irwin, University of Auckland, Auckland, New Zealand. Lecturer in mathematics education at the University of Auckland. Works mainly with practising mathematics teachers toward advanced degrees, although also teaches preservice primary school teachers. Supervisor of several research projects exploring classroom practices.

Barbara Jaworski, Department of Educational Studies, University of Oxford. Co-director of Centre for Mathematics Education Research. Works with teachers in Initial Teacher Education and Continuing Professional Development. Supervises doctoral students mainly in qualitative studies involving the teaching and learning of mathematics.

Konrad Krainer, Associate Professor, Center for Interdisciplinary Research and Development of Austrian Universities, Austria. Head of the Department 'School and Professional Development' at the Center for Interdisciplinary Research and Development of Austrian Universities. Works in the fields of mathematics education, professionalization of teachers and principals, and school development.

Cristina Loureiro, Escola Superior de Educação, Instituto Politécnico de Lisboa, Portugal. Teacher of Mathematics Education, working in preservice and inservice education for primary and middle school teachers. Main interest in teacher knowledge in mathematics, especially in geometry and discrete mathematics.

Zvia Markovits, Head of the Center for Mathematics Education Oranim School of Education, Tivon, Israel. Head of the Center for Mathematics Education at Oranim School of Education. In the last 10 years involved in preservice and inservice teacher education, teaching and research. Conducted a five-year project for improving mathematics teaching and learning in all eight elementary schools in a development town in Israel, and conducting now a similar project in another town.

Phillip Mnisi, South Africa. Currently works as a curriculum researcher for the National Department of Education, South Africa. When he wrote this paper with his colleagues, he was employed in a Non-Governmental Organisation (NGO) inservice project which worked collaboratively with primary mathematics teachers in Soweto.

Hanlie Murray, Faculty of Education, University of Stellenbosch, South Africa. Lectures in mathematics education for undergraduate and postgraduate students at primary and middle school level. Involved in inservice training and professional development of college lecturers and teachers of historically disadvantaged communities. As Associate Researcher (Research Unit for Mathematics Education) involved in the articulation and refinement of the problem-centred approach to learning, curriculum design and generation of materials.

Alwyn Olivier, Faculty of Education, University of Stellenbosch, South Africa. Senior lecturer in mathematics education, teaching preservice courses at both primary and secondary school level. Through the Research Unit for Mathematics Education involved in the problem-centred learning project. Director of Mathematics Malati (Learning and Teaching Initiative), a curriculum and teacher development project.

John Richards, Senior Vice President, Turner Learning, Inc., USA. Turner Learning is the educational arm of the Turner networks, including CNN, TNT, Turner Classic Movies and Cartoon. Working with teachers to incorporate multiple media into their curricula, particularly using news and current events as a source of authentic, collaborative problem-solving.

Pamela Rodwell, Plettenberg Bay, South Africa. When the chapter was written, Pamela worked as a materials developer in a Mathematics NGO which worked with teachers to develop and research appropriate learner-centred ways of teaching mathematics in large, under-resourced classes. She is now retired from education.

Lurdes Serrazina, Escola Superior de Educação, Instituto Politécnico de Lisboa, Portugal. Teacher of Mathematics Education, working in preservice and inservice education for pre-school, primary and middle school teachers. Main interest in teacher development and teacher knowledge in mathematics, especially primary mathematics.

A.I. Weinzweig, Professor of Mathematics at the University of Illinois at Chicago, USA. Active in the preparation and enhancement of teachers; worked extensively with children and teachers in school and classroom settings, particularly in inner-city schools. From 1984–89, directed The Institute for the Learning and Teaching of Mathematics, an inservice project for Chicago Elementary School teachers. From 1991–94, director of the MathPET Project for the mathematical preparation of elementary school teachers.

Terry Wood, Professor of Mathematics Education, Department of Curriculum and Instruction, Purdue University, USA. Teaches mathematics education courses for undergraduate preservice teachers in elementary education and graduate students in mathematics education. Works with inservice elementary teachers developing approaches to teacher education. Director of the Recreating Teaching Mathematics in Elementary Schools project.

Index